"There is a sad state of affairs in the quality of many books about writing… It isn't only that they are not especially well written—they are downright boring. Adios breaks out of this unfortunate mold with spectacular style. The writing is clear, clever, and engaging. It respectfully pokes fun at established traditions while providing invaluable tools for communicating in a way that will capture the imagination of aspiring writers…"

Danny Iny, **author of** *Ordinary Miracle: Harness the Power of Writing*

"This book has re-energized my classroom!!!!!… This book is so well written that my students actually read it on their own time for FUN!!!?? How many times does that happen with a composition textbook???? What this has done so much better than a traditional 'writing' textbook is take my students out of relying on a Barney-fied' 3-point thesis/5- paragraph format and inspire them to be bolder, more lively writers. I KNOW this book has changed the way I think about writing and the teaching of writing!"

Lisa Edmunds, a.k.a. "The Grammar Goddess" on amazon.com

"Having had the pleasure of not only reading the Hoffmans' book, but also being a student in their classes, I have to fully express my satisfaction with the book. It is my new bible for English. What first struck me as unusual (considering the bland, tasteless writing I had been taught most of my educational career) was merely fulfilling my craving for originality. I wholeheartedly enjoyed the text, and constantly refer to it for enhancement in all my communications."

amazon.com reader, Costa Mesa, California

"Just when the reader thinks the Hoffmans need a sound dose of Strunk and White for casting too far out of the mainstream, the Hoffmans not only explain clearly how to achieve that notion, they also justify it with a colorful tapestry of examples from high and low, literary and scientific. Readers will end each section renewed with an eager-to-try-it spirit."

Donna Barnard, *inside english, The Journal of the English Council of California Two-Year Colleges* and author of *Sparks: A Reader to Energize Writing*

"Before I was not able to describe the intangible element of good writing... Now, thanks to Adios, I have a means of articulating my answer, which is sometimes as simple as 'no flow; no pause' or 'awkward twist tie.' If these terms sound unfamiliar, they are meant to be. The Hoffmans promise, and deliver, a textbook without what they call 'teacherese.'"

Leigh Ann Weatherford, professor of English
From "This is Wondrous Strange" in *Pedagogy*,
Duke University Press

"*Adios, Strunk and White approaches writing with such playfulness and creativity that writers, non-writers, and people of all ages would have fun... In fact, I sent an extra copy to my daughter who volunteers her time at Highland Elementary School in Boise...*"

Margaret Gratton, college president

"The Hoffmans' solution is to invent a terminology that labels the effects, rather than the mechanics, of rhetorical technique... Their result is fascinating. The Hoffmans' book is comprehensive, undogmatic, and evocative. I bought it because the title filled me with glee; I keep it on my desk because I find the content valuable."

Sandra in Australia from "Thus Strunk the Prophet"
in *Connectives*

"Hoffman and Hoffman expose the secret weapons every good writer uses but might not even know they know. Adios gives even experienced writers a blueprint for improvement."
Audrey Davidow, senior editor, *Angeleno Magazine*

"I've been a professional writer for twenty-five years...writing style is too often the product of habit. Adios provides practical— yet highly creative—advice and counsel."
Jim Carnett, community relations director

Adios, Strunk and White

Fourth Edition

Gary & Glynis Hoffman

VERVE PRESS

Adios, Strunk and White, fourth edition by Gary and Glynis Hoffman

ISBN-10: 0-937363-40-5 ISBN-13: 978-0-93763-40-9
Library of Congress Catalog Card Number: 2007928279
Printed in the United States of America
Published by Verve Press, P.O. Box 1997, Huntington Beach, California, 92647

Printing: Birmingham Press
First Edition Printing   1997
Second Edition Printing   1999
Third Edition Printing   2003
Fourth Edition Printing   2007

Cover Design: Gary Hoffman
Graphic Designs: Gary Hoffman
Graphic Enhancement: Darby's Type & Design, Inc.
Page Layout: Darby's Type & Design, Inc.

Library of Congress Cataloguing-in-Publication Data
Hoffman, Gary
    Adios, Strunk and White / Gary and Glynis Hoffman,—4th ed.
p. 256   cm.

ISBN-10: 0-937363-40-5 ISBN-13: 978-0-937363-40-9
            1. English language—Style
            2. English language—Composition and exercises
            3. English language—Rhetoric
            4. English language—Grammar
            5. Critical Thinking   I. Hoffman
Glynis   II. Title
PE 1408 .H656 2007   2007928279
808.042   LC CIP

Horatio: O day and night, but this is wondrous strange!

Hamlet: And therefore as a stranger give it welcome.
There are more things in heaven and earth, Horatio,
Than are dreamt of in your philosophy.

Hamlet, Act I. scene v.

CONTENTS

An about-the-authors acknowledgement preface

INTRODUCTION
The Church of English Teachers
Writing Before Reading
Neither a Trade Book Nor a Textbook Be
The Strunk and White Tradition
A Warning

An about-the-authors acknowledgement preface

You may ask yourself, "Well? How did I get here?" — *David Byrne*

Nothing has affected me as a professor of English more than attending the School of Architecture at the University of California at Berkeley when I was eighteen. The school was influenced by Walter Gropius's Bauhaus movement centered on the axiom "form follows function" and established a parallel teaching theory— learning through problem solving. I remember working on a typical Bauhaus assignment: to design a shell that could be used as a roof for a building; that could be dragged over snow by huskies; that could carry a specific amount of bagged cement on top of it; that when raised off the ground could collect enough rainwater in the spring (based on the area's average rainfall) to mix with the cement to create the remainder of the building in the summer. Several years later (after switching to English and art at UCLA, and then as a PhD candidate in English at the University of Southern California) I had no idea that Bauhaus thought had become more essential than James Joyce to my English-major self. To start with, the Bauhaus idea of total immersion in a problem while simultaneously jettisoning past formulaic solutions influenced how I read literature: I learned to give myself over to someone else's language and story without too much dependence on a Jungian, Freudian, feminist, Marxist, or any other critical template.

The Bauhaus had an even greater influence on me as a teacher. At twenty-four and just finishing my first year as a full-time, tenure-track instructor at Orange Coast College, I had a nightmare. I had a vision of a career stretching at least thirty years ahead, made miserable not so much by thought-sloppy, language-tangled student essays (I expected those), but surprisingly by the boredom of reading "A" papers propped up by grammatical correctness and safe English-teacher formulas such as the five-paragraph essay. This was an unexpected dread. I remember asking what those "A" papers had to do with Joan Didion's incisive voice. Where were Norman Maileresque fire flashes? Having students write about their passions helped give their papers detail and sincerity, but their papers lacked the music of professional essayists. To get that, I realized I would need to design teaching strategies, ones pulled by fresh huskies that would drag the students through the snow of their past writing educations, not to mention my own.

This realization started an unimaginable process. I was opening up views into professional writing I had never been taught: how to write with different styles, how to take advantage of different organizational strategies, how to create voice and attitude for different audiences. I designed; my designs informed my own writing; my own writing informed my reading of great essayists, which in turn helped me to revise my designs or come up with new ones—a continuous cycle of learning and doing. The cycle forced me to break out of sanctioned, academic molds and gave me confidence to talk with students about how to become strong writers. My faith in the cycle might have withered if not for the encouragement of my colleague and best friend,

Gary Freeman, himself a syndicated satirist and accomplished essay writer, who constructively criticized what I did while helping me to kick away the pressure I received from the threatened, academically correct world. After thirteen years of teaching, I turned my designs into a book called *Writeful*.

Four years after *Writeful* and after I was divorced, Glynis was a student in my Humor as Literature course. Aside from enthralling me by writing an imaginative "Q-and-A-ing" between Chaucer's wife of Bath and Dr. Ruth, a syndicated television sex advisor, Glynis, during a casual finals-week office conversation, stripped everyone in the class naked, articulating personality quirks that I was just beginning to glimpse even though I had the advantage of reading their papers. Her unvarnished insights trumped anything else (well, almost anything else) I could have wanted in a girlfriend. One cannot use personality templates to discover the kind of fine distinctions Glynis brought to her analytical descriptions. She was a Bauhaus girl.

Furthermore, before I knew her, Glynis believed style was more than just attitude; it shaped content. When she opened *Writeful,* she told me, she saw a truth she always knew—form followed function. Glynis tells the story this way:

The stereotypic snapshot of someone who grows up to be an English teacher is, I would suppose, a picture of a kid who always had her nose in a book, a person in love with ideas and who could lose herself in the imaginary world of a novel. That wasn't me. I did love reading, but more than being in love with the ideas or an intricate story (elaborate plots still confuse me), what I liked best about reading were the rhythms and cadences, the word choice and distinct voices—what I now call style—that created the singular voice of a narrator, character, or writer. I tried to imitate these voices by using their diction and register. And sometimes I could stumble on the syntax and recreate, by instinct, a specific tone—usually a funny or witty voice that was full of punch and shock, but writing by ear or instinct was not always reliable and I was often frustrated when I couldn't get the voice I wanted. I had assumed that writing classes in school would address how to analyze and recreate voice, but in academic settings the reading and writing connection (what we read and what we wrote) focused mostly on summarizing main ideas, identifying the theme, and producing a topic sentence. Sometimes I was inspired and could write "A" papers; other times I couldn't find my way into the writing and might barely pass a class. What I wanted to talk about and write about in a composition or literature class was not the "what" but the "how," how the writer got his or her ideas to resonate, but I didn't know how to talk about the "how."

After taking classes at community colleges for eight years, I ended up in a Humor in Literature class and the how was finally addressed. The professor had his own little book called Writeful *and as we plowed through the literature—*Gulliver's Travels, Catch 22, Metamorphosis, *the film* Nashville, Canterbury Tales—*he asked us to respond to the literature using strategies from his book,* Writeful, *a handbook on the hows: here's how to write a long sentence to create different kinds of* *rhythms; here's how to use punctuation to create dramatic pause; here's how to weave together two different but related narratives; here's how to get original definitions from abstract concepts; here's how to compose a letter that you could never really send. I became obsessed with* Writeful. *I turned myself over to the strategies, having faith that by concentrating on the style and organization of my writing, my content and ideas would come through loud and deep and clear. I fell in love with* Writeful, *and because I fell in love with this book on writing, I fell in love with writing, and then I fell in love with the writer of* Writeful *for making me fall in love with writing, and then I seduced that writer, Gary, my professor; I unwittingly seduced him through my writing, seduced him with the verve and passion I put into to the* Writeful *strategies, and, I believe, these seductive papers made him fall just a little in love with me, and then I became a teacher of writing. And after working with* Writeful, *first as a student then as a teacher, I learned quickly how to analyze writing for style and to figure out ways to imitate and then teach those tones. I reworked some of Gary's strategies and then came up with a few of my own—Netting, Quote Sandwiching, Thesauruscoping—techniques that are used by professional writers all the time and modeled after essays I love. Gary can tell you how we collaborated to create* Adios.

After Glynis finished degrees in English at California State University, Fullerton, and entered the teaching profession at several campuses, she visited my writing courses, dragging me outside during breaks to kiss me and then to explain how my designs needed renovations. When she started teaching at Orange Coast College, Glynis revised many of the designs and finally began to Bauhaus some of her own. Thirteen years after I had written *Writeful*, thinking I would never write a book about writing again, Glynis and I rewrote *Writeful* into *Adios, Strunk and White*.

We are still discovering ways to improve *Adios* and want to share those with our colleagues and students. Over the years, they have given us helpful feedback and we like to think this work is a way of thanking them. We also want to give special thanks to Diane Duncan who was this edition's copyeditor. Diane's expertise and precision have made our ideas more clear.

Despite all our improvements, Glynis and I know there will always be readers of *Adios* who will end up worse off than before they picked up the book. Somehow any kind of advice can be misconstrued and send people into worlds of babble. But we also know that the boring, academically correct "A" papers are gone when a paper is *Adios*-good, a paper that is a joy to read because it enters a world where most writing instructors and their students do not dare to tread.

Gary and Glynis Hoffman

Professors of English

2007

INTRODUCTION

The Church of English Teachers
Writing Before Reading
Neither a Trade Book Nor a Textbook Be
The Strunk and White Tradition
A Warning

The church of English teachers. Learning to write is the result of being smacked or blessed by English teachers. However, in their various interpretations of The Gospel of the Word, English teachers have rewritten the catechism several times: In the 1950s and early 1960s, writing instructors pinched content into strict formats (a bone-dry burden resulting in lifeless student papers); in the late 1960s and 1970s, they revolted against this dogma by encouraging touchy-feely journals and free-writing cluster balloons (a laying-on-of-hands resulting in awkward, self-indulgent papers); in the 1980s, they overreacted to ill-disciplined students by sending these sinners into the Purgatory of Back-to-Basics. The 1950s relics had risen from the dead.

After the dogma failures of previous eras, English teachers, in the 1990s, armed with the New Gospel of Peter and Pablo (Peter Elbow and Pablo Freire) began a Revival called "process writing," a self-discovery approach that considers instruction "too prescriptive," and thus an "oppressive" force, a dictatorial pedagogy that prohibits students from stumbling onto strong writing through trial and error. Trial and error is always part of writing, but faith that students (often depending on peer feedback) would enthusiastically unlock the sacristy of composition on their own time has often resulted in the blind leading the blind. Playing hide-and-seek with the writing tabernacle means students have had less time to activate and practice the written word's vast potential.

Teaching dogma has kept writing teachers preoccupied in the rules/no rules religious wars for so long they have forgotten to pose an essential question about writing instruction: Why have students enjoyed learning in welding, computer graphics, music, culinary, fashion design, and physical education classes but not in writing classes? The reasons are clear. First, students need to know experts' tools, not ones teachers fabricate to make grading easier (rules like "no long sentences" or "never use first person in an academic essay"), writing conventions that result in the never-to-be-subverted canon. Secondly, the tools must appeal simultaneously to both the rational and imaginative parts of a writer's mind. Thirdly, writing students cannot be asked to accept these tools on faith but must immediately see the magic each tool has in crunching, reshaping, and reviving a written piece. This book tries to fulfill these tenets.

Writing before reading. Writers—taking advantage of complex writing tools in their own work—become adept, sensitive readers, less likely to get lost in the complex style and form of strong essays. As with all endeavors—sports, drawing, acting, or surgery—without practice and personal engagement, it is extremely difficult to appreciate, let alone even recognize, what a skilled master is doing. If someone has never written a sentence with multiple subjects, then never expanded each of those subjects with a relative clause, and then compounded that sentence with an ironic afterthought, that person may be

11

easily confused, even intimidated, when he or she reads one. Learning to use complex style and form enables new writers to comprehend the music and rhythms of writing, an exciting nexus similar to that made by a computer animation student learning how to pace action frames, see the magical results, and thereafter recognize the brilliance of pacing in professional work.

After one learns to write with complexity, reading other expert writers becomes an essential part of reinforcing and enjoying those writing skills. Choosing writers to read presents another problem. Many English teachers have placed a gag order on style and innovative forms, feeling compelled to force-feed students with politically correct topics (too often rejecting writers who are not topical), while others reject writers who do not neatly lock into a standard essay form or who have strong personal voices. Good essays are energized. Often these are topical, politically correct, or traditionally formatted, *but not necessarily.* Shelby Steele, for instance, in his essay "On Being Black and Middle Class," challenges the notion of entitlement by tossing out a textbook management of the issue and allowing his personal voice and experiences to blend with style and form techniques, some even associated with fiction. The result is neither strictly personal nor purely academic, neither entirely sociological nor wholly literary. It is all of these. Publishers such as Houghton Mifflin with their *Best American Essays* and magazines like *Harper's* have done much to promote this kind of writing.

Neither a trade book nor a textbook be. This book does not pretend to fit narrowly defined target markets: It is neither a committee-toned textbook for students, nor an insider trade how-to book for would-be professional writers, nor a personalized resource book for writing instructors, but something that lives in the groove between all of these. Some of the approaches here have appealed to elementary school teachers and many of the approaches to professors teaching graduate seminars. This pleases us because we believe that using this book should be a function of the user's personality. The idea of an instructor's manual that pretends to tell instructors how to use a textbook makes us ill.

The Strunk and White tradition. In 1919 William Strunk Jr. at Cornell self-published his textbook entitled *The Elements of Style*, which he copyrighted in 1935. E .B. White, who later wrote *Charlotte's Web* and many essays for *The New Yorker*, was a student in Strunk's class and, in 1975, after Strunk died, Macmillan Publishing Company had White revise the book. For most of the twentieth century, *The Elements of Style* has been the touchstone for professionals, amateurs, teachers, and students. White always admired the brevity of the book and also Strunk's "kindly lash" that made the book a series of sharp commands. We like to think our book pays homage to the compactness and uniqueness of that spirit. In most ideological ways we have departed from Strunk and White. Writing has too. In the last part of the twentieth and into the twenty-first centuries, essay writing has expanded farther than either Strunk or White could have dreamt of in their instructional philosophies. The techniques for writing demand new explanations, especially for a more visual-oriented, cyberspace-writing generation. In order to do this, we have no choice—*Adios*, Strunk and White.

A warning. The advice in this book can be abused, misused, or followed without complete understanding. Strong writers always take calculated risks. However, advice in this book must be practiced over and over again, drafts must be constantly revised, and writing must also be tempered by the writer's maturity in knowing when to apply certain writing devices in this book and when not to. Individuals are responsible for what they write, regardless of where they get advice or what they intend to say. We take only partial credit or blame for the brilliance or gibberish that results from *Adios, Strunk and White*.

1
STYLE

FLOW
PAUSE
FUSION
OPT

Style Before Structure

Style is writing's soul. After reading a magazine article, newspaper column, short story, a personal letter, or a historical account, our minds tend to pin the overall idea or message onto one or two well-turned sentences that capture the essence of the writing. When style is neglected, the fire of an essay vanishes, and ideas and structure linger only to haunt a spiritless composition. While a speaker injects style through voice inflection and body language to convey passion and sincerity that persuades and provokes an audience, a writer's style seems more elusive, emanating from a mysterious "writing" underworld or from a writer's DNA. Because its sources seem obscure, English teachers avoid teaching style, placing emphasis on thesis and supporting details and acting like there is only one correct style.

However, it is misleading to pretend that writers can travel from an introductory thesis statement to a conclusion by simply grafting one supporting example to another, with no attention to voice. The notion of a single, official style has become passé for several reasons: First, students and professors from diverse backgrounds bring their own sensibilities, represented by unique style, to writing. Second, many scholars have devoted serious critical thought to popular culture, encouraging writers such as Camille Paglia and William Gass to blend words and images

14

from pop culture with the literary allusions and priestly voice of traditional academia. Third, word processing allows writers to spend less time outlining and pre-planning essays and more time revising, deleting, and inserting to shape subtext and craft voice.

The elements that make up written style are tangible and can be taught. The writer's voice, like the orator's, relies on inflection and gesticulation, created through careful use of sentence structure, punctuation, metaphor, word choice, and point of view. The problem is that the traditional grammar rules for describing these elements can be overwhelming. Even when the rules are memorized, they are hardly ever discussed in terms of their emotional or psychological impact on the reader, nor are developing writers shown where great essayists purposely break rules, not out of laziness but intentionally for a desired effect. This section boils down many grammatical rules and melts them into new concepts, accessible to the playful, expressive parts of the mind. All writers—scientific researchers, business correspondents, critics, journalists, and personal essayists—use these newly defined techniques. Purpose, audience, and DNA govern what they do with them, but all are using the same notes and color wheels.

FLOW:
Ways to Speed and Smooth

Freighting
Telescoping

≡ ||||

By the time we get out of first grade we can write, maybe with misspellings, "He throws the ball." But at six or seven years old we can say so much more than we can write:

> Bill, the guy who is always getting me in trouble and never listens to the teacher—but she always says 'He's trying'—and John, the guy who fed the rat to Kurt, the python at school, both got sick and started throwing up all over the floor, the desks, and Mr. Skumawitz, the new principal everyone calls Skoomie.

As adults we are afraid to write and use long sentences; but until we can *Flow*, we never have that complete repertoire that makes for energetic writing. Length-stunting probably stems from English teachers—weary from correcting length-related entanglements—discouraging students from long sentences, by red-inking them as *run-ons*. (The irony is that short sentences can be run-ons: *He ate the cake she ate the pie.*)

Despite our length apprehensions, some sentences *have to be long.* The sentence about Bill and John must be long in order to capture the characters, actions, and sub-thoughts that work together to describe an exhausting reality as fraught with sideshows as the actual event, all descriptive details we don't hesitate to include when we speak. The sentence amasses reality's *Flow*, recreating the elongated experience; short sentences would shatter the content, compromising if not losing the energy of the incident:

> Bill is always getting me in trouble. Bill never listens to the teacher. The teacher always says, "he's trying." Bill has a

friend John. John fed the rat to the school python. The python is called Kurt. Both Bill and John got sick.

Enough. You get the idea. *Freighting* and *Telescoping* are two visual methods to build *Flow* while avoiding grammatical mistakes. Eventually you will combine both methods to create a variety of voices that serve a multitude of purposes.

Freighting

Freighting offers a way to *Flow* by visualizing a simple sentence as flatbed freight cars, each one capable of having more similar material piled vertically on top of it. This material is then snapped onto the top of its appropriate freight load with commas (,) or, when the loads are long and complicated, with semicolons (;). For instance, in the simple sentence "Bill chewed a red apple," there are essentially four freight cars: "Bill," "chewed," "red," and "apple." *Freighting* requires the writer to look more and more carefully at the reality the sentence can describe.

Loading. Begin to lengthen by *loading*. Ask whether people other than Bill chewed the apple. If so, they are snapped on top of the "Bill" car:

> Bill, my aunt Tina, and all their cronies chewed a red apple.

Next, one looks more closely at the situation and asks if the apple was only chewed or whether it suffered any other fates and then snaps these actions on the "chew" car:

> Bill, my aunt Tina, and all their cronies chopped, chewed, and pulverized the red apple.

The writer never stops observing. Maybe the apples were not just red, and maybe more than apples filled the food trough. Using commas, the writer snaps more material on top of the "red" and "apple" cars. The final freight train could look like this:

> Bill, my aunt Tina, and all their cronies, chopped, chewed, and utterly pulverized the red, hard, juicy, candied apple and the

mud-brown, crumbling cookies, scatter-shot with chocolate chips.

Any phrases attached to the main sentence may also be viewed as freight cars. For example, if the sentence above opened with the phrase "While opening the door, Bill chewed a red apple," it might eventually read as follows:

> While opening the door, tiptoeing across the threshold, and wondering if his life had any future, Bill chewed the red apple.

The final question the writer asks is whether any of the one-word entries can grow into phrases or have phrases attached to them, adding even more information to the *Flow*. For instance, "Bill, my aunt Tina, and all their cronies" may weigh in as:

> Bill, whom you can count on to sniff out the best groceries; my aunt Tina, who is a freeloader; and all their cronies, who show up only when the larder is full . . .

Connecting. The *Flow* can grow. Sentence trains can be switched onto a second track which has its own train and, if the two trains are closely related in idea, they can be bolted together with *connecting* words such as "and," "but," "or," "besides," "because," and others, including the semicolon (;).

Kinks. *Freighting* is not an excuse to language-scribble in a million directions. All the items on the subject car must stay together and must share all the words on the verb car. The *Flow* will become inarticulate if the writer forgets which freight car is being stacked: if items that belong together separate, each subject item pulling its own verb off the verb car, the writer will create *run-on sentences* (Bill chewed the apple Tina pulverized the apple) or *comma splices* (Bill chewed the apple, Tina pulverized the apple). When these kinks occur in a long sentence, the sentence runs out of control and stops making sense.

English Teacherese. A less playful explanation of *Freighting,* by a grammar tyrant, might sound like this: A *freighted* sentence uses multiple subjects, and/or verbs, and/or objects (direct or indirect), where each of the multiple subjects or objects might be expanded with either a relative adverbial clause (where, when, why) or relative pronoun clause (who, whose, whom, that, which), participial phrase (the boy *eating* butter), and/or prepositional phrase *(in, under, above* the house), and/or the verbs might be expanded with an adverbial clause (*after* dinner). The sentence sometimes uses either a subordinating conjunction—usually adverbial (where, when, because)—or a coordinating conjunction (and, but, or, so) to connect with another independent clause that could be expanded like the first part of the sentence.

Your turn. Review the sentences below and make a case for how the subject matter is complemented by length. Then write ten *Freighting* sentences, each one six lines long, each one with a *connecting freight.* (See *connecting* above.) Use content, which benefits from the flowing form: your passions, complaints, interests, expertise, and reaction to films, books, music, and philosophical considerations.

Flows of Freighting:

I fought a migraine then, ignored the warnings it sent, went to school and after to work in spite of it, sat through lectures in Middle English and presentations to advertisers with involuntary tears running down the right side of my face, threw up in washrooms, stumbled home by instinct, emptied ice trays onto my bed and tried to freeze the pain in my right temple, wished only for a neurosurgeon who would do a lobotomy on house call, and cursed my imagination. (From *The White Album* by Joan Didion)

You can brick up your heart as stout and tight and hard and cold and impregnable as you possibly can and down it comes in an instant, felled by a woman's second glance, a child's apple breath, the shatter of glass in the road, the words, "I have something to tell you," a cat with a broken spine dragging itself into the forest to die, the brush of your mother's papery ancient hand in the thicket of your hair, the memory of your father's voice early in the morning echoing from the kitchen where he is making pancakes for his children. (From "Joyas Voladoras" by Brian Doyle in *The American Scholar*)

It wasn't unusual to see naked women hosing ice cream off their bodies in the kitchen pot sink (the Howard Stern event); sinister Moroccan food tasters packing heat (Royal Air Maroc party); Ted Kennedy in a kitchen walk-through eerily reminiscent of RFK's last moments; our drunken crew, in a hostile mood, bullying a lost Mike Myers into "doing that Wayne's World *Ex*-cel-lent thing," Rosie Perez hanging on the sauté end, fitting right in as if she worked with us, sitting on a cutting board, "What's good to eat in here, boys?"; clit-piercing on stage (Stern again); Madonna fans trying to sneak through the kitchen from the hotel (she brings her own eggs for Caesar salad); concerts, swimsuit models, hard-core hip-hoppers, go-go boys. (From "Sous-Chef" by Anthony Bourdain in *Kitchen Confidential*)

The members of my family, close and distant relations, have found themselves dispersed across the globe, along the rolling rivers of China, at the feet of its impassive mountains, centered in the din of Taiwan's cacophonous cities, radiated beneath the neon of Hong Kong, and outside of Asia altogether, across the great seas, near the steaming jungles of Brazil and Costa Rica, lost in the multitudes of New York City, walking the roads of North Carolina, and living in a two-story duplex, on a quiet cul-de-sac, in the suburb of Buena Park, California. Here I sit. (From "Personal Flow" by Gary Liu for a student assignment)

If, for example, you are working on a book, and it is not yet finished—it has not yet become an object separate from the process of its making—you may think to yourself, when somebody asks you to tell them about the book, that it would be best to avoid the question, that simply to speak the name of that which exists but does not yet exist, that whose existence has not yet been confirmed by its presence, could cause it to disappear, and so you change the subject or shrug and say things like, *I don't know, it's a book,* or, *it's about this and that,* and then you feel nervous and unclean for the rest of the day or night until you can sit down again and work and remember what it feels like and know that it is still there. (From "I'll Not Go On: The End of Javier Marías" by Eli S. Evans in *N+1*)

Academic encouragement, easy jesting, an affectionate epithet—all of what used to be the currency of good fellowship as well as teaching—have become cause for vigilance, fodder for complaint, the stuff of suits. One of the oddest developments in this story is that a movement such as campus feminism, which began with the aim of giving women more power—more faith in their own resources; greater enfranchisement, sexuality, and independence—has ended by infantilizing them to this extent, sensitizing them to slights they never felt, making them alternately ridiculous . . . and irrelevant (me) in their own sexual-harassment tales, and training them to see themselves as resourceless victims of resourceful men. It has ended by teaching them to run to their elders and fear the dark; to distrust male appreciation and demonize male attraction—to revert, in sum, into the shrinking, swooning, sex-spooked maidens we thought we'd left behind in a darker age. (From "The Higher Yearning: Bringing Eros Back to Academe" by Cristina Nehring in *Harper's Magazine*)

Then she looked around the Salon and made the encompassing shrug-and-pout-and-flex-your-hands-from-the-wrist French gesture that in that context meant that the apparent absurdity of the act of fanning yourself in the cold is no more absurd than the whole enterprise of traveling to Paris to look at clothes that you will never wear, displayed on models to whom you bear no resemblance, in order to help a designer get people who will never attend shows like this to someday buy a perfume or a scarf that will give them the consoling illusion that they have a vague association with the kind of people who do attend shows like this—even though the people who attend shows like this are the kind who fan themselves against July heat that happens not to exist. (From "Couture Shock" by Adam Gopnik in *The New Yorker*)

He [Robert Chapman, modern editor of *Roget's International Thesaurus*] transformed, altered, and caused the transmutation of the stuffy, dull, ill-ventilated compendium of synonyms and antonyms into a hip, cool, with-it collection of words and associations, not only piquing the intellects of language lovers but saving the behinds, fannies, and GPAs of countless late-night collegiate essay writers (see also Indolent, Slothful, Procrastinating). (From "A Thesaurist Leaves, Exits" by the editors in *The Los Angeles Times*)

So descended the Lem, weird unwieldy flying machine, vehicle on stilts and never before landed, craft with a range of shifting velocities more than comparable to the difference from a racing car down to an amphibious duck, a vehicle with huge variations in speed and handling as it slowed, a vehicle to be flown for the first time in the rapidly changing field of gravity, and one-sixth gravity had never been experienced before in anything but the crudest simulations, and mascons beneath, their location unknown, their effect on moon gravity considerable, angles of vision altering all the time and never near to perfect, the weight of the vehicle reducing drastically as the fuel was consumed, and with it all, the computer guiding them, allowing them to feel all the confidence a one-eyed man can put in a blind man going down a dark alley, and when, at the moment they could take over themselves to fly it manually, a range of choices already tried in simulation but never in reality would be open between full manual and full computer. (From *Of a Fire on the Moon* by Norman Mailer)

We are only now beginning to appreciate how strange and splendid it is, how it catches the breath, the loveliest object afloat around the sun, enclosed in its own blue bubble of atmosphere, manufacturing and breathing its own oxygen, fixing its own nitrogen from the air into its own soil, generating its own weather at the surface of its rain forests, constructing its own carapace from living parts: chalk cliffs, coral reefs, old fossils from earlier forms of life now covered by layers of new life meshed together around the globe, Troy upon Troy. (From "The Corner of the Eye" by Lewis Thomas in *Late Night Thoughts on Listening to Mahler's Ninth*)

In *The Seventh Seal*, film director Ingmar Bergman elucidates his complex concepts of God through Antonius, a knight who returns to his homeland questioning and searching for God anywhere, even in the eyes of a suspected witch, hoping that by seeing the Devil in her stare he will know God exists; Jon, Antonius's squire, an agnostic who is more occupied with living life in the moment and believes life is a mess; Joseph, who views his baby son and the baby Jesus as pure and remains hopeful and positive about the meaning of life; Jon's quiet housekeeper, who exhibits the blind, long-suffering faith of those who wait for this life to be "finished"; and finally Death, without whom even the most faithful would doubt the existence and purpose of God. (From "Critique of *The Seventh Seal*" by Christine Allcorn for a student assignment)

Telescoping

Telescoping is another *Flow* technique that stresses close observation by the writer. Unlike *Freighting*, a sentence envisioned as vertical stacks of material piled upon freight cars, the *Telescoping* sentence keeps extending, moving closer and closer to ideas in the previous clause. A writer who is *Freighting* may take the sentence "Billy Faulkner chewed a red apple" and *Flow* by asking who else chewed (more subjects), or what other actions were performed on the apple (more verbs), or what other objects beside the apple were acted upon (more objects). Yet, when *Telescoping* the writer replaces the period at the end of the sentence with a comma, thus beginning the *Flow*.

Zooming. The comma replacing the period works like a telephoto lens, signaling an upcoming *zoom*, a new clause generated by the material in the initial sentence. In this example, "Billy Faulkner chewed a red apple," the comma allows the writer to *zoom* up closer on any of the items mentioned, and provide more details about "Billy," or about "chewed," or about "apple." If the writer decides to *zoom* up on "apple," the sentence might read:

> Billy Faulkner chewed a red apple, the apple's skin marked with dark imperfections.

The sentence and clause seamlessly flow together without the use of a conjunction. The period ending this two-part sentence may also be replaced with a second comma, but now the writer may only *zoom* onto one of the details from the last phrase—"skin," "marked," "dark," or "imperfections." Since the sentence has *zoomed* up on the apple's skin, the writer cannot skip back and *zoom* onto details from the first part of the sentence; otherwise the sentence might have a *dangling modifier*. For instance, if the writer now skipped back, incorrectly having Billy in the lens for this *telescope*, the writer might *mistakenly* write this:

> Billy Faulkner chewed the red apple, the apple's skin marked with dark imperfections, his mouth missing several teeth.

The reader might think the skin turned into a surreal cartoon and grew a mouth of its own. By restricting the *zoom* to items in the very last clause, the writer might create the following *correct* sentence:

> Billy Faulkner chewed the red apple, the apple's skin marked with dark imperfections, the fruit's flaws representing attempts by worms to beat Billy to the apple's goodness.

In summary, the writer *Flows* like this: "Billy Faulkner chewed the red apple," (*zoom* up closer to the apple) "the apple's skin marked with dark imperfections," (*zoom* up closer to those imperfections) "the imperfections representing whatever." Incidentally, the "whatever" might have been something less physical than "attempts by worm," the writer substituting a metaphysical concept such as "representing the fact that nothing in life is perfect."

Panning. At this point, the writer could use a third comma, and a fifth, a fiftieth, so long as each *zoom* focuses on a detail from the previous clause. Most writers stop after only one or two *zooms*. If the sentence needs to contain more details, the writer would likely use a *connecting* word ("and," "but," "while," "since," "because," "when") to "*pan* over" or "pull back," interrupting the *zoom* and focusing on a newly introduced idea or revisiting an *unzoomed* subject from an earlier clause. In effect, the *panning* is a way to connect two sentences, creating one *compound* sentence. This new shot starts over with its own complete verb and *Telescopes*. Using "and" to *pan*, the writer could connect these two sentences:

> Billy Faulkner chewed the red apple, the apple's skin marked with dark imperfections, the imperfections representing the fact that nothing in life is perfect, and Aunt Tina ate prunes, each one carrying with it the hope that her days of constipation would soon be over, those days beginning to suggest that life was becoming very regular in its irregularity.

Closure. If the writer decides not to *pan* but instead has one *Telescoped* clause after another, finally ending, arbitrarily on a *Telescoped* clause, a rhythm of gradual dissipation takes over the sentence. Psychological *closure* is denied. If the effect is unwelcome, a writer has several options: One way to give *closure* is to move the original sentence with the complete verb to the end of the sentence:

> A red apple, the apple's skin marked with dark imperfections, the imperfections representing the fact that nothing in life is perfect, tempted Billy Faulkner.

A second solution is to end with a *connecting* word such as "which" or "that" and this phrase's own complete verb:

> Billy Faulkner chewed the red apple, the apple's skin marked with dark imperfections, the imperfections representing the fact that nothing in life is perfect, which was a sentiment Aunt Tina had expressed earlier in the day.

Finally a third approach is a very short *pan* (compound) ending:

> Billy Faulkner chewed the red apple, the apple's skin marked with dark imperfections, the imperfections representing the fact that nothing in life is perfect, yet Aunt Tina said she found a perfect peach.

Kinks. *Telescoping* sentences can bad-grammar your writing. If the *zoomed* parts are described with complete verbs, then the sentence becomes a *comma splice,* an error created by splicing together complete sentences with commas instead of separating with periods, semicolons, or *connecting* words. To avoid splices, make sure only one of the clauses is a complete sentence and all the phrases that *zoom* have incomplete verbs, or verbs omitted where possible. The sample sentence would be spliced if it were written like this:

> Billy Faulkner chewed the red apple, the apple's skin *was* marked with dark imperfections, the imperfections represent*ed* the fact that nothing in life is perfect.

Every section of the sentence can be disconnected with periods instead of commas and read separately because "was" turns "marked" into a complete verb and the "-ed" instead of "-ing" on "represent" makes that a complete verb. The sentence now has two comma splices so is grammatically incorrect. Always read each *zoom* phrase and make sure it cannot stand on its own as a complete sentence; if it can, revise the verb.

English Teacherese. As with *Freighting*, when it comes to explaining *Telescoping* from the technical perspective, forget it. Here's why the explanation would stop a student cold: The sentence has an independent clause (a structure that contains both a subject and predicate that can stand as a complete sentence) and several dependent clauses (structures containing both a subject and predicate that are unable to stand independently as sentences) and/or nominative absolutes (a modifier with a nonfinite verb, a verb form lacking a necessary auxiliary to denote tense, usually a present participle, which is a verb form using -ing or past participle, which is a verb form using -en or -ed), and the sentence connects these dependent clauses or nominative absolutes so as not to create misplaced or dangling modifiers. Some of the sentences use a subordinating conjunction—usually adverbial (where, when, because)—or a coordinating conjunction (and, but, or, so) to connect with another independent clause and dependent clauses constructed the same way as the first part of the sentence.

Your turn. For each of the sentences below, follow each scope, noting what idea or description is being enhanced by the next phrase. *Telescope* five important scenes today.

Sightings with Telescoping:

A two-day storm has scrubbed the sky clean of haze and left the orchard bare, dead leaves spread in soggy puddles of russet and yellow at the trees' feet like vender's ware. (From "Seeing in the Dark" by Timothy Ferris in *The New Yorker*)

The power of the mound is at least sexual, the arched back of earth rising in desire here to as much of the sky as the mountains ever have to offer, announcing itself when we are in its presence as the center of all, the long grassy meadow strewn about it in the droopy shapes of detumescence. (From "Nacoochee Indian Mound: Helen, Georgia" by Steven Harvey in *In Short, A Collection of Brief Nonfiction*)

Marriage is so unrealistically depicted in the minds of naïve people, the dreamers believing that taking life-long vows will reap eternal bliss, this bliss lasting, at most, a few years, soon giving way to the many trials that face all couples, these unsuspecting couples inevitably mistaking commonplace difficulties for the loss of love, this erred thought bringing on further discontent and eventual destruction of the relationship; therefore, I find it crucial that people realize that marriage needs to be constantly worked on together. ("Who Am I?" by Nisleen Montrivisai for student assignment)

People sidle toward [suicidal] death, intent upon outwitting their own bodies' defenses, or they may dramatize the chance to make one last, unambiguous, irrevocable decision, like a captain scuttling his ship—death before dishonor—leaping toward oblivion through a curtain of pain, like a frog going down the throat of a snake. (From "Heaven and Nature" by Edward Hoagland in *Harper's Magazine*)

The minimalist tendency to offer the anguished facts and allow the seeker to supply the emotional caption is culminated in a stark and dark modern monument, the Vietnam Veterans Memorial, a black wall furnished with no rhetoric, simply the names and dates, row on row, achieving, below ground level, the monitory and pathetic impact of that archaic epitaph on a Greek cliff top: When my ship sank, the others sailed on. (From "Why Stop" by Mary Hood in *The Gettysburg Review*)

The Grimm Brothers' "The Frog Prince" uses a frog as analogous to someone offering a helping hand and expecting a reward of companionship in return, the princess offering this reward reluctantly, a debt of gratitude she fulfills only because her father orders her to, the princess taking the frog onto her table and sharing her meal with him, the frog afterwards requesting to be taken into her bed, but the princess finally throws the frog at a wall, this action breaking a curse on the frog, the act, a symbolic smashing of the frog's ego, an ego that made him appear ugly, his appearance now changing to a noble, handsome prince who is suitable for love. (From "Wishes and Nightmares" by Andy Stuart for Critical Thinking About Literature)

Is man at heart any different from the spider, I wonder: man thoughts, as limited as spider thoughts, contemplating now the nearest star with the threat of bringing with him the fungus rot from earth, wars, violence, the burden of a population he refuses to control, cherishing again his dream of the Adamic Eden he had pursued and lost in the green forest of America. (From "The Hidden Teacher" by Loren Eisely in *The Unexpected Universe*)

With a snubby, rust-covered oyster knife, he popped the thing open and handed it to me, everyone watching now, my little brother shrinking away from this glistening, vaguely sexual-looking object, still dripping and nearly alive. (From "Food Is Good" by Anthony Bourdain in *Kitchen Confidential*)

The feeling of standing there on that border—a border that had been raided four times, resulting in the deaths of many more people than even the large number reported by the press—in the darkness, the bullets crashing into my shirt, bursting through my back with a fist-sized lump of flesh and clotted blood, my body dropping into the sand by the light of a fizzing lantern, the men standing over me and firing into my inert body, my head broken open . . . It was unbearable. (From *Sunrise with Seamonsters: Travels and Discoveries* by Paul Theroux)

The American settlers' version of creationism in Genesis is fraught with choreographed temptation of the forbidden fruit, temptation giving way to knowledge, wisdom blooming into history-altering shame stemming from creative use of fig leaves, that shame breaking over stories such as one by the Cherokee, a myth acknowledging mankind's naiveté about who created the earth, this unknown creator fastening the earth "to the sky with four cords," threads symbolizing the earth's vulnerability; while both Christian and native American stories were acceptable to ready-to-make-peace Indians, Christians were compelled to dismiss native beliefs, the missionary in Ben Franklin's "The Savages of North American" declaring the native American myths "fable, fiction, and falsehood," insults instead of icebreakers. (From "America Anew" by Tara Vavere for American Literature Before 1900)

Seeing the radiating minerals is a beautiful visual experience, which is even more fascinating when integrated with our knowledge of nature's submicroscopic happenings, high-energy ultraviolet photons impinging on the surface of the minerals, causing the excitation of atoms in the mineral structure. . . . (From *Conceptual Physics* by Paul G. Hewitt)

The entire genius of evolution had gone into crafting *asva*, as it was called in Sanskrit, this verb made flesh, this thing whose every atom wanted to run, from the giant nostrils, drawing huge drafts of air into the cavernous heart and lungs, to its long powerful hindquarters. (From "Horseman, Pass By" by John Jeremiah Sullivan in *Harper's Magazine*)

PAUSE:
Ways to Slow and Emphasize

Very Short Sentences
Melted-together Words
Hieroglyphics
Super-literalism

△ △ △ △

Being able to flow, smoothing together details and implications that belong together to accurately depict reality, works best when *Flow* has brakes. Effective writers know how to pause in order to emphasize or dramatize special thoughts that otherwise would blend into larger language clusters. *Pause* may occur after *Flow*, or in the middle of *Flow*. *Pause* tools might seem easier to learn than *Flow* techniques, but they are best appreciated after mastering *Flow* because *Flow* provides a backdrop for *Pause*. There are many ways to create *Pause*. The following four essential techniques all possess an important visual dimension that quickly heightens a reader's consciousness. All strong writers, whether they are business, scientific, fiction, academic, or media writers, make some use of the following *Pause* techniques.

Very Short Sentence

The two-to-five-word sentence is something we learn to write in the first grade. Later, we vaporize it. Maybe we abandon it because we associate longer sentences with having more mature, sophisticated ideas, or perhaps by college we feel pressured to run together masses of details from textbooks and lecture notes. When a *Very Short Sentence* does appear in an essay, it takes us by surprise. A reader pauses. While composing a *Very Short Sentence* (*VSS*) requires only a modicum of grammatical expertise, there are considerations for maximizing dramatic effect.

Zen. Since there are so few parts in the sentence, each word carries more weight than in a long sentence. In addition to choosing a word based on meaning, a writer test-drives the word's consonants and vowels to see how they will ride in a reader's mouth. The combination of sound and context of each determines the pausing quality of the *Very Short Sentence,* creating a variety of effects: It can reinforce a revelation or it can communicate expectation, sarcasm, certitude, edginess, shock, hopefulness, or finality. Consider the difference in the following *Very Short Sentences:* one sharp, edgy, and shocking, (and elliptical), the other affirmative and certain:

> William, my aunt Tina, and all their cronies ate clam pudding, pork soufflé, and apple pizza, chased by a corn-dog shake. It was a barf buffet.

> William, my aunt Tina, and all their cronies ate clam pudding, pork soufflé, and apple pizza, chased by a corn-dog shake. This was extraordinary chow.

Geography. A writer must explore all options when positioning the *VSS* inside a paragraph, pitching it where it will offer the most dramatic pause—at the beginning, end, or smack in the middle of the paragraph. Surrounded by stubby, medium-length sentences, a *VSS* recedes into the rest of the text; however, when bordered by a long *Freighting* or *Telescoping* sentence, the *VSS* pops off the page. Notice how the meaning of the information changes when the *VSSs* above are positioned at the beginning of the flow, emphasizing negative expectation in the first set and positive anticipation in the second set:

> It sucked. Billy, my aunt Tina, and all their cronies ate the apple.

> You'd have loved it. Billy, my aunt Tina, and all their cronies ate the apple.

Rebels. Often professional writers will purposefully commit a grammatical error known as a *sentence fragment.* Breaking rules is justified when the end product is stunning. A tailored, poised *Very Short Sentence* fragment will not be mistaken for ignorance of sentence-boundary rules. Note the effect of stringing together *VSSs*, one a fragmented short sentence, to sputter the information to a gasping halt:

> Billy, my aunt Tina, and all their cronies ate the apple. Not a good thing. Unless you like gas.

Flashes of Very Short Sentences:

In the Amazon, on the other hand, should you have had too much to drink, say, and inadvertently urinate as you swim, any homeless candiru, attracted by the smell, will take you for a big fish and swim excitedly up your stream of uric acid, enter your urethra like a worm into its burrow, and, raising its gill cover, stick out a set of retrose spines. Nothing can be done. The pain, apparently, is spectacular. (From "Amazon Adventure" by Redmond O'Hanlon in *Granata*)

If you are a member of an average American college-grad household, you are richer than 99.9 percent of the human beings who have ever lived. You are stinking rich. (From "Why the U.S. Will Always Be Rich" by David Brooks in *The New York Times Magazine*)

My Filipino family is one that celebrates its unique culinary culture by indulging in such tasteful delicacies: chopped pork snout simmered in the dark blood of a pig (also popularly referred to as *Vampire Stew*); oxtail and tripe soaked in diluted peanut butter sauce; broiled cow tongue drizzled with countless seasonings; pig's feet marinated in vinegar and topped off with banana leaves; and of course the ever-so-famous half-developed chicken egg which comes fully loaded with eyes, a beak and feathers. I like rice. (From "Flow About Me" for a freshman composition assignment by Bryan Malinis)

I hate hope. It was hammered into me constantly a few years ago when I was being treated for breast cancer: Think positively! Don't lose hope! Wear your pink ribbon with pride! A couple of years later, I was alarmed to discover that the facility where I received my follow-up care was called the Hope Center. Hope? What about a *cure?* At antiwar and labor rallies over the years, I have dutifully joined Jesse Jackson in chanting "Keep hope alive!"—all the while crossing my fingers and thinking, "Fuck hope. Keep us alive." (From "Pathologies of Hope" by Barbara Ehrenreich in *Harper's Magazine*)

David Pimentel, an expert on food and energy at Cornell University, has estimated that if all the world ate the way the United States eats, humanity would exhaust all known global fossil-fuel reserves in just over seven years. Pimentel has his detractors. Some have accused him of being off on other calculations by as much as 30 percent. Fine. Make it ten years. (From "The Oil We Eat" by Richard Manning for *Harper's Magazine*)

In the Koran, Allah asks, "The heaven and the earth and all in between, thinkest thou I made them in jest?" It's a good question. (From *Pilgrim at Tinker Creek* by Annie Dillard)

Camouflaged toilet paper is a must for the modern hunter, along with his Bronco and his beer. Too many hunters taking a dump in the woods with their roll of Charmin beside them were mistaken for white-tailed deer and shot. Hunters get excited. (From "The Killing Game" by Joy Williams in *Esquire*)

All the same, if a cure were found, would I take it? In a minute. I may be a cripple, but I'm only occasionally a loony and never a saint. Anyway, in my brand of theology God doesn't give bonus points for a limp. I'd take a cure; I just don't need one. A friend who also has MS startled me once by asking, "Do you ever say to yourself, 'Why me, Lord?'" "No Michael, I don't," I told him, "because whenever I try, the only response I can think of is 'Why not?'" If I could make a cosmic deal, who would I put in my place? What in my life would I give up in exchange for sound limbs and a thrilling rush of energy? No one. Nothing. I might as well do the job myself. Now that I'm getting the hang of it. (From "On Being a Cripple" by Nancy Mairs in *Plaintext: Deciphering a Woman's Life*)

Your time of decay may be distant, but it will surely come, for even the White Man whose God walked and talked with him as friend with friend, cannot be exempt from the common destiny. We may be brothers after all. We will see. (From "Reply to Governor Stevens" by Chief Seattle, translated by Henry A. Smith)

I have neither heard nor read that a Santa Ana [wind] is due, but I know it, and almost everyone I have seen today knows is too. We know it because we feel it. The baby frets. The maid sulks. I rekindle a waning argument with the telephone company, then cut my losses and lie down, given over to whatever it is in the air. (From *Slouching Towards Bethlehem* by Joan Didion)

It's all in the ears. When Mickey Mouse was born in 1927, the world of early cartoon animation was filled with two-legged zoomorphic humanoids, whose strange half-black faces were distinguished one from another chiefly by the ears. (From "The Mystery of Mickey Mouse" by John Updike in *Arts and Antiques*)

The man [Saddam Hussein] was undoubtedly a villain, a brutal psychopath who murdered children and poisoned village wells, stored biological weapons in hospitals, subjected his enemies to unspeakable torture, and imprisoned his friends in the cages of perpetual fear. Not a nice fellow. (From "The Road to Babylon" by Lewis Lapham in *Harper's Magazine*)

Melted-together Words

By melting together a group of words with hyphens, a writer can produce a new word. For instance, the words "blue" and "green" denote two different colors but when they are melted with a hyphen into "blue-green" they create a new word and a new color. Students are rarely taught to snap together their own original *Melted-together Words,* but all professional writers know the value of using this tool for imparting playful *Pause.* Because of their uniqueness, cleverness, and heavy content load, *Melted-together Words* (*MTWs*) slow a sentence's flow and focus attention on their content. The more original they are, the more they become show-stoppers, spotlighting material that might otherwise blend away into the cast of lackluster clauses and redundant sentences, as in the following:

> Aunt Tina made the candy apples. Bill chewed the red apple, which had been candied the night before.

In editing for *Pause*, the writer melts a phrase from the first sentence and the essential information from the second sentence to produce two new adjectives:

> Bill chewed the red, candied-the-night-before, made-by-Aunt-Tina apples.

By combining the two sentences and transforming the "which" phrase into a *Melted-together Word*, the descriptive information about the apples begins to resonate in the reader's mind.

Kinks. *Melted-together Words* can be tricky to craft, initially. Note that in the sentence above there is not a hyphen after "red" because any adjective that modifies "apples" on its own cannot be melted into the other newly melted words. For the same reason, no hyphen is used to join the two *Melted-together Words* into one big one; each operates as a separate adjective, describing "apples." Also, there is not a hyphen after "Tina" because "apples" is the noun that all three adjectives modify. Finally, *MTWs* can only function where word pairs or clauses have been transformed into a single word and where the new word has changed its form and shifted its place in the sentence; *MTWs* cannot function by simply hyphenating existing word pairs or sequences within a sentence, as in the following: "Bill chewed the candied apple which-had-been-made-the-night-before."

More Kinks. A confident writer does not surround *MTWs* ("candied-the-night-before") with quotation marks, a guilt-ridden, I-know-this-word-does-not-really-exist signal to the reader, unless the writer is intentionally drawing attention to the *MTW* as an overused expression or thought:

> Aunt Tina always chimes in with her "an-apple-a-day-keeps-the-doctor-away" dime-store maxims.

However, drawing attention to a cliché by transforming it into a *MTW* is different from using clichéd *MTWs*—a phrase that has already lost its *Pause* power: Tina has an in-your-face attitude. Clichéd *Melted-together Words* are quickly chewed up and spit out by the reader's brain and thus have no dramatic potential.

Dazzles with Melted-together Words:

[Dickerson, a black woman and Harvard graduate, is describing the person who shot her nephew for no apparent reason.] . . . a brother did it. A non-job-having, middle-of-the-day malt-liquor-drinking, crotch-clutching, loud-talking brother with many neglected children born of many forgotten women. (From "Who Shot Johnny?" by Debra Dickerson in *The New Republic*)

In the internship year, we came very close to a divorce. Your basic doctor-in-training-meets-gorgeous-nurse-and-wants-to-leave-his-wife-and-small-baby story. (From "A Portrait of the Puttana as a Middle-Aged Woolf Scholar" by Louise De Salvo in *Between Women*)

This is not to say that all penises are, according to Pound's dictum, moral. Indeed, a gratuitously shocking penis, an extraneous-to-our-story penis, a hey-look-at-me-for-the-sake-of-nothing-but-me penis, however imposing, is literally immoral (that is, incompetent), because by jarring the reader from the narrative or argumentative flow into a mood of "What's this stupid penis doing here?" the author has undermined the greatest truth of this tale: i.e. our ability to immerse ourselves in it. (From "Toxins in the Mother Tongue" by David Duncan in *The Los Angeles Times Magazine*)

The dominant fiction projected by commercial society is that you can gratify yourself at no cost except to your wallet or your pocketbook, and *Sex and the City* has taken that illusion for reality. The show sublimates actual sex into ideal sex-in-an-emotional-vacuum in the same way that sitcoms from the 1950s sublimated actual family relations into ideal family relations. *Sex and the City* is *Leave It to Beaver* after dark. (From "Relationshipism: Who is Carrie Bradshaw Really Dating?" by Lee Siegel in *The New Republic*)

The hate group that started this whole mess—Orange Unified's board of trustees, which banned the Gay-Straight Alliance from campus in December, only to have a federal court later reverse that—continued its take-away-all-our-marbles-and-go-home-if-we-don't-get-our-way fit by banning all nonacademic campus clubs on February 10. (From "A Clockwork Orange" by Matt Coker in *The Orange County Weekly*)

The case that gave rise to the "Fire!"-in-a-crowded-theater analogy, Schenck v. United States, involved the prosecution of Charles Schenck . . . attempting to cause insubordination among soldiers who had been drafted to fight in the First World War . . . urging draftees not to "submit to intimidation" . . . (From "Shouting 'Fire!'" by Alan Dershowitz in *The Atlantic*)

Atheists aren't by nature of one mind. There's a godless organization for every wrinkle of nonbelief—the prayer-never-hurt-anyone, live-and-let-live atheists; the prove-the-God-fearing-world-wrong, keep-America-secular atheists; and the contrarian, I-don't-believe-in-God-but-don't-call-me-an-atheist's atheist. (From "A Time of Doubt for Atheists" by Gina Piccalo for *The Los Angeles Times*)

I stood in awe as the lady from behind the counter casually went into a how-to-tell-if-a-vibrator-is-good-for-you speech. Before the eyes of three other people, including a man, she used me as her mannequin, first gently and then roughly, demonstrating on my pelvic area the pros and cons of each vibrator. (From "Betty and Celina Get Wired: Part I" by Betty Boob in *The Bust Guide to the New Girl Order*)

Hieroglyphics

Powerful writing relies on *Hieroglyphics*. These signals establish the subtle relationships between details and ideas in an essay by inflecting tone. Most people know a comma slows a flow with a soft, slightly breath-catching pause and a period abruptly ends the flow. But between the comma and the period an essayist can choose from an array of visual gestures which modulate *Pause* and help the reader to interpret the writer's music: The semicolon (;), the colon (:) or single dash (—), parentheses ( ) and dash skewer (—internal clause—). There are many rules of usage for these punctuation tools; the *Hieroglyphics* in this chapter focus on the tone-inflecting punctuation.

Semicolon. The *semicolon* (;) can be used to create punctuated *Pause* between two closely related sentences, replacing the less emphatic connector words such as "for," "and," "nor," "but," "or," "yet," "so," (FANBOYS). Two complete sentences can be smoothly combined with a conjunction and a comma:

> Bill and his cronies ate the apple, but Tina refused even a single bite.

However, when a writer swaps the conjunction for a *semicolon*, the same words communicate a different meaning:

> William chewed an apple; Tina refused even a single bite.

The *semicolon* sharpens the *Pause* with a wait-until-you-see-what-aunt-Tina-did anticipation, subtly suggesting her more satisfying experience. Assuming a sensitive reader, a tenor who reads the music of punctuation notes, the writer considers the tone and attitude of the sentence and the essay in opting to switch out the connecting word for a *semicolon*.

Semicolons occasionally replace commas, but not just any commas, usually just those that separate items in a series. *Semicolons* are particularly useful in *Freighting* sentences where commas— already being used to modify the different items on the freight car—easily become mixed up with those commas being used to separate all the items on the freight car, confusing the reader as to where the modifying phrase stops and a new item in the freight begins. For instance, imagine how confusing it could be to read the following sentence if commas, which would still have been grammatically correct, were used instead of the *semicolons*. With a comma after "story," for a split second the reader might think the story is about Aunt Tina:

> Several people ate the red apple: William, a person whom you can always count on for a good story; my aunt Tina, a tiresome smart-ass who thinks she knows more than she does, a person who has learned very little from everything she has suffered; and their three best cronies, all patient and tolerant friends with many problems of their own.

Colon and Single Dash. Though the *colon* may look similar to the *semicolon*, the *colon* is more closely related to the *single dash*. In fact, *colons* (:) and *dashes* (—) perform the *exact* same *Pause*-creating functions. Either punctuation mark is used to connect a second part to the first sentence. The second part can be another complete sentence, a clause, sentence fragment, or a list. *Colons* and *single dashes* act as stand-ins for expressions that set up examples, replacing phrases such as "such as," or "for instance," or "for example," or "as follows." Notice the abrupt pause created by substituting a *colon* in place of "for example" in the following sentence:

> William, my aunt Tina, and all their cronies ate some very strange food: clam pudding, pork soufflé, and apple pizza, chased by a corn-dog shake.

In the first example, the *colon* gives emphasis to the general statement about who ate what kind of food so that this statement does not get de-emphasized in a long sentence where the examples could overwhelm the reader's attention.

A more dramatic purpose for *colons* and *single dashes*, however, is to launch a clever or metaphorical restatement, to deliver a pert summation or a shrewd elaboration, or to dispatch a sardonic observation, an aside commenting on the first part of the sentence as in the following example:

> William, my aunt Tina, and all their cronies ate clam pudding, pork soufflé, apple pizza, chased by a corn-dog shake: a barf buffet.

The *colon* and attached commentary emphasize the list of unusual fare. Since there is an abrupt stop with the *colon* (instead of the blend that would be created with "for example"), what follows the *colon* gets read with more snap. Both sentences can be written with *single dashes* to produce the same effect. *Colons* and *dashes* are interchangeable, but many writers make a subtle distinction in their usage: *Dashes* are casual and make writing more conversational; *colons* are more polished, more academic, and subtler.

Dash Skewer and Parentheses. A *dash skewer*—two *dashes* used to enclose an internal clause—is a versatile *hieroglyph*. With the post-modernist's preoccupation for subtext—ideas that are implied below the surface of the text—and with the writer's impulse to pay closer attention to information a reader might mistakenly consider mundane, beside the point, or non-crucial, writers need to signal readers they are entering a parallel reality without totally exiting the surface one.

A writer's first instinct might be to use a set of commas to enclose an internal or interrupting clause or a parenthetical statement within a sentence:

> William, my aunt Tina, and their cronies, avowed carnivores who adamantly avoid fructose, chewed the red apple.

Using a set of commas to enclose the internal clause, the writer blends together the surface information and the subtext material. The information inside and outside the commas is read and regarded as of equal importance. However, the writer who wishes to de-emphasize the internal clause (or treat the clause as a secret revealed) might choose to lower the volume with a set of *parentheses*:

> William, my aunt Tina, and their cronies (avowed carnivores who adamantly avoid fructose) chewed the red apple.

By choosing *parentheses*, the writer indicates that the internal clause is less important, that the information is a digression from the main point of the sentence, or that a secret is being divulged. (Also, sometimes *parentheses* are used to whisper sideline comments as in the Kusz example below.) But, a writer who wants to create the opposite effect—emphasizing the parenthetical statement—will employ the *dash skewer*.

> William, my aunt Tina, and their cronies—avowed carnivores who adamantly avoid fructose—chewed the red apple.

Here the internal clause, *skewered* by *dashes*, is forcefully raised to the surface, getting at least as much, if not more attention as the main sentence, stressing the contrast between the information within the *dashes* and that which surrounds the punctuation, thus communicating irony.

With all three enclosures, a sentence is begun, then temporarily suspended by the delivery of an internal clause, and after the interruption, the main sentence is finally completed. A writer can test the grammatical integrity of the *dash skewer* by temporarily omitting the enclosed comment to make sure that what is left forms a complete sentence. Use *dash skewers* to suspend or interrupt a sentence, but avoid using the *dash skewer* to join three separate and complete sentences:

> William and my aunt Tina, have many cronies—they are

avowed carnivores and adamantly avoid fructose—but they all chewed the red apple.

Music of Hieroglyphics:

In an amazing miscalculation, we seem to have thought that God was a sort of Aladdin's genie: If you rub him the right way, he will make more fish after we've sieved out the ocean; more topsoil if we've stripped it off and paved it over; more drinking water as we siphon dry the aquifers. Manlike, he will respond to pious stroking, and if the poles melt and the oceans brim, he'll throw us a rope, build us an ark. (From "That Sense of Falling" by Edward Hoagland in *Preservation*)

The clichés of earlier love poetry—bleeding hearts, cheeks like roses, and lips like cherries, Cupid shooting the arrows of love— appear in Donne's poetry only to be mocked, or in some ingenious transmutation. The tears which flow in "A Valediction: Of Weeping" are different from, and more complex than, the ordinary saline fluid of unhappy lovers; they are ciphers, naughts, symbols of the world's emptiness with the beloved; or else, suddenly reflecting her image, they are globes, worlds, they contain the sum of things. (From "John Donne" by Robert Adams and George Logan in *The Norton Anthology of English Literature*)

Im Kaleem was not a true prostitute, however, because she did not charge for her services—not even for the coffee and tea (and, occasionally, the strong liquor called arrack) that she served the men. . . . Im Kaleem was no slut either—unlike some women in the village—because she loved all the men she entertained, and they loved her, every one of them. In a way, she was married to all the men in the village. Everybody knew it—the wives knew it; the itinerant Catholic priest knew it; the Presbyterian minister knew it—but nobody objected. Actually I suspect the women (my mother included) did not mind their husbands' visits to Im Kaleem. (From "The Telephone" by Anwar F. Accawi in *The Boy from the Tower of the Moon*)

A first-time visitor to any college campus can easily differentiate between tenured and nontenured faculty by keeping in mind a learning institution's two main expectations: (1) that a young professor will spend her first several years on the job proving herself indispensable (sucking up), working to advance the interests of the college (sucking up), and making a name for herself in her field of study (sucking up); and (2) that a senior, tenured professor, having achieved indispensability . . . will thereafter lend her widely recognized name to the school's public relations office, which will use that name to attract prospective new students and faculty, who will in turn be encouraged to call on senior professors for the purpose of asking deep, scholarly questions (sucking up). (From "Ring Leader" by Natalie Kusz in *Allure* magazine)

As borders crumble and cultures mingle, more and more of us are becoming hyphenated. I, perhaps, am an increasingly typical example: entirely Indian by blood, yet unable to speak a word of any Indian language; a British citizen, born and educated in England, yet never having really worked or lived in the country of my birth; an American permanent resident who has made his home for two thirds of his life in America, in part because it feels so little like home; and a would-be resident of Japan. (From "The Contagion of Innocence" by Pico Iyer in *New Perspectives Quarterly*)

To begin with, I am honest; she is not. Or, to spare her a moral lecture (But why should I? What has she ever spared *me?*), let me put it that she is a fantasist and I am not. (From "The Break" by Cynthia Ozick in *Antaeus*)

Two animal populations can look quite different from each other –Great Danes and Chihuahuas, for instance—yet remain closely related genetically. Or they can look very much alike—the orangutans from Borneo and those from Sumatra are a good example—even though they diverged from the same ancestral stocks many thousands or even millions of years ago. (From "Gorilla Warfare" by Craig Sanford in *The Sciences*)

In a world of canned dog food, a smooth consistency is a sign of low quality—lots of cereal. A lumpy, frightening, bloody, stringy horror is a sign of high quality—lots of meat. (From "No Wonder They Call Me a Bitch" by Ann Hodgman in *Spy*)

Bingham [a professional photographer] subsequently became [Muhammad Ali's] closest male friend and has photographed every aspect of Ali's life: his rise and fall three times as the heavyweight champion; his three-year expulsion from boxing, beginning in 1967, for refusing to serve in the American military during the Vietnam War ("I ain't got no quarrel with them Vietcong"); his four marriages; his fatherhood of nine children (one adopted, two out of wedlock); his endless public appearances in all parts of the world—Germany, England, Egypt (sailing on the Nile with a son of Elijah Muhammad's), Sweden, Libya, Pakistan (hugging refugees from Afghanistan), Japan, Indonesia, Ghana (wearing a dashiki and posing with President Kwame Nkrumah), Zaire (beating George Forman), Manila (beating Joe Frazier) . . . and now, on the final night of his 1996 visit to Cuba, he is en route to a social encounter with an aging contender [Fidel Castro] he has long admired—one who has survived at the top for nearly forty years despite the ill will of nine American presidents, the CIA, the Mafia, and various militant Cuban Americans. (From "Ali in Havana" by Gay Talese in *Esquire*)

The strange lies were mine. All the attacks, the hateful rhetoric, the dark alliances and strange conspiracies, an eye for an eye, nuts and sluts, defending Pinochet, throwing grenades, carpet bombing the White House, Bob Bork, Bob Tyrell, Bob Dornan, Bob Barley, Bob Barr—it all led right here: I lost my soul. (From *Blinded by the Right: the Conscience of an Ex-Conservative* by David Brock)

The pursuit of a theory of everything and a viable quantum theory of gravity is predicated on a simple fact: Extrapolations from experimental data imply that at a scale of energy known as the Planck scale—some eighteen orders of magnitude beyond what even the most powerful particle accelerators can generate— the gravitational force of the universe at large and the two forces of the microscopic universe, known as the electroweak force and the strong force, would be equally strong and potentially indistinguishable. (From "String Theorists Find a Rosetta Stone" by Gary Taubes in *Science*)

And in that unforgettably sweet moment in my personal history [as a young boy agreeing to eat an oyster], that one moment still more alive for me than so many of the other "firsts" that followed—first pussy, first joint, first day in high school, first published book or any other thing—I attained glory. (From "Food Is Good" by Anthony Bourdain in *Kitchen Confidential*)

I am probably better informed about Indian life than most Americans ever thought of being, but not informed enough for a thoughtful reader and writer. My resistance has taken the form of a mixture of pride and contempt: pride that I already know more than these books can tell me, and contempt for the white liberal intellectual's romance with all things Indian. . . . Whatever my romantic notions were about the ideal forms of American Indian wisdom—closeness to the land, respect for other living creatures, a sense of harmony with the natural cycles, a way of walking lightly in the world, a manner of living that could make the ordinary and profane into the sacred—I learned that on the reservation I was inhabiting a world that was contrary to all these values. (From "Wounded Chevy at Wounded Knee" by Diana Hume George in *The Missouri Review* 1990)

Super-literalism

Reducing words or phrases to their most taken-for-granted elements is a powerful *Pause* technique. To do it, writers will treat a simple word like "apple" as if it were abstract terminology, shocking the reader by reducing the word to an even more down-to-earth reality. In the sentence, "Bill, my aunt Tina, and all their cronies chewed the red apples" the word "apples" does not draw any special attention. However, when the writer becomes super-literal, substituting "apples" with words that pin point what apples really are, the reader is caught off guard and has to pause and rethink reality. Here's an example: "Guillermo, my aunt Tina, and all their cronies chewed the *shiny red seed pods.*"

Super-literalism is not metaphor: It does not compare unlike things. Describing apples as red blimps is metaphoric, not literal. *Super-literalism* is a counter to euphemistic language (see the *Scrub* section), which attempts to make reality more pleasing or politically correct. By reminding us of the vulnerable, simpler, animalistic or manufactured core that is hidden by numbing, common words, *Super-literalism* can shake up our worldview. When interjected into an essay with an abstract, intellectual, or a sophisticated tone, *Super-literalism* abruptly rubs the reader's nose down into the authentic world.

Since *Super-literalism* is a powerful stun tool, it needs to be used sparingly to be effective. When a writer knows it is a tool, all language comes under playful scrutiny and so overall expression becomes clearer. This is a tool that can add much clarity, honesty, irony, and humor, but is rarely discussed by English teachers.

Your turn. Rewrite the following examples *without Super-literalism* and then write two sentences with your own *Super-literalism*.

Shocks with Super-literalism:

I belong to a Clan of One-Breasted Women. My mother, my grandmothers, and six aunts have all had mastectomies. Seven are dead. The two who survive have just completed rounds of chemotherapy and radiation.

I've had my own problems: two biopsies for breast cancer and a small tumor between my ribs diagnosed as "borderline malignancy." (From *Refuge* by Terry Tempest Williams)

Swims-carrying-stick: beaver; lump-raiser: mosquito; long-claws: grizzly bear; bird-who-carries-mud-in-mouth: swallow; bird-who-vexes-air: humming bird. (From "Lakota language glossary" by Ruth Bebe Hill in *Hanta Yo*)

A farm field appropriates that energy [built up layers of topsoil made of dead organic matter], puts it into seeds we can eat. Much of the energy moves from the earth to the rings of fat around our necks and waists. (From "The Oil We Eat" by Richard Manning for *Harper's Magazine*)

At the very least, I believe in two [extremes] that were articulated some years ago by the theologian Paul Tillich, those being "the absolute concreteness of every situation in which a moral decision is required" and "the command not to treat a person as a thing." Presumably, the latter of these would preclude vitalizing the body of a vegetative person (of which there are at least 15,000 in this country at any given time) by plugging him into a wall like a Mr. Coffee machine . . . (From "Life Everlasting: The religious right and the right to die" by Garret Keizer in *Harper's Magazine*)

As Aristotle put it, the beginning of philosophy is wonder. I am simply amazed to find myself living on a ball of rock that swings around an immense spherical fire. . . . But what really gets me is that almost all the substance of the substance of this maze [of life], aside from water, was once other living bodies—the bodies of animals and plants—and that I had to obtain it by murder . . . . I exist solely through membership in this perfectly weird arrangement of beings that flourish by chewing each other up. (From "Murder in the Kitchen" by Alan Watts in *Does it Matter?*)

For at least 100 years, the rendering industry has been converting dead animals into food supplements for livestock, but the advent of high-milk-yielding cattle and rBGH has increased the demand for this animal protein in cow fodder. Cows have been turned into carnivores, even cannibals. (From "Unethical Contexts for Ethical Questions" by David Ehrenfeld in a lecture at Yale University)

From the standpoint of reproduction, the male body is a delivery system, as the female is a mazy device for retention. Once delivery is made, men feel a faint but distinct falling-off of interest. Yet against the enduring female heroics of birth and nurture should be set the male's superhuman frenzy to deliver his goods: he vaults walls, skips sleep, risks wallet, health, and his political future all to ram home his seed into the gut of the chosen woman. (From "The Disposable Rocket" by John Updike in *Michigan Quarterly Review*)

I am eating what I love: the unendurable places, the bone-stuff, the ground. The same electrolytes that dance their vital dance in my blood—sodium, calcium, potassium, carbonate, chloride—are there in the evaporates at the fringe of desert marshes and ephemeral lakes: sulfates, carbonates, and chlorides crystallized on basin rims as white residues as though boiled dry. . . . Our body fluids contain 0.9 percent salt, nowadays, very likely the exact salinity of whatever ancient sea we managed to crawl out of, a sea we could leave because we had learned, first of all, to contain it. (From "Salt" by Diana Kappel-Smith in *Orion*)

A wavering heat, which the bomber pilots said they had felt through the sides of their planes [on bombing raids over Germany], continued to rise from the smoking, glowing mounds of stone. . . . Horribly disfigured corpses lay everywhere . . . doubled up in pools of their own melted fat, which had sometimes already congealed. (From "A Natural History of Destruction" by W. G. Sebald in *The New Yorker*)

The classroom's sidewall is not noise-insulated from the adjacent restrooms. . . . This noise is both distracting and disruptive, not to say unpleasant, and frequently doesn't allow us to conduct serious, intense discussions when we all can hear faucet taps being opened, bowels being evacuated, bladders being released, toilets being flushed, and doors being slammed. (From draft of "Memo to Campus Operations" by Geoffrey Bellah, college professor)

Man is albuminoid, proteinaceous, laked pearl; woman is yolky, ovoid, rich. Both are exuberant bloody growths. I would use the defects and deformities of each for my sacred purposes of writing, for I know that it is the marred and scarred and faulty that are subject to grace. (From *Mortal Lessons: The Art of Surgery* by Richard Selzer)

Ted [Williams] took his time leaving the world, and he's not quite out of it yet. He is cryonically frozen in Arizona, drained of blood and upside down but pretty much intact. . . . To those of us who saw him at the plate, he seemed the concentrated essence of baseball . . . snapping the slender implement of Kentucky ash back and forth, back and forth, in his impatience to hit the ball . . . (From "The Batter Who Mattered" by John Updike in *The New York Times Magazine*)

I'm killing the four hours between when I had to be off the cruise ship and when my flight to Chicago leaves by trying to summon up a kind of hypnotic sensuous collage of all the stuff I've seen and heard and done. . . . I have smelled what suntan lotion smells like spread over 21,000 pounds of hot flesh. . . . I, in dark moods, viewed and logged every type of erythma, keratinosis, pre-melanomic lesion, liver spot, eczema, wart, popular cyst, potbelly, femoral cellulite, varicosity, collagen and silicone enhancement, bad tint, hair transplants that have not taken—i.e. I have seen nearly naked a lot of people I would prefer not to have seen nearly naked. (From "Shipping Out" by David Foster Wallace in *Harper's Magazine*)

FUSION:
Ways to Spark and Compress

Slang Tang
Break-ups
Mix Masters

Essentially there are two kinds of language systems that we all use—literal and metaphoric. Literal language is straightforward, dictionary-defined language, necessary for communicating and survival. In an emergency we want an unembellished, literal signal: "Fire!" If we were in a burning theatre and someone attempted to warn us by shouting "A liquid sun tumbles upon us," we would curse that person's creativity. Although metaphoric language is a nightmare at a fire escape, metaphor in an essay works magic.

For instance, in capturing the "personality" of a blaze (suppose it were capricious, not planned, smelled like rotten eggs, and so large as to seem cosmic but laughable in its absurdity), an effective expression might be "the evil gods have farted." Metaphors work quickly and intuitively by fusing two seemingly unlike things, here a fire and the gods' farts. This figurative language flash-fuses three dimensions: It captures the reader's attention, *fine-tunes* the writer's attitude towards the content, and *compresses* explanations, meanings, or descriptions.

A reader does not usually analyze a metaphor's three dimensions: choice metaphors appeal to the subconscious, fitting smoothly into a piece of writing and eliciting the reader's fleeting smile or brief wince. Virtually all good writing—fictional, historical, journalistic, business, social science, theological, political, scientific, philosophical—uses metaphor. Without it, the reader drowns in a sea of literalism. *Slang Tang, Break-ups,* and *Mix Masters* are all ways to generate metaphors, but any of the approaches could end up discovering a metaphor that one of the others might have yielded. English teachers usually downplay the use of metaphors in essay writing because there are no rules to evaluate metaphors (they can only be evaluated in terms of their contexts) and writers must be playful to create them. Mixing intellectual analysis and play is not the forte of academia.

Slang Tang

Regardless of the lack of decorum, filthy slang is many people's first exuberant encounter with metaphor. During adolescence, slang shrink-wraps sexual embarrassment by cartooning genitalia, or slangy figurative language bubble-packs social insecurities by making fun of outsiders. An adolescent would not be interested in the sentence "Bill, my aunt Tina, and all their cronies ate the apple" unless it was rewritten to make fun of their own repressed concerns:

> Bill, who smells like someone crawled up his ass and died; my aunt Tina, who keeps scratching her fur burger; and all their uber-geek cronies ate the apple, which later caused them all to up-chuck and break wind.

This sentence does not meet everyone's literary, moral, or social tastes, but neither do Geoffrey Chaucer's references to medieval Bible students who take pride in "grinding their corn." Slang, as opposed, to metaphorical devices found in most essays, is often secretive and has value only within a narrow social group: "We're looking at a package that's going to make this town weep" makes sense to a movie producer; "Getting jumped in by being good from the pockets and the shoulders" makes sense to a gang member; and "I'm burning it for ten fucking *minutos, pinche tortuga,* so you can radar it if you have to and give it a squirt of the green jiz" makes sense to a sous-chef.

This primal love of slang can kick up the heat for an essayist. But there are problems. Aside from adjusting pitch for a specific audience and making sure the slang metaphor carries its intended associations, overuse of favorite terms fries inventive slang into clichés. Instead of capturing the reader's attention, forcing the reader to rethink reality, the cliché lets the reader's imagination go on a coffee break. Following are ways writers often engage their brains' slang-creating fuel cells to come up with good metaphors.

Similes. The first way is simple. In order to capture the essence of the "apple" in the sentence "Bill, my aunt Tina, and all their cronies ate the apple," the writer creates a mini-*analogy* to the apple called a *simile*, using "like" or "as" to connect an image to the apple that clarifies its essence. Creating apt analogies and similes can be challenging, since these metaphorical comparisons draw overt attention to themselves: "the apple looked like a red ball." Similes can fall flat, be too predictable, clichéd, or forced.

To create a simile, first list all the objects that share some quality of the apple (taste, color, texture, shape, size). For now we will limit our choices to objects similar in color and basic shape: red balloon, blood cell, red pill, rising sun, flesh bump. Next, the writer extends the list by looking these words up in the thesaurus: blimp, sphere, globe, bulge, growth, dilation, enlargement. Finally, the writer is ready to fuse the apple with one of the words from either list that captures both the physical attributes of the apple and what the apple represents.

Using "bulge" would suggest that the apple is disconcertingly misshapen; using "red balloon" would make the apple seem lightweight; "pill" would underscore a bitter or tart taste but remind readers of the therapeutic qualities of the apple; "red bump" would turn the apple into an aberration and make eating it surreal. Realize that a writer can remove "like" or "as" and replaces "apple" with the list-word itself: "Bill, my aunt Tina, and all their cronies ate the red blimp." In this case, the context of the passage surrounding the sentence would need to clarify that the blimp was an apple, but "red blimp" gets so much attention without being part of a simile that a group might start using it as slang.

Piece. A variation of the above is to use a *part* of the apple itself as a substitute for the whole apple, what rhetoricians call *synecdoche*. Again, it is important to make lists and then determine which item on the list has the desired associations for the piece of writing: stem, skin, core, seeds, juice, pulp. "Skin" would be more appropriate than "pulp" if the writer wishes to emphasize the sour, between-teeth unpleasantness of the apple: "Bill, my aunt Tina and all their cronies ate skins." Context would flesh out that these were apples. Some writers go so far as to use objects *related* to, but not part of, the subject to replace the subject. This is called *metonymy*. An example is "Bill, my aunt Tina, and all their cronies ate the orchard's back forty" or "ate the juice factory."

Solder. Another way to use the thesaurus to create *Slang's Tang* is for the writer to solder one of the words from the lists above with another word or part of another *subject-related* word. This has unlimited possibilities. For instance, the writer might combine thesaurus-discovered words for eaters and then solder them with words from the above lists to characterize "Bill, my aunt Tina, and all their cronies" instead of referring to the apple directly. Someone who eats can be a consumer, devourer, feeder, chewer, grinder, wolfer, gobbler, pecker, snapper, grazer, or nibbler. A word created by melting of two words without a hyphen is called a *portmanteau* word, although sometimes a hyphen-melt works better. The writer might write, "Bill, my aunt Tina, and all their cronies were pulp-peckers," or "red-spot-snappers," or "orchard-skinners." Sometimes connecting a list-word with a Roman or Greek *suffix* or *prefix* opens possibilities: "Bill, my aunt Tina, and all their cronies got applerrhea," "rrhea" being a Greek suffix meaning "abnormal discharge." You can find lists of Greek and Latin suffixes and prefixes in books about the history of the English language.

Your turn. Using the different techniques discussed above, change all the metaphors in the following sentences so they become nastier, more polite, more academic, or more street-wise. Create *Slang Tang* for six things you do in your own life.

Flashes of Slang Tang:

Live on broken phrases and syllable gristle, telegraphese and film reviews. No one will suspect . . . until you speak, and your soul falls out of your mouth like a can of corn from a shelf. (From *Habitation of the Word* by William Gass)

It would be years before I heard the word "transvestite," so I struggled to find a word for what I'd seen. "He-she" came to mind . . . . "Burl's" [a restaurant's name] would have been perfect like "boys" and "girls" spliced together. (From "Burl's" by Bernard Cooper in *The Los Angeles Times Magazine*)

Goldstein's lab [at UC, San Diego] found a family of gene mutants that cause the movement of materials through the cell to be disrupted. The obvious names were chosen: roadblock, gridlock, Sunday driver. [Other names for genes mentioned in the article are Ken and Barbie (causes flies to lack external genitalia), Maggie (development is arrested in mutants, as seems to have happened with Maggie Simpson), Cleopatra (lethal when found with another gene variant named asp), Lot (mutant that tolerates large quantities of salt as Lot's wife in the Bible was turned into a column of salt).] (From "Playing the Name Game" by Thomas H. Maugh II in *The Los Angeles Times*)

Although the erstwhile pipeline company had certainly become more skilled at pumping debt into subterranean partnerships than at earning money by pumping petroleum, it was clear that any of Enron's bosses had in fact overstepped the bounds Congress had set for the conduct of their business. But then this was not the first time our elected representatives had publicly chastised one of their children for smashing the car, knowing full well that they themselves had liquored the kid up beforehand and slipped him the keys. (From "Unmade in America: the true cost of a global assembly line" by Barry Lynn in *Harper's Magazine*)

In the desert, the muscular texture of agaves is a welcome contrast to the fine leaves of acacia. . . . Agaves also give structure to beds of wispy wildflowers. Penstemon and desert marigold look twice as flowery and feminine with a few of these macho characters in their midst. (From "Living Sculptures" by Sharon Cohoon in *Sunset Magazine*)

Blamestorming n. A meeting whose sole purpose is to discuss why a deadline was missed or a project failed and who was responsible.

Guyatus n. A hiatus from guys. ("Thanks, but no thanks. I'm kind of on a *guyatus*.")

Teenile adj. Used to describe someone who is way too old for what she is wearing. ("That 45-year-old woman is wearing low-cut jeans. Is she crazy or just *teenile*?")

Yellular adj. The loudness you adopt in response to a bad cellphone connection, in the misguided hope that talking will improve the connection. ("I'm so embarrassed. I went totally *yellular* at the restaurant last night.")
(From "Chickspeak" by Dany Levy in *The Los Angeles Magazine*)

Meanwhile, the legendary mansion parties have become legendary again, stocked like trout ponds with A-list celebrities, athletes and camera-hungry hotties. . . . Hefner's primary role in all this is to be the living, still-breathing embodiment of the brand—the Colonel Sanders of hot chicks, if you will. (From "Rake's Progress" by Dan Neil in *The Los Angeles Times Magazine*)

Just as raging surf forces a would-be wader out of the ocean and onto the beach, the jangled polar-field lines can shove cosmic rays away from the sun and back into the outer heliosphere. (From "Shooting the Solar Breeze" by Edward Smith and Richard Marsden in *The Sciences*)

The menu says the cinnamon bun is "legendary." Bunyanesque in size, it is a full meal and then some . . . the big fry bread is split open like a clam shell and loaded with chunks and shreds of utterly scrumptious, deeply seasoned roast beef. . . . Nonetheless, Frito pie (known among local connoisseurs as a "stomach grenade") is one of the most beloved dishes of the real people in and around Santa Fe. (From *Roadfood* by Jane and Michael Stern)

The "remember whens" faltered, finally, and I think it occurred to all three of us at the same time that we really were rather big to be up in a tree. . . . We looked at the bare branches around us receding into obscurity, and suddenly, there was nothing up there for us. Like Adam and Eve, we saw our own nakedness, and that terrible grown-up question "What are you *doing*?" made us ashamed. (From "A Lovely Sort of Lower Purpose" by Ian Frazier in *Outside* magazine)

Break-ups

An assortment of metaphorical images in an essay can scatter the reader's mind in too many directions. For instance, sample the myriad metaphors in the following sentence:

Sugar-glazed Bill, my crumbling aunt Tina, and all their wooden, laminated cronies murdered the apple.

The figurative language stretches from metaphorical adjectives of food and then wood, to a homicidal verb. A writer might revise the sentence keeping the metaphors consistent:

Soft varnished Bill, my splintered aunt Tina, and all their wooden, laminated cronies power-drilled the apple.

Deriving all the metaphors from woodworking imagery communicates a more unified tone.

One way to generate theme-related metaphors is to ask, "What image or object captures the mood of the subject but is not overtly related to it?" Instead of using the wood-related content in the sentence above, the writer might want to imply that the apple-eating activity was noisy and busy—though not chaotic—but more organized like a symphony: an orchestra might appropriately capture the mood of the action. The writer then *Breaks-up* the subject matter of a symphony into parts to create a *Break-up* list:

Woodwind Section	French Horn	Measures
Tuba	Clarinet	B Flat
Harpsichord	Kettle Drums	F Sharp
Cello	Snare Drums	Beethoven
Oboe	Trombone	Mozart
Chorus	Frets	Sound Board
Ensemble	Opus	Finger Board
Cymbals	Musical Notes	Turning Pegs
Philharmonic	Harmony	Don Giovanni
Madame Butterfly	Tenor	Musical Scores

All the listed items should be nouns (people, places, and things) or nouns accompanied by adjectives (words that describe or modify nouns). The longer the list, the more choices the writer will have when constructing metaphors. The list can then be used to create figurative language—metaphorical adjectives, nouns, and verbs.

Break-up Adjectives. In sprinkling figurative language into one's essay, a writer's first impulse may be to use the items in the *Break-up* list as similes:

> Bill, who reminds me of a trombone; my aunt Tina, who has a nose shaped like a cello; and all their cronies, who comment and criticize like a chorus in a musical ensemble chewed an apple that was a lot like a snare drum.

Though all the metaphors are consistent, the use of so many similes calls too much attention to the figurative language rather than blending into the sentence. The metaphors are overdone. However, these heavy-handed similes can be converted into metaphorical adjectives by removing "like" or "as" and then lining up any of the choices from the list in front of the literal nouns. *Break-up adjectives* are more confident than similes, resulting in seamless metaphorical imagery. Other items from the list can then be converted into adjectives to modify other people, places, and things in the sentence, producing the following sentence:

> <u>Trombone</u> Bill, my <u>cello-nosed</u> aunt Tina, and all their <u>chorus</u> cronies ate a <u>snare-drum</u> apple.

For a quick metaphorical adjective, without creating a *Break-up* list, consider placing a human quality before an inanimate noun (called *personification*) such as a bashful apple" or by doing the opposite—placing an adjective that is usually reserved for non-living objects in front of a live or animate noun, as in "stainless steel cronies."

Break-up Nouns. The writer can also use the same *Break-up* list for turning literal nouns into metaphorical nouns that are possessed by something literal:

> Billy, <u>the trombone of our family</u>, Aunt Tina the B flat of the family, and all their wind ensemble cronies, chewed on <u>the sound board of the apple.</u>

Or, if the writer prefers a more succinct style, the metaphors can be expressed as possessive nouns by adding an apostrophe "s" to the literal noun—

Billy, <u>our family's trombone</u>, Aunt Tina, the family's B flat, and all their wind-ensemble cronies chewed <u>the apple's sound board.</u>

Break-up Verbs. The literal verb phrase "chewed the apple" can be replaced with a *Break-up* list word, turning one of the nouns into a metaphorical verb: "*we finger-boarded the apple*" or "*we harpsichorded the apple.*" The metaphorical verbs capture the noisy but musical way in which the apple is eaten. In converting the verb to a noun, note that an ed or -smay need to be added to the noun to make the newly created verb agree with the tense and form of the replaced verb. These *Break-up verbs* could then be accompanied by literal verbs that are consistent with the symphony imagery: "strum," "croon," "chant," "perform," "harmonize," and "orchestrate." The revised sentence might read,

> Trombone Billy, my cello-nosed Aunt Tina, and all their wind-ensemble cronies <u>harmonized</u> and <u>Don-Giovannied</u> the snare-drum apple.

Making use of the *Break-ups* gives the sentence coherence; but mixing metaphors can cause a disjointed effect. Despite English-teacher uproar over mixed metaphors, an innovative writer will always consider generating two separate *Break-up* lists, combining and juxtaposing images from both lists to create *purposefully* irregular or jarring images.

As with all metaphors, *Break-up adjectives, nouns, and verbs* carry a load of descriptive associations and so become an editing tool. For instance, to write the last sentence with only literal language, one would have to add many wordy clauses:

> Bill, a big and booming guy, who, despite his large frame, remains in the background, sliding around everyone; my aunt Tina, who has a long nose bridge that gives way to flaring nostrils which emit low snorting noises; and all their cronies, who make a lot of clamor including belching and other unsavory sounds that do not have much meaning, ate an apple in a way that was both synchronized—each taking turns chewing—and with gusto, the group appreciating the sensual experience of consuming the juicy ripe fruit which had a smooth, tight skin that made a jarring sound as it was pierced by their teeth.

Metaphors are economical—they communicate an enormous amount of information, meaning, tone, and attitude in a compressed space.

Your turn. Find the *Break-up* adjectives, nouns, and verbs in the following sentences. Then offer replacement metaphors to change the information, meaning, tone, and attitude of the sentences.

Kaleidoscopes of Break-ups:

Here's the Hummer on a city street: a swollen Jeep; an SUV with a bad thyroid and a bloated ego. The city's a restaurant, and over there is a wealthy man gigantic at his table; he's full of wine, sweetbreads, and a sense of self; he stands up, shouts a cough of satisfaction into his napkin, weaves toward the bar, and rubs people wrong as he travels. Hummers annoy people. (From "High Mobility" by Colin McAdam in *Harper's Magazine*)

Spring jitterbugs inside me. (From "Spring" by Gretel Ehrlich in *Antaeus*)

Rugged shrub-land of agaves and yuccas marks the Chihuahuan [desert], and the wildly diverse Great Basin is sagebrush basins in one spot, a hive of bare canyons and cliffs in another. These places are where you come to see what the inside of your planet looks like—the ribs, scapulas, and tender membranes brought to the surface. I've spent decades piecing together a *Gray's Anatomy* of the desert, filling notebooks. (From "Water from a Stone" by Craig Childs in *Outside* magazine)

There are also so-called hit-and-run infections, in which a pathogen or its products disrupt the body's immunological surveillance system; once the microbes are gone (or when they are present in such low frequency as to be undetectable), the immune response stays stuck in the "on" mode, causing a lingering inflammation. (From "A New Germ Theory" by Judith Hooper in *The Atlantic Monthly*)

Fifty years ago, schoolchildren memorized Emily Dickinson and the taffy-sweet quatrains of Marlow and Burns and Lovelace. Poetry was easy and portable popular entertainment, the iPod of literacy. (From "Poetry for the Rest of Us" by Dan Neil in *The Los Angeles Times Magazine*)

Mated birds in Audubon are not slaves of instinct but married couples; they are always in cahoots. Or else his birds are alone in fancy dress and become worldly types: the senatorial pelican, the demagogic shrike, the seigniorial blue heron, the outlaw vulture. (From "Audubon's Passion" by Adam Gopnik in *The New Yorker*)

Most vulnerable are the "little emperors," those legions of only children born under China's strict population-control policy. These children came of age during the miracle years of economic reform, and their stomachs are treasure chests into which parents have stuffed their newfound wealth. (From "China's Wealth Goes to Youths' Waistlines" by Ching-Ching Ni in *The Los Angeles Times*)

Oil is water with bad nerves. Instead of advancing fluidly and unproblematically like water, oil insinuates itself and minces along. Oil is water with hips. . . . Exactly the same distinction exists between a nail and a screw. A screw is morose and circumspect, like oil. It is like a lubricated nail, manufactured to be mindful of other materials and to get along with them. . . . In a screw the brusque commands of a nail have been transmuted into dialogue and negotiation. . . . In place of hostile takeover there is gentle infiltration. A nail is heroic and exciting. It moves in an epic world. A screw is ugly, torpid, asthmatic, having little initial impact and betraying to eagerness, no feeling whatsoever. But therein lies its strength. (From "The Yearning of the Screw" by Fabio Morabito in *Toolbox*)

Shrimp Cancun broiled inside thick flak-jackets of bacon and ham, then blanketed with melted cheese, may seem ghastly in concept but actually sort of works like an *hors d'oeuvre* bombarded with mutant radiation in a '50s monster flick. . . . Huachinango relleno is a complex work of culinary engineering but may be a little too weird to eat: a crisp-skinned, grilled fish, split and filled with a mixture of shrimp and octopus, drenched with a quart or so of 40-weight cheese sauce . . . and surmounted with toothpick-mounted olives that jut from the snapper's flank like eye stalks from a crab. (From "Veracruzing East L.A." by Jonathan Gold in *The Los Angeles Times*)

Clint Eastwood is a tall, chiseled piece of lumber—a totem pole with feet [;]. . . he's tense and clenched, anally vigilant. (From "Is That A Gun in Your Pocket?" by James Walcott in *Vanity Fair*)

Overall, the car has a profoundly geriatric feeling about it. Like it was built with a swollen prostate. To drive this car is to feel the icy hand of death upon you, or at least the icy hand of Hertz, because it simply screams rental. (From "A Senior Moment" by Dan Neil in *The Los Angeles Times*)

Small arms and light weapons—such as pistols, assault rifles, and hand-held grenade launchers—are the T-shirts of the twenty-first century. Countries that in the past may have counted on a nascent garment or shoe industry to kick-start development now turn to producing for the low end of the arms market. (From "Making a Killing" by Ted C. Fishman in *Harper's Magazine*)

[At the dentist] it is not the local pain that causes dread, but the greater pain: the loss of speech, the pinioning, the drool tides coming and washing out, the marooning of the brain. For two hours, the brain is Robinson Crusoe alone in the bone cup of the skull, peering out at faraway chrome implements and rubber-sheathed fingers and cotton cylinders red with blood, peering out but forbidden to signal for help. (From "The Crime of the Tooth: Dentistry in the Chair" by Peter Fruendlich in *Harper's Magazine*)

My mother almost shattered me once, with that instinct mothers have—blind, I think, in this case, but unerring nonetheless—for striking blows along the fault-lines of their children's hearts, by telling me, in an attack on my selfishness, "We all have to make allowances for you [who has MS], of course, because of the way you are." (From "On Being a Cripple" by Nancy Mairs in *Plaintext: Deciphering a Woman's Life*)

This flower [*Selenicereus plerantus,* which blooms only at night] touches your face, it kisses your ear, its tongue slides across your crotch. The flower is shameless, absolutely shameless. When it opens its white jaws, the petals span a foot and lust pours out into the . . . black evenings when the air is warmer than your body and you cannot tell where your flesh ends and the world begins. (From "The Bone Garden of Desire" by Charles Bowden in *Esquire*)

I invited a young diabetic woman to the operating room to amputate her leg. . . . There upon her foot was a Mississippi Delta brimming with corruption, sending its raw tributaries down between her toes. (From *The Art of Surgery: A variation of the art of writing* by Richard Selzer)

The struts and girders of inequality, the cantilevers of effort, are no longer covered by molded-steel cladding or plastic coating. The guts of craft and luck and error, of exploitation and hype and deceit, are now spilling out. They have their own particular beauty: not the easy, comfortable beauty of smoothness, but the much more demanding beauty of truth. (From "Against Smoothness" by Mark Kingwell in a convocation address)

I thought, he looks like the flayed skin of St. Bartholomew in the Sistine Chapel. As soon as I had the thought, I knew that it was dishonorable. To think about anything outside the moment, outside Gary (a boy who drowned), was a crime of inattention. I swallowed a small, sour piece of self-knowledge: I was the sort of person who, instead of weeping or shouting or praying during a crisis, thought about something from a textbook (H.W.Janson's *History of Art*, page 360). (From "Under Water" by Anne Fadiman in *The New Yorker*)

The most inclusive description of the art is that, termite-like, it feels its way through the walls of particularization, with no sign that the artist has any object in mind other than eating away the immediate boundaries of his art, and turning these boundaries into conditions of the next achievement. (From 'Termite Art" by Manny Farber in *Negative Space*)

I had always been under my father's supervision, idolizing my distant mother, a seductive, formidably ambitious woman, alternating warmth and glacial narcissism, with whom I had seldom even shared a meal until I came into her charge. (From "The Work of Mourning," by Francine du Plessix Gray in *The American Scholar*)

The questions that Carrie asks are easy to deride, with their silly self-centeredness, their marketing-executive idiom, their coin-operated impersonality. (From "Relationshipism: Who is Carrie Bradshaw Really Dating?" by Lee Siegel in *The New Republic*)

[Priests'] real serenity or asceticism I no longer expect, and I take for granted the beefy calm that frequently goes with Catholic celibacy, but I am watching for the marks of love and often see mere resignation or tenacity. (From "Heaven and Nature" by Edward Hoagland in *Harper's Magazine*)

Mix Masters

Finally, here is a game that everyone can play, at parties or in class, regardless of one's lack of imagination. This game turns out to be a metaphor generator and teacher. Everyone in the group needs at least fifteen cards or pieces of scratch paper. On each side of the cards each person writes down the most important thirty words in his or her life, expressed as one specific noun unless it is a title: food items, songs, perfumes, vacation images, films, fictional characters, clothes, designs, good and bad things, past and present experiences. Most of the words must be *concretions*, words known through touch, sound, sight, smell, and taste, except for three words, which can be *abstractions* (God, humor, anger, kindness). If playing the game often, you can change the nature of the lists, grouping the thirty words by an historical period, political situation, a novel, or a work place—anything a group of people is studying or writing about.

Mixing. Ideally, people should be in groups of four although it is possible to play by oneself or in a larger group. One person shuffles his or her "cards" and deals three of them off the top, at random, into the center of the group. That person, and everyone else in the group, must use all three words to write a sentence that will make metaphorical sense. It cannot be literal. Here are the other rules: (1) You may change the form of any of the words (by adding -ing, -ed, -s); (2) You can use as many articles as needed (a, an, the); (3) You may add *one* preposition (words that denote place such as in, over, under, near); (4) You may add any other word whatsoever—a verb, noun, adjective, adverb—but only *one*. These rules ensure spontaneity, and nudge writers into using all the fusion techniques—*Slang Tang, Line-ups, Break-ups.*

Suppose the three words a person lays out from his or her deck are "sprinklers," "gossip," and "mowed grass" (words that could easily appear in the deck of a young person who grew up in the desert). One person adds the word "about" to write "The sprinklers gossiped about mowed grass," while a second person melts words together and unintentionally creates a line-up meta-phor by writing "The mowed-grass gossip used the sprinkler." This sentence actually has two metaphors since "gossip" cannot use a sprinkler and there is no such thing as a "mowed-grass" gossip. The extra word is "used." Another person writes, "Gossip sprinklered over the mowed grass," probably unconsciously changing sprinkler into a break-up verb metaphor.

As soon as one person in the group writes a complete, legible sentence, everyone else in the group must finish within sixty seconds. Time pressure forces people to be unintentionally creative. As soon as everyone is finished, all must read their sentences aloud to the rest of the group, and the group takes a minute or two to discuss the profundity or absurdity of each sentence before going on to the next person in the group and writing from that person's three cards. The game can continue around the group several times. The game teaches writers to have confidence in being playful and making the most of time pressure.

Mastering. After mixing for a while, the game can become more complex. To better understand the genius compression of these sentences, the group takes some of the most intriguing ones and masters them one at a time. Mastering the sentence is a three-part process that is boot-camp training in how to analyze anything: To start, everyone writes down the same sentence that one of the players wrote earlier. For step two everyone, individually, writes down the metaphor(s) in the sentence. There can be more than one. For instance, in the sentence "The sprinklers gossiped about mowed grass," a player could decide "gossiped" is literal and therefore "sprinklers" and "mowed grass" must be metaphors for some type of people; or the player could decide "gossiped" is metaphoric, making the sentence literally about sprinklers doing something to mowed grass.

Once the metaphors are chosen, each player writes them down separately from the original sentence, and after each metaphor lists all the universal associations most people have when they read that word, staying away from personal associations that others would not understand. For example, if "gossip" is the metaphor, the player might write down "gossip: whisper, secretive, usually about something personal that is untruthful or unkind, information that changes as it is passed along." Avoid anticipating step three as you make this list.

Step three is the most challenging. Now the player looks at both the original metaphoric sentence of step one and the associations of step two in order to write the metaphor *out* of the sentence and, instead, compose a sentence that makes *literal, non-metaphoric* sense; the new sentence actually interprets the metaphor. Since metaphors compress so many associations, this literal sentence will be longer than the original metaphoric one and may have more complicated structure. The player may use new words that closely parallel any of the associations from step two in order to do the translation. Sometimes the writer can simply plug the association word into the sentence to make it literal, but sometimes the sentence will continue to be metaphoric as in "The sprinklers whispered about mowed grass."

In this sentence, the literal part is going to be about the sprinklers doing something to the mowed grass under certain conditions, but these will have to be expressed with parallel words such as "quiet" for "whisper," "when no one is around" for "secretive," "damage" for "untruthful and unkind," "changing its appearance" for "the information changes as it is passed along." The player must use as many of the words, or parallels to the words, as possible to explore the whole potential of the metaphor. There will be different translations depending on the player, but here is one possibility given the above connections: "When no one was around, the quiet sprinklers damaged the mowed grass, adversely changing its appearance." When the first person is finished writing all these steps out legibly, everyone else in the group has three minutes to finish, and then everyone should read his or her sentences out loud for the group to decide on the closest translation.

Usually the best one will be written by a player who had no idea what the sentence implied when it was first playfully created and only thought the sentence sounded interesting. The player will also be one who does not anticipate step three while doing step two, so all the associations with the metaphor are explored without holding back on these because they might not fit in step three. The player will also be imaginative enough to sometimes find parallels to these associations. Good analysis of *Fusion* is always a matter of step-by-step discovery. If a person can analyze these sentences, he or she will be close to analyzing the metaphorical implications of anything.

Your turn. Have a party and *Mix Master.*

OPT:
Ways to Wield Point of View

Personalizing Lens
Humbling Lens
Distancing Lens
Martianing Lens

The phrase "point of view" can refer to either a person's philosophical position or a writer's relationship to subject matter and audience. But point of view can also refer to *Style*. A stylistic point of view of can be first person (I, we), second person (you), or third person (he, she, it, they). And now, for the first time, we offer a variant of the others called *Martian* point of view. All these perspectives offer a variety of reality-trapping advantages, just as different photography lenses capture different views. A telescopic lens can catch close-up shots but make objects seem nearer than in reality; a wide-angle lens captures great horizontal scope but makes distances seem farther than in reality. Writers have similar advantages and disadvantages with different points of view. Sometimes English teachers believe that first person is too personal, that second person is too didactic, and that third person is totally objective, and probably have not even considered the *Martian* "person." These teachers need to take their lens caps off.

Personalizing Lens

When writing a personal memoir or autobiography, a writer naturally opts to use first-person point of view The writer knows that readers accept in good faith the authenticity of personal details of the "I" perspective because what is personal is assumed to be subjective. But when an essayist appropriates the use of first person (I or we) to recount incidents for which he or she was not present—Jesus' crucifixion or the writer's own birth—or for nonpersonal compositions such as research and criticism, academicians bristle. In nonpersonal writing, invoking the "I" perspective is discouraged because its familiarity undermines the objectivity assumed in third-person point of view (one, it, he, she, they). Readers regard details disseminated in the third person as less subjective and self-centered than what comes from first person. But this notion is only an illusion.

In rethinking critical theory, feminists questioned the supposed objectivity of third person when analyzing texts; instead they celebrated the "I" bias and emphasized the personal experience inherent in all studies, which the feminists maintain should be honestly represented by use of first person in academic writing. Despite seeming less objective, the *Personalizing Lens* keeps reality from drying out by reconstituting historical events, aesthetic analyses, political commentary, and scientific speculation.

The editors of *American Heritage* magazine considered this revitalizing advantage when they enlisted authors and scholars to comment on history from a first person, fly-on-the-wall perspective. One such historian, Walter Lord, stepped into the Golden Spike ceremony at Promontory Point, Utah, in 1869 to celebrate the first time the nation was linked coast to coast with a railway. Using imagery from A. J. Russell's famous photographs of the ceremony as a stimulus, Lord places himself into the moment. Writing through the first-person *Lens* enables him to focus on background people, include some humorous speculation, and consider the psychology of those in the photo. The *Personalizing Lens*, when paired with present tense narration (see *Pulsing the Tense*) further accents the drama of the nonfiction details, endowing an event with a sense of immediacy or creating dreamlike ambiance.

Your turn. Because the writer is using first person, he or she has taken "poetic license" with some of the details. Separate those details from actual "facts" in the excerpts below. Then identify which words and phrases are used "poetically" to make the details more intimate.

Intimacies of First Person:

I want to mix with that boisterous crowd of tracklayers, soldiers, dishwashers, gamblers, and strumpets. I want to listen to the 21st infantry band thumping away. I want to watch the cowcatchers touch. I want to sample the bottle of champagne held out by the man standing on the Central Pacific's locomotive Jupiter. I want to know who the lady is in the exact center of the preliminary photograph, but who vanishes in the final, climactic shot. I want to know the identity of the one man in the picture who turned his back to the camera. Was he just inattentive, or was his likeness perhaps posted as "WANTED" in every post office in the West? I want to watch Leland Stanford swing his hammer—and miss the gold spike. (From "I Wish I'd Been There" by Walter Lord in *American Heritage* magazine)

Standing in the crowd of distressed and jeering citizens of Jerusalem, I am thankful that a stranger presses Jesus' shoulders to brace his cross-loaded shoulders, but I can tell from the steadiness of his eyes, the calmness of his mouth, and the vertical strength of the his body that he can carry his burden without anyone's help. (From "Sienna's Giovanni di Paolo's painting 'Christ Carrying the Cross, 1426'" by Julie Jenkins for a freshman composition assignment)

Should I call it a nose—this immense membranous organ that picks up all smells, even the most private ones? I'm referring to the grayish lump, with white scabs, that starts out at my mouth and descends as far as my bull's neck.... I am not pitiful, and I do not want others to feel sympathy for me. I am what I am and that's enough for me. To know that others are worse off is a great consolation. (From "Head One" by Mario Vargas Llosa about a grotesque portrait painted by Francis Bacon in *Harper's Magazine*)

I have the power to scheme and to construct—a power that time has eroded in her, a power that she [the writer's twin alter-ego] regards as superseded, useless. Null and void. Whatever shreds remain of her own ambitiousness embarrass her now. She is resigned to her failures. She is shamed by them. To be old and unachieved: Ah . . . . Perhaps she labored for the sake of fame, who knows?... [It] is fruitfulness I am after: despite the unwantedness of it—and especially despite her—I mean to begin a life of novel-writing.... I have decades to squander.

As for her: I deny her, I denounce her, I let her go. Whining, wizened, hoary fake, with her cowardice, her fake name! (From "The Break" by Cynthia Ozick in *Antaeus*)

Shadows from the open door are printed upon the floor. And there lay I on the kitchen table, dragged wet from my fetal world, tiny, bundled, blind, my heartbeat continent upon a series of vascular valves which are as fragile as the petals of a flower and not yet, quite, unfolded. Where, you ask, is the Malvern pudding, weighted with its ancient stone? It has been set aside, as my mother's cookery book. They will not be seen again in this story. I am swaddled in—what?—a kitchen towel. Or something, perhaps, yanked from Clarentine Flett's clothesline, a pillowslip dried stiff and sour in Manitoba sun. My mouth is open, a wrinkled ring of thread, already seeking, demanding, and perhaps knowing at some unconscious level that that filament of matter we struggle to catch hold of at birth is going to be out of reach for me. (From *The Stone Diaries* by Carol Shields)

My name was Salmon, like the fish; first name, Susie. I was fourteen when I was murdered on December 6, 1973. In newspaper photos of missing girls from the seventies, most looked like me: white girls with mousy brown hair. This was before kids of all races and genders started appearing on milk cartons or in the daily mail. It was still back when people believed things like that didn't happen. (From *The Lovely Bones* by Alice Sebold)

It is the Texas Zephyr at midnight—the woman in a white suit, the man in a blue uniform; she carries flowers—I know they are flowers. The petals spill and spill in the aisle and a child goes past this couple who have just come from their own wedding— goes past them and past them, going always to the toilet but really just going past them; and the child could be a horse or she could be the police and they'd not notice her any more than they do, which is not at all—the man's hands high up on the woman's legs, her skirt up, her stockings and garters, the petals and finally all the flowers spilling out into the aisle and his mouth open on her. My mother. My father. I am conceived near Dallas in the dark while a child passes, a young girl who knows and doesn't know, who witnesses, in glimpses, the creation of the universe, who feels odd hurt as her own mother, fat and empty, snores with her mouth open, her false teeth slipping down, snores and snores just two seats behind the Creators. (From "Oranges and Sweet Sister Boy" by Judy Ruiz in *Iowa Woman*)

Surely chaos is a capacious area of common ground. I am convinced that my own mind spends much of its waking hours, not to mention its sleeping time, in a state of chaos directly analogous to that of the cricket hearing the sound of the nearby bat. But there is a big difference. My chaos is not induced by a bat; it is not suddenly switched on in order to facilitate escape; it is not an evasive tactic set off by any new danger.... The chaos that is my natural state of being is rather like the concept of chaos that has emerged in higher mathematical circles in recent years.... When we are lucky, and the system operates at its random best, something astonishing may suddenly turn up, beyond predicting or imagining. Events like these we recognize as good ideas. (From "Crickets, Bats, Cats, & Chaos" by Lewis Thomas in *Audubon*)

Humbling Lens

The second-person point of view (you) when used with command-form verbs has often been the domain of "How-to" manuals, process essays, advice columns, and personal letters. However, when used in unexpected ways, in a biography on a controversial figure or in a passionate plea to an anonymous audience, second-person point of view establishes an up-close-and-personal relationship between writer and reader, wiping out the comfort zone provided by the third person. We make use of this in-your-face intensity during emotional exchanges if we suspect a person is being unsympathetic: "How would you feel if Aunt Tina did this to you?" Our accusations are often accompanied by literally aiming our forefinger at the other person. In a written piece, when trying to gain readers' empathy or get them to accept responsibility, an essayist can figuratively finger-point without breaching etiquette by addressing the reader as "you."

One essayist, Joy Williams, employs the *Humbling Lens,* avoiding referring to her target in a third-person general "they," instead replacing the pronoun with the second person: "you just want and want and want." By singling out "you," Williams thwarts attempts by her readers (we conspicuous consumers who want to think of ourselves as environmentally conscientious) to escape culpability. Williams is not accusing *them*; she is reproaching *you*.

The *Humbling Lens* can be used for purposes other than just reproaches; it can be instructive, guiding an audience through an unusual "how-to" essay that commands readers to identify with a maligned media personality, an infamous historical figure, or the inner workings of an enigmatic individual. In "How to be Marcia Clark," Danna Schaeffer anticipates her audience's unwillingness to "relate to" the sharp-edged prosecutor. The use of imperative voice, in tandem with the intimate and poignant details of Clark's life, helps to create a more sympathetic portrait by compelling the audience to slip into Clark's shoes. To avoid repeating the pronoun "you," Schaeffer exploits command-form verbs ("Don't grow up rich," "Marry," "Turn"), which carry an implied second-person point of view.

Your turn. For each of the excerpts below identify key details that resonate and shock. Then explain how those details communicate the purpose or thesis. Write in second person a short biography about someone you know well or a researched famous person. Or attack a group by addressing, in second person, a mock-up of a typical member in that group.

Humblings of Second Person:

When you find out about the moving cursor, or hear statistics about AIDS in Africa, or see your 947th picture of a weeping fireman, you can't help but become fundamentally indifferent because you are exposed to things like this all the time, just as you are to the rest of your options. At breakfast. In the waiting room. Driving to work. At the checkout counter. *All the time.* I know you know this already. I'm just reminding you.... But, once again, the issue isn't what you *can* do when I call your attention to it. The real issue is *do* you do it as a matter of routine processing? Or do you rely instead on a general immunity that only numbness can provide, an immunity that puts the whole flood in brackets and transforms it all into a play of surfaces—over which you hover and glide like a little god, dipping in here and there for the moving experience of your choice, with the ultimate reaches of your soul on permanent remote? (From "The Numbing of the American Mind" by Thomas de Zengotita in *Harper's Magazine*)

I don't want to talk about *me*, of course, but it seems as though far too much attention has been lavished on *you* lately—that your greed and vanities and quest for self-fulfillment have been catered to far too much. You just want and want and want. (From "Save the Whales, Screw the Shrimp" by Joy Williams in *Esquire* magazine)

Yell when you are born. Don't grow up rich. Learn to work hard and crave victory. Do well in school. Develop an Old Testament sense of justice. Turn into a beautiful woman but don't think of yourself as sexy. Marry someone who's not right for you. Go to law school and discover your fabulous memory stands you in perfect stead. Finish law school. Divorce. Marry again. Take a job with a criminal-defense firm. (From "How to Be Marcia Clark" by Danna Schaeffer in *Mirabella*. Aside from her infamous role as the lead O.J. Simpson prosecutor, Clark also successfully prosecuted the murderer of actress Rebecca Schaefer, Danna's daughter.)

The thing you always suspected about yourself the minute you became a tourist is true: A tourist is an ugly human being. . . . An ugly thing, that is what you are when you become a tourist, an ugly, empty thing, a stupid thing, a piece of rubbish pausing here and there to gaze at this and taste that, and it will never occur to you that the people who inhabit the place in which you have just paused cannot stand you, that behind their closed doors they laugh at your strangeness . . . they collapse helpless from laughter, mimicking the way they imagine you must look as you carry out some everyday bodily function. They do not like you. *They do not like me!* That thought never actually occurs to you.

Still you feel a little uneasy. (From *A Small Place* by Jamaica Kincaid)

You know those white pulpy strings that hold tangerines into their skins? Tear them off. Be careful. . . . After you have put the pieces of tangerine on the paper on the hot radiator, it is best to forget about them. Al comes home, you go to a long noon dinner in the brown dining-room, afterwards maybe you have a little nip of *quetsch* from the bottle on the *armoire*. Finally he goes; of course you are sorry, but—On the radiator the sections of tangerine have grown even plumper, hot and full. You carry them to the window, pull it open, and place them for a few minutes on the packed snow of the sill. They are ready. . . . The sections of the tangerine are gone, and I cannot tell you why they are so magical. Perhaps it is that little shell, thin as one layer of enamel on a Chinese bowl, that crackles so tinily, so ultimately under your teeth. Or the rush of cold pulp just after it. Or the perfume. I cannot tell.

There must be some one, though, who knows what I mean. Probably everyone does, because of his own secret eatings. (From *Serve it Forth* by M.F.K. Fisher)

You cannot serve God and mammon. . . . Do not throw your pearls before swine, lest they trample them under foot and turn to attack you. . . . Enter by the narrow gate; for the gate is wide and the way is easy that leads to destruction, and those who enter by it are many. For the gate is narrow and the way is hard, that leads to life, and those who find it are few. (Jesus in Matthew 5:1 – 7:28)

You cannot possibly teach quantum mechanics without mathematics, to be sure, but you can describe the strangeness of the world opened up by quantum theory . . . that there are deep mysteries and profound paradoxes. . . . Do not teach that biology is a useful, perhaps profitable science; that can come later. . . . Teach ecology early on. Let it be understood that the earth's life is a system . . . held in an almost unbelievably improbable state of regulated balance. (From "The Art of Teaching Science" speech by Lewis Thomas reported in *The New York Times*)

Your name is Sherwood Anderson and you know that life in a small town is not as tranquil and simple as most people suppose it to be. You decide that very short stories about all the people who live in a town called Winesburg will allow you to enter their private lives, dramatizing their secret aspirations and perverse emotional needs. These people would realistically intersect each other's lives and so you realize some would have to enter each other's separate stories. This in turn could potentially make the stories seem hectic so you decide to create George Willard, a reporter who would naturally intersect several people's lives at different times in his life. But you do not want the reader to fall into the trap of thinking that the most noticed character in either one's life or stories is necessarily the touchstone of morality or reality so you create a second character named Dr. Reefy who . . . (From "How to Create the Collection *Winesburg, Ohio: An Analysis*" by Sally Shapiro for an assignment in American literature)

Dear Customer: As soon as you put on the state-of-the-art headgear, body-suit, and electronic sensors, you find yourself in the bunker's living room. Late April 1945. . . . He comes towards you with such warmth, his smile tired, his arms open to embrace you. Remember—you are Eva. When Hitler closes his arms around you, the view darkens and you are surrounded by his presence. You are almost overwhelmed with titillation when you feel the whiskers of that famous little facial tuft tickle your ear and the back of your neck. (From *Live and Die as Eva Braun: Hitler's Mistress, in the Berlin Bunker and Beyond* by Roee Rosen)

Distancing Lens

Third person (he, she, it, they) dominates academic writing because it builds an illusion of objectivity that the writer's presentation suggests an unbiased, distant perspective. But this seemingly objective *Lens* does have more imaginative purposes. Third-person point of view is so impersonal that Ernest Hemingway used it without an *antecedent* (a reference to a person's name), a method to highlight the main character's value-empty identity and to underscore "him" as everyman. For instance, in his "A Very Short Story," the very first sentence is

"One hot evening in Padua they carried him up onto the roof and he could look out over the top of the town." The reader never finds out this person's name (and it takes a second to understand that "they" refers to other soldiers) as "he" goes through a humiliating affair with a woman named Luz, a nurse whom "they all liked." By contrast, knowing Luz's name empowers her and magnifies her subtle manipulations.

Third person, or the *Distancing Lens,* can also create a composite that turns a group of individuals into a satiric cartoon. By assigning a long list of identifying particulars—habits, traits, behaviors, expressions—to a single "he" or "she" that in reality exists among several individuals in the target group, the writer magnifies those undesirable qualities. In the example below, Germaine Greer shatters the stereotypical self-indulged woman by assigning all the items that these women desire as a group to a single, indefinite "she," an archetypal representative from the spoiled women's caucus. For a second the reader thinks of all the listed items weighing on one person, this tonnage rendering the subject grotesque, a cosmic vacuum cleaner, sucking up all that the natural world has to offer.

To use this *Distancing Lens* pick five different individuals from your target group and list them vertically down one side of a table or grid. Horizontally across the top of the grid, list all categories important to all five individuals: foods each one likes, clothes each one wears, expressions each one uses, material items over which they obsess, absurd fantasies on which they dwell, where they hang out and other relevant lifestyle details— pet peeves, flaws, and foibles. As you write a draft using a third-person singular pronoun (he, she, it), each time you write about one of the categories, list all the five entries from all five individuals as if now they belong to only one person. The discrepancy between what are clearly characteristics of a spectrum of people in the group, heaped on a single person, turns the group into a cartoon.

Your turn. In the examples below, identify which details make it clear that despite the use of third-person singular, the writer is really describing a group of people who generally share these traits.

Portraits with Third Person:

She is the crown of creation, the masterpiece. The depths of the sea are ransacked for pearls and coral to deck her; the bowels of the earth are laid open that she might wear gold, sapphires, diamonds, and rubies. Baby seals are battered with staves, unborn lambs ripped from their mothers' wombs, millions of moles, muskrats, squirrels, minks, ermines, foxes, beavers, chinchillas, ocelots, lynxes, and other small and lovely creatures die untimely deaths that she might have furs. (From *The Female Eunuch* by Germaine Greer)

He is the superior jock star, the emperor of the in-crowd, leader of the band, director of fads, do-as-I-say home commander, and the ultimate hero of family chaos. He takes up all the space at the three point line on the basketball court, at the tight end spot on the line of scrimmage, behind the net at the tennis court, in front of the goal on the soccer field, on top of the pitcher's rubber, and next to the breaking point at the ocean's edge—allowing only his buddies to enter. Shelf space at video stores stock only games that he has approved worthy of his time: Master of the Universe, Dragon Fighter, Mario III, and Zelda. . . .

He and his youth associates cruise through town on a girly hunt—their bodies resembling four-legged creatures who are unable to carry on conversations because their tongues are too big for their mouths—cruising in a whispering Dodge, a monster Mustang, a midnight Bronco, an oversized Hummer, and a fat Harley Davidson. He fuels his own tank with afternoon snacks of four irritable bean burritos, cozy Big Mac super-sizes, cranky pepperoni pizzas. . . (From "Teenage Boys" by Sharron Perez for a freshman composition assignment)

The fanatic is stubborn, obstinate, dogmatic: Everything for him is black or white, curse or blessing, friend or foe—nothing in between. He has no taste for or interest in nuances. . . . . He is immune to doubt and to hesitation. Intellectual exercise is distasteful, and art and beauty of dialogue alien to him. He is never bothered by difficult problems: A decree or bullet solves them . . . immediately. . . . The fanatic derides and hates tolerance, which he perceives as weakness, resignation or submission. That is why he despises women: their tenderness is to him a sign of passivity. He has a goal and is ready to pay any price to achieve it. Or more precisely: He is ready to make *others* pay any price in order to achieve it. The fanatic feels important, for he presumes being capable of altering—and dominating—the course of history. (From "How Can We Understand Their Hatred?" by Elie Wiesel in *Parade Magazine*)

He lives in his mother's basement with furniture rented at an astronomical interest rate, the exact amount of which he does not know. He has a car phone, an $80 monthly cable bill, and every possible phone feature but no savings. He steals Social Security numbers from unsuspecting relatives and assumes their identities to acquire large TV sets for which he will never pay. On the slim chance that he is brought to justice, he will have a colorful criminal history and no coherent explanation to offer for his acts. His family will raucously defend him and cry cover-up. Some liberal lawyer just like me will help him plea-bargain his way to yet another short stay in a prison pesthouse that will serve only to add another layer to the brother's sociopathology and formless, mindless nihilism. We know him. We've known and feared him all our lives.

As a teenager, he called, "Hey, baby gimme soma that boodie!" at us from car windows. Indignant at our lack of response, he followed up with, "Fuck you, then, 'ho!" He calls me a "white-boy-lovin' nigger bitch oreo" for being in the gifted program and loving it. (From "Who Shot Johnny?" by Debra Dickerson in *The New Republic*)

He worked himself to death, finally and precisely, at 3:00 A.M. He was a perfect type A, a workaholic, a classic. . . . He worked like the Important People. He had no outside "extracurricular interests," unless of course you think about a monthly golf game that way. . . . He always ate egg salad sandwiches at his desk. He was, of course, overweight, by 20 or 25 pounds. He thought it was okay, though, because he didn't smoke. . . . He worked six days a week, five of them until eight or nine at night. . . . His second child is a girl, who is twenty-four and married. . . . They had nothing to say to each other. (From "The Company Man" by Ellen Goodman in *Close to Home.*)

Imperfections are intolerable. And so a picture frame on the wall with its corners two-and-a-half degrees off perpendicular with the lint-less, dust-free, over-reflective shiny, triple-waxed wooden floor is by no means exempted from justice. Whenever we come over to her place, an unavoidable sense of shame takes us over as she guides us through her sanctum of labeled cabinets, alphabetized movie collection, categorized-by-frequency-of-being-read magazine compilation, polished shelves and freshly mopped-looking floor, while apologizing "I haven't had time to clean up," heads towards the fridge, reaches past the color-coded Tupperware items and selects a can of soda from its single fine alignment of military precision to serve her guest. . . . Her motto: Life is messy; clean it up. In fact this has evolved into more than just an aphorism and beyond a habit, but into a sort of code of honor—an addiction. . . . She's perfect—too perfect, to the point where we just want to grab a book from section A in her alphabetized bookshelf and shove it into a random spot in section P. (From "The Perfectionist" by Chau Tran for freshman composition).

Martianing Lens

The *Martian* point of view emerges from a combination of innocence and bewilderment, a *Lens* of a being shocked at everything he or she notices. The being, of course, is the writer who asks the reader to imagine something from this other-worldly perspective and in doing this, uses the second-person command point of view: (you) "imagine," "conceive," "think for a moment." The *Martian* is usually not literally from outer space but from a different inner space. This *Martian* may have expectations of what should exist, and in not finding a list of "what should be" existing, implies the disappointing prevalence of "what is not." (See *The Unexpected Minority* below.)

Other times, the *Martian* might be a worldly person, such as an anthropologist or sociologist who sees the present world as if he or she were living in the future and looking back, the contemporary world turning into something unrecognizable, needing to be restudied and reclassified as if it were an ancient world. Trying to make sense out of what we take for granted by relabeling it, sometimes with euphemisms (see under *3 Headwork*), the present becomes strange and absurd, a good way to satirize or show the absurdity of the way we live (See "Body Rituals Among the Nacirema" below.)

Or instead of an anthropologist, imagine an incredibly naïve person with a flat, indifferent voice, reporting absurd, even atrocious, behavior as if it were nothing unnatural. The person hearing the report would be the *Martian*, reacting with utter astonishment to everything reported, another way to reveal the absurd activities we revere without giving them much thought. (See *Gulliver's Travels* below.)

Your turn. Pick a subject that has injustices or absurdities that are taken too much for granted and that you would like the viewer to perceive as unnatural rather than normal. Think about the setting where this subject takes place, the attitudes of the people involved, actions that you see as grotesque. Make long lists of details of all these things before you start writing. Model after the examples below; notice most examples are using second-person command. You need to choose an overall tone: are you listing what someone expects to find, implying or stating what they find instead; or are you looking back at the present from a future position like an anthropologist and inventing euphemisms that make fun of what we take for granted; or are you innocently, with a matter-of-fact voice, describing what goes on now? For this last stance you need to use *Super-literalism*. (See the *Pause* section under *1 STYLE*.)

Spooks from Martians:

Imagine a country in which millions of apparently successful people nonetheless have come to believe fervently that they are really lost souls—a country where countless adults allude matter-of-factly to their "inner children," who, they say, lie wounded and in desperate need of relief within the wreckage of their grown-up selves. Imagine the celebrities and opinion-makers [having] these people talking nightly on TV and weekly in the magazines not about their triumphs but about their victimization, not about their power and fame but about their addictions and childhood persecutions.

Imagine that this belief in abused "inner children" dragging down grown-up men and women has become so widespread as to exert considerable influence over the policies of such supposedly practical bodies as corporations, public hospitals, and boards of education—which, in turn, have taken to acting as if the greatest threat facing their various constituencies is a nexus of addictions and other self-destructive "behaviors," ranging from alcoholism and drug addiction to the more nebulous, if satisfyingly all-encompassing, category of "codependency," a term meaning, in essence, any reliance for one's sense of self on the opinion of someone else, someone more often than not plagued by his or her own addiction. One would be imagining a place, then, where nearly everyone is identified—is identifying himself or herself—as some sort of psychological cripple. (From "Victims, All?" by David Rieff in *Harper's Magazine*)

The justification for the total scope of the responsibility to exercise is health. . . . The person, who does not exercise, in our current conception, is a slow suicide. . . . Conceive of a society in which it was believed that the senses could be used up. Eyesight worsened the more vivid sights you saw. Hearing worsened the more intense sounds you heard. It would be inevitable that such a conception would bleed into people's whole pattern of life, changing the way they spent their days. Would they use up their powers on the most saturated colors, listening to the most intoxicating sounds? Or might its members refuse to move, eyes shut, ears covered, nursing the remaining reserves of sensation? We, too, believe our daily lives are not being lived but eaten up by age. And we spend our time desperately. From the desperate materialist gratifications of a hedonistic society, commanding immediate comfort and happiness, we recoil to the desperate economics of health, and chase a longer span of happinesses deferred, and comforts delayed, by disposing of the better of our lives in life preservation. (From "Against Exercise" by Mark Greif in *N + 1*)

To begin with, the traveler [from an advanced industrial society that genuinely respected disabled people] would take for granted that a market of millions of children and tens of millions of adults would not be ignored. He would expect to find many industries catering to the special needs of the handicapped. He would look for cheap automobiles that could be safely and easily driven by a paraplegic or a quadriplegic. . . .

Overhearing discussions of America's energy crisis, he would expect to find that proposals for long-term energy strategies took into account the special needs and concerns of handicapped people. As he read our newspapers, magazines, journals, and books, as he watched our movies, television shows or went to our theaters, he would expect to find many reports about handicaps, many fictional characters who were handicapped, many cartoon figures . . . who were handicapped. (From *The Unexpected Minority: Handicapped Children in America* by John Gliedman and William Roth)

Nacirema culture is characterized by a highly developed market economy, which has evolved in a rich natural habitat. . . . The fundamental belief underlying the whole system appears to be that the human body is ugly and that its natural tendency is to debility and disease. Incarcerated in such a body, man's only hope is to avert these characteristics through the use of the powerful influences of ritual and ceremony. Every household has one or more shrines devoted to this purpose. . . . Most houses are of wattle and daub construction, but the shrine rooms of the more wealthy are walled with stone. . . . The Nacirema have an almost pathological horror of and fascination with the mouth, the condition of which is believed to have a supernatural influence on all social relationships. Were it not for the rituals of the mouth . . . their lovers [would] reject them. They also believe that a strong relationship exists between oral and moral characteristics. For example, there is a ritual ablution of the mouth for children, which is supposed to improve their moral fiber. (From "Body Ritual Among the Nacirema" by Horace Miner in *American Anthropologist*)

In hopes to ingratiate my self farther into his majesty's [the king of Brobdingnag's] favor, I told him of an invention discovered between three and four hundred years ago to make a certain powder; into a heap of which the smallest spark of fire falling would kindle the whole in a moment . . . that the largest balls thus discharged would not only destroy whole ranks of an army at once; but batter the strongest walls to the ground; sink down ships with a thousand men in each, to the bottom of the sea . . . dashing out the brains of all who came near. . . . This I humbly offered to his majesty, as a small tribute of acknowledgment in return of so many marks that I had received of his royal favor and protection. The king was struck with horror at the description I had given of those terrible engines, and the proposal I had made. He was amazed how so impotent and groveling an insect as I (these were his expressions) could entertain such inhuman ideas. . . .

He was perfectly astonished with the historical account I gave him of our affairs during the last century; protesting it was only a heap of conspiracies, rebellions, murders, massacres, revolutions, banishments; the very worst effect that avarice, faction, hypocrisy, perfidiousness, cruelty, rage, madness, hatred, envy, lust, malice and ambition could produce. . . . [At another audience saying] you have clearly proved that ignorance, idleness, and vice are the proper ingredients for qualifying a legislator. The laws are best explained, interpreted, and applied by those whose interest and abilities lie in perverting, confounding, and eluding them. . . . What I have gathered from your own relation, and the answers I have with much pains wringed and extorted from you; I cannot but conclude the bulk of your natives, to be the most pernicious race of little odious vermin that nature ever suffered to crawl upon the surface of the earth. (From "A Voyage to Brobdingnag" by Jonathan Swift in *Gulliver's Travels*)

2
FORM

Structure as Shuffled Forms

Form is an essay's bones. English teacher dogma insists upon an "ideal" *Form* to be used to organize an essay: Start with a thesis statement, divide the support for the thesis into three body sections, and restate the thesis in a concluding paragraph. While this structure is easy for teachers to evaluate, its application is limited to in-class, timed writings, in which a thin skin is grafted to a set structure. Spirited writers know this pre-cast skeleton protrudes, dehydrating energetic ideas and passionate style into essay carcasses. Instead, innovative writers use a variety of shaping devices, letting the essay's different purposes or functions dictate the *Form*.

The *Forms* used to organize sections or paragraphs within an essay are responses to specific articulation problems: The challenges faced when narrating factual events and describing non-fictional experiences are addressed in *Time Warping*. The difficulties with defining abstract concepts are tackled in *Encircling*. Solutions for disarming opponents in an argument are offered in *Bursting*. Tactics for intensifying key sections in an essay are listed in *Punching Up*. All of these remedies can then be combined and connected using the strategies in *Transitioning* to form the larger organizational structure.

TIME WARPING:
Ways to Narrate

Anecdoting
Pulsing the Tense
Splitting the Second
Problem Making

In an article for *American Educator*, Edward O. Wilson, a professor of zoology at Harvard University, observes that, "of the hundreds of fellow scientists I have known for more than 50 years, from graduate students to novelists, all generally prefer at random moments of their lives to listen to gossip and music rather than to scientific lectures." Wilson concludes (and neuroscientists and cognitive psychologists have theorized) that our gray matter is wired for narratives. Because readers struggle with less concrete subjects, including an authentic (or invented) mini-story in an academic essay awakens audiences to the potential imagery and drama of philosophical, historical, scientific, or business topics. Using a short narration to support a point requires *Anecdoting*, a strategy for smoothly weaving a story into an essay. *Pulsing the Tense* resurrects and intensifies past events through present tense narration. *Splitting the Second* slows down time to detail and highlight key moments. *Problem Making* divides a dramatic illustration, elevating a conflict and withholding resolution to serve as a thrilling climax.

Anecdoting

With the exception of in-class essay exams, most apprentice and professional writers would probably never construct a nonfiction exposition by first flatly serving up a thesis statement and then offering three dry proofs to support the argument. Those who are passionate about their subject matter—whether personal, scientific, historical, or philosophical—intuit the need to warm up the audience before delivering a thesis and anticipate a responsibility to flush out and explain raw evidence. These requirements can be met with *Anecdoting*, a miniature story within a nonfiction piece or argument that can fulfill a variety of functions.

Once the thesis is on the table, an essayist needs supporting side dishes to bolster the argument. Data and statistics gathered from research are always strong support, but a "just-the-facts-ma'am" approach can fail to convince a reader or appeal to an audience's *pathos*. *Anecdoting* also is a potent form of evidence.

Plotting. Whether using *Anecdoting* as a startling introduction to an essay or as dynamic evidence inside the body to firm up abstract ideas, the events within the mini-story cannot be oversimplified; instead, a writer adds and omits details to enhance the account. Such detailing involves borrowing fictional devices—building a suspenseful plot with a climax and a dénouement, establishing symbolic settings, forming vivid imagery, constructing revealing dialogue, molding intriguing characterizations, and shaping analogies and metaphor. However, there is an important difference between a fictional narrative and an anecdote in a nonfiction essay: In *Anecdoting*, the story is accompanied by an overt interpretation of the story and an explanation connecting the anecdote to major or minor ideas in the essay.

Framing. When *Anecdoting*, the main frame of the essay is temporarily suspended while the writer plunges into a story that relates a scene or an event, literally acting out an intangible concept. Once the narrative ends, the writer resurfaces to the larger frame of the essay. This jump-cutting can be accomplished with smooth, flowing transitions that gently escort the reader to and away from the *Anecdoting* (see *Twist Ties* in the *Transitioning* chapter). Other times, an essayist shifts with a heading or headline that sets the scene by titling the section with time and place (see *Captions* in *Transitioning*). Playing off the shock value of the anecdote, a writer may omit a transition altogether and abruptly move into the subnarrative (see *Double Exposure,* also in *Transtioning*).

Your turn. Identify the topic in each of the anecdotes below. Then write your own anecdote on one of those same subjects that might articulate a different point of view of that topic.

Overheard Anecdoting:

In my junior year in college I rode to a debate tournament with three white students and our faculty coach, an elderly English professor. . . . Halfway through the trip the professor casually turned to me and, in an isn't-the-world-funny sort of tone, said that he just refused to rent an apartment in a house he owned to a "very nice" black couple because their color would "offend" the white couple who lived downstairs. . . . His comment pressured me to choose between my class identification, which had contributed to my being a college student and a member of the debating team, and my desperate desire to be "black." I could have one but not both; I was double-bound. . . . I punished [the professor] not according to the measure of his crime but according to the measure of my vulnerability. . . .

   Seeing myself as a victim meant that I clung all the harder to my racial identity, which in turn, meant that I suppressed my class identity. This cut me off from all the resources my class values might have offered me. In those values, for instance, I might have found the means to a more dispassionate response, the response less of a victim attacked by a victimizer than of an individual offended by a foolish old man. (From "On Being Black and Middle Class" by Shelby Steele in *Commentary*)

Earlier this had happened: we had gone to a store where the Prince of Wales has his shirts made. . . . [The salesman] was very pleased with these, he said, because they bore the crest of the Prince of Wales, and the Prince of Wales had never allowed his crest to decorate an article of clothing before. There was something in the way he said it; his tone was slavish, reverential, awed. . . . I said, my husband and I hate princes; my husband would never wear anything that had a prince's anything on it. My friend stiffened. The salesman stiffened. They both drew themselves in, away from me. My friend told me that the prince was a symbol of her Englishness, and I could see that I had caused offense. I looked at her. She was an English person, the sort of English person I used to know at home [in Antigua, a former British colony, populated by descendents of African slaves], the sort who was nobody in England but somebody when they came to live among the people like me [an African American]. There were many people I could have seen England with; that I was seeing it with this particular person, a person who reminded me of the people who showed me England long ago as I sat in church or at my desk, made me feel silent and afraid, for I wondered if, all these years of our friendship, I had had a friend or had been in the thrall of a racial memory. (From "On Seeing England for the First Time" by Jamaica Kincaid in *Transition*)

With the help of the ice cubes I have been trying to think, because *The American Scholar* asked me to, in some abstract way about "morality," a word I distrust more every day, but my mind veers inflexibly toward the particular.

Here are some particulars. At midnight last night, on the road in from Las Vegas to Death Valley Junction, a car hit a shoulder and turned over. The driver, very young and apparently drunk, was killed instantly. His girl was found alive but bleeding internally, deep in shock. I talked this afternoon to the nurse who had driven the girl to the nearest doctor, 185 miles across the floor of the Valley and three ranges of lethal mountain road. The nurse explained that her husband, a talc miner, had stayed on the highway with the boy's body until the coroner could get over the mountains from Bishop, at dawn today. "You can't just leave a body on the highway," she said. "It's immoral."

It was one instance in which I did not distrust the word, because she meant something quite specific. She meant that if a body is left alone for even a few minutes on the desert, the coyotes close in and eat the flesh. Whether or not a corpse is torn apart by coyotes may seem only a sentimental consideration, but of course it is more: one of the promises we make to one another is that we will try to retrieve our casualties, try not to abandon our dead to the coyotes. If we have been taught to keep our promises—if, in the simplest terms, our upbringing is good enough—we stay with the body, or have bad dreams.

I am talking, of course, about the kind of social code that is sometimes called, usually pejoratively, "wagon-train morality." (From "On Morality" by Joan Didion in *Slouching Toward Bethlehem*)

The cradle rocks above an abyss, and common sense tells us that our existence is but a brief crack of light between two eternities of darkness. Although the two are identical twins, man, as a rule, views the prenatal abyss with more calm than the one he is heading for (at some forty-five hundred heartbeats an hour). I know, however, of a young chronophobiac who experienced something like panic when looking for the first time at homemade movies that had been taken a few weeks before his birth. He saw a world that was practically unchanged—the same house, the same people— and then realized that he did not exist there at all and that nobody mourned his absence. He caught a glimpse of his mother waving from an upstairs window, and that unfamiliar gesture disturbed him, as if it were some mysterious farewell. But what particularly frightened him was the sight of a brand-new baby carriage standing there on the porch, with the smug, encroaching air of a coffin; even that was empty, as if, in the reverse course of events, his very bones had disintegrated. (From "Perfect Past" by Vladimir Nabokov in *Speak, Memory*)

So in the following American years, my blissfully remarried mother would continue to evade every mention of my father [who had been killed in World War II], wipe away every trace of the warrior lying in his military grave thousands of miles across the ocean. Like my stepfather, she geared all activity to goals of social advancement and career, worked prodigiously hard, gambled, laughed, dined and entertained the years away as she sought out the company of the powerful, talented, and wealthy. (The dead are none of these; snobs are seldom good at mourning.) And within a year or two, I began to play her game; I began to forget with her, for it was by far the easier and lazier plan. . . . I collaborated like a traitor; I soon transferred to my charming, generous stepfather the affection I had borne for the dead warrior. I came to know the euphoria of burying the ancestral past rather than burying the dead. . . . Only decades later did I grasp the link between Ismene's limp obedience to Creon [in Sophocles' play *Antigone*] and my own cowardice about the rites and rights of a dead one lost in war. Only recently have I realized that the role of Ismene, "that beauteous measure of the ordinary," as Kierkegaard describes her, was the one my mother and I had played together for some years. (From "The Work of Mourning" by Francine du Plessix Gray in *The American Scholar*)

Pulsing the Tense

When discussing important moments from our past or notable historical events, we use the past tense: People in the past *smiled, suffered, preserved dignity, consumed love and devoured the land, were oppressed and became liberated.* Poignant and painful memories recounted in the past tense allow an audience to psychologically relax, creating a comfortable distance by implying the agonizing events and tender moments are over and done. But when relegated to these outskirts of time, remarkable incidents can lose their heat-of-the-moment momentum in past-tense verbs. The past becomes freeze-dried. This "correct" tense may not be the most dramatically advantageous.

Separating. When it comes to writing about past personal events, one might argue that using present tense makes the narrative more objective. George Kennan, one of the first American ambassadors to the former Soviet Union, uses present tense when writing about history in order to "stress the responsibility of these memories in speaking for themselves and to distance the young [person] who received the experiences from the elderly one who now recalls them." A writer who explores past events in the present tense allows readers into a very special realm where details seem both unreal—haunted by a backwards movement through time possible only in dreams—and super-real—outlined with a clarity obtained only when considering events in retrospect. Past events that appear to unfold in the present create still-warm happenings that demand the reader's attention.

Pulsing. In revising a personal memory or an account of a significant historical event, one begins by reworking the verbs since they control tense. Instead of describing a moment from the past as, "*Ten years ago I walked into my lover's house; everyone was watching,*" one *Pulses the Tense* by writing, "*It is ten years ago and I am walking into my lover's house; everyone is watching.*" (See *Personalizing Lens* in *Opt.*) As the writer works through the process of revising the tense, a strange phenomenon starts to happen: the writer, now thinking of the event in the present moments, begins to remember or notice small but significant details that help to give depth and verisimilitude to the narration.

There is one more important use of present tense. When writing on a work of literature, there is a tendency to describe the fictional actions in the past tense because our experience reading the work is finished. However, literary experiences are always living: when we close the book, someone else immediately opens it. Describing poems, stories, dramas, and films in the present tense keeps that reality alive.

Your turn. In the excerpts below, identify what details become more intense because of the present tense narration. Then research an historical event or use a personal memory as the basis for practicing present-tense narration.

Revisits with Pulsing:

The purges [Communist political trails of 1937] are now at their height. The Ambassador is invited to attend the second of the three great public purge trials—the visible tip of the immense iceberg of terror and cruelty, which is now crushing Soviet society. He takes me with him as his interpreter, and I, sitting next to him, whisper into his ear what I can of the proceedings. He understands nothing of what is really going on. He even thinks the accused are genuinely guilty of the preposterous charges to which they are confessing, and he sententiously pronounces this opinion, during the intermission, to the assembled American journalists. But I do know what is going on; and the sight of these ashen, doomed men, several of them only recently prominent figures of the regime but now less than twenty-four hours away from their executions—the sight of these men standing there mumbling their preposterous confessions in the vain hope of saving themselves, or perhaps the members of their families, from disaster, the sight of their twitching lips, their prison pallor, their evasive downcast eyes—is never to leave my memory.

(From "Flashbacks" by George Kennan in *The New Yorker*)

Suddenly I see the past, superimposed on this hot moment. I've seen it before, again and again, cars full of little Indian kids in the heat of summer on the sides of roads. I glance again, see the woman in the front seat, know that she's their mother or their aunt. She looks weary and resigned, not really sad. She expects this.

And then in another blink it's not only that I have seen this woman; I have *been* this woman, my old car or someone else's packed with little kids who are almost preternaturally quiet, wide-eyed and dark-skinned and already knowing that this is a big part of what life is about, sitting in boiling back seats, their arms jammed against the arms of their brother, their sister, their cousin . . . (From "Wounded Chevy at Wounded Knee" by Diana Hume George in *The Missouri Review*)

After all, a long time ago, in Freud's Vienna, the crazy man was seen as someone close to creativity, Van Gogh's stars stuffed in his twilit skull. . . . I trace the loss of these views to the rise, in the late 1950's, of Humanistic Psychology and the work of Abraham Maslow. Maslow believed in what he called a Hierarchy of Basic Needs. . . . In the Maslowian model, which dominates modern psychiatric treatment, the very weight of the psychotic illness, with its attendant terrors and confusions, would likely subsume striving of a higher sort.

And yet, as I begin to listen to the men in my group, as week after week goes by, I think I start to see glimmers of higher-level capabilities. Oscar's delusions have an awful lot to do with girl-friends who turn into lizards. . . . Do these delusions, I wonder, possibly reflect a mature desire for intimacy in such seemingly immature minds? I'm not sure. I need to push things, explore a little.

It is late August now, and I've been leading the group for two months. . . . Pieces of madness cling to me like lint, and I can't shake them off. (From *Welcome to My Country* by Lauren Slater)

My father is the driver for the rich old white lady up the road. Her name is Miss May. She owns all the land for miles around, as well as the house in which we live. All I remember about her is that she once offered to pay my mother 75 cents for cleaning her house, raking up piles of her magnolia leaves, and wash-ing her family's clothes, and that my mother—she of no money, eight children, and a chronic earache—refused it. But I do not think of this in 1947. I am two-and-a-half years old. I want to go everywhere my daddy goes. . . . It is Easter Sunday, 1950. I am dressed in a green, flocked scalloped-hem dress. . . . When I rise to give my speech I do so on a great wave of love and pride and expectation. People in church stop rustling their new crinolines. They seem to hold their breath. I can tell they admire my dress, but it is my spirit, bordering on sassiness (womanishness) they secretly applaud. (From "Beauty: When the Other Dancer Is the Self" by Alice Walker in *In Search of Our Mothers' Gardens*)

[In an imagined, old film] it is Sunday afternoon, June 12th, 1909, and my father is walking down the quiet streets of Brooklyn on his way to visit my mother. . . . My father thinks of my mother, of how lady-like she is, and of the pride which will be his when he introduces her to his family. They are not yet engaged and he is not yet sure that he loves my mother, so that, once in a while, he becomes panicky about the bond already established. But he reassures himself by thinking of the big men he admires who are married: William Randolph Hearst and William Howard Taft, who has just become the President of the United States. My father arrives at the house. . . . It is evident that the respect in which my father is held in this house is tempered by a good deal of mirth. He is impressive, but also very awkward. (From "In Dreams Begin Responsibilities" by Delmore Schwartz)

Carol Smith is lecturing on Virgina Woolf's *To the Lighthouse*. She is talking about the relationship between Mr. And Mrs. Ramsay in "The Window" section of the novel. I have never in my life heard such genius. I am taking notes, watching her talk, and watching her belly. She is very pregnant. She is wearing a beige maternity dress. I take down every word, while watching to see when the baby she is pregnant with will kick her again. (From "A Portrait of the Puttana as a Middle-Aged Woolf Scholar" in *Between Women*)

In my dream the night is as pure and dark as a blackened negative. . . . As I cross the field, taking slow and careful steps but determined to reach the ominous yet familiar stone building at any cost, I become aware that the entire sloping field has been blanketed with enormous soft round pads of cow manure. They are round as flagstone, thick as the width of a man's hand on edge, spongy within and thickly encrusted without, soft and resilient and yet able to bear the full weight of a heavy man, though there is always the possibility of piercing the crust and sinking into the slime within. . . . But suddenly I know that the shapes lying like dark and spongy land mines beneath my feet are composed not of cow dung, as I had thought, but of congealed blood. (From *Death, Sleep, & the Traveler* by John Hawkes)

My friend and I, two women obviously engrossed in conversation, are sitting at a corner table in the crowed Oak room of the Plaza at ten o'clock on a Tuesday night. A man materializes and interrupts us with the snappy opening line, "A good woman is hard to find."

We say nothing, hoping he will disappear back into his bottle. But he fancies himself as our genie and asks, "Are you visiting?" Still we say nothing. Finally my friend looks up and says, "We live here." She and I look at each other, the thread of our conversations napped, our thoughts focused on how to get rid of this intruder. In a minute, if something isn't done, he will scrunch down next to me on the banquette and start offering to buy us drinks.

"Would you leave us alone, please," I say in a loud but reasonably polite voice. He looks slightly offended but goes on with his bright social patter. I become more explicit. "We don't want to talk to you, we didn't ask you over here, and we want to be alone. Go away." This time he directs his full attention to me—and he is mad. . . . When he passes our table on the way out of the room, this well-dressed, obviously affluent man mutters, "Good-bye, bitch," under his breath.

Why is this man calling me names? Because I have asserted my right to sit at a table in a public place without being drawn into a sexual flirtation. Because he has been told, in no uncertain terms, that two attractive women prefer each other's company to his. (From "Unfair Game" by Susan Jacoby in *The New York Times*)

Splitting the Second

Describing a brief, poignant moment of heightened reality—the fleeting passion of a lover's kiss, the lightening quickness of a great basketball player moving down court to score, the exhilaration of seeing two mountain lions appear on the trail and then disappear, the transitory confusion upon awakening from an intense dream—presents a challenging narrative task for the essayist: Without glossing over the event so quickly in writing-time, the writer must grapple with capturing swift actions so that the event's worth can be fully savored by the reader. Inevitably the written piece will take much longer to experience than the actual event, yet the intensity of the event must not dissipate.

Splitting. To purposefully draw out a pertinent moment, the essayist must chop larger, more general actions or motions into smaller sections, literally *Splitting the Second* for the reader. For instance, in the description below by N. Scott Momaday, the general action—two eagles flying overhead—is slow-motioned, revealing more subtle movements, resulting in many descriptive verbs: "cavorting, spinning, and spiraling." These playful actions and the form of the verbs used to describe them, with their lilting "ing" endings, begin to suggest a distinct mood.

Toning. Once the action has been *Split* and the mood begins to emerge, a specific tone can be further enhanced through carefully selected verbs and adjectives that both unify the event and suggest mood without the writer ever explicitly stating it. Strong essayists stay away from qualifying or judgmental terms or abstractions such as "beautiful," "ugly," or "unfair" and allow the details and the style to simultaneously describe and be the proof for the thesis or mood.

For instance, Momaday filters the scene by using colors such as blue, silver, copper, clear, or golden, all gleaming visuals that suggest an ethereal tone. In the example which follows Momaday's (also about flight), Annie Dillard includes sensory details, not just of what she sees, but kinesthetic details that register panic: "I forced myself to hold my heavy head up against the G's and to raise my eyelids, heavy as barbells," and nerve-rattling acoustic details: "everything made noise and shook" and "somebody shouted at me." These sensory details also help *Split* the swift action and focus the event's blur.

Fusing. Both Dillard and Momaday include details about a snake, but each has different metaphorical implications: Momaday's snake flickers "like a bit of silver thread," becoming a symbol of the sun, and is a shared object of play which unites the male and female in a mating dance; Dillard's snake seen from the airplane is "in the green shallows" and is unexpected, an ominous reminder of life on the ground. *Flow* and *Pause* also become metaphorical, underscoring the thesis mood: placing emphasis on *Flow* in the Momaday *Split* suggests a calming, light, or ponderous mood; accenting *Pause* in the Dillard piece announces a tense, disquieting, or fearful tone.

Your turn. Study the *Flow*, *Pause*, *Fusion*, and details in the excerpts below; then label each passage by its overall thesis-mood. Note what details correspond to the senses—sight, smell, sound, touch, and taste. After studying the passages below, describe a fleeting experience. Title your passage with a specific mood. Never mention that mood in the passage, but sustain it in over two pages of description.

Glimpses of Splitting the Second:

They were golden eagles, a male and a female, in their mating flight. They were cavorting, spinning and spiraling on the cold, clear columns of air and they were beautiful. They swooped and hovered, leaning on the air, and swung close together, feinting and screaming with delight. The female was full grown, and the span of her broad wings was greater than any man's height. There was a fine flourish to her motion; she was deceptively incredibly fast, and her pivots and wheels were wide and full bloom. But her great weight was streamlined and perfectly controlled. She carried a rattlesnake; it hung shining from her feet, limp and curving out in the trail of her flight. Suddenly her wings and tail fanned, catching full on the wind, and for an instant she was still, widespread and spectral in the blue, while her mate flared past and away, turning around in the distance to look for her. Then she began to beat upward at an angle from the rim until she was small in the sky, and she let go of the snake. It fell slowly, writhing and rolling, floating out like a bit of silver thread against the wide backdrop of the land. She held still above, buoyed up on the cold current, her crop and hackles were gleaming like copper in the sun. The male swerved and sailed. He was younger than she and a little more than half as large. He was quicker, tighter in his moves. He let the carrion drift by; then suddenly he gathered himself and stooped, sliding down in a blur motion to the strike. He hit the snake on the head, with not the slightest deflection of his course or speed, upward in a great pendulum arc, riding out his momentum. At the top of his glide he let go of the snake in turn, but the female did not go for it. Instead she soared out over the plain, nearly out of sight like a mote receding into the haze of the far mountain. The male followed, and Abel watched them go, straining to see, saw them veer once, dip and disappear. (From *House Made of Dawn* by Natachee Scott Momaday)

Pitching snow filled all the windows, and shapes of dark rock. I had no notion which way was up. Everything was black or gray or white except the fatal crevasses; everything made noise and shook. I felt my face smashed sideways and saw rushing abstractions of snow in the windshield. Patches of cloud obscured the mountainside for another pass, which was made, apparently, on our rear, and fell away. If a commercial plane's black box, such as the FAA painstakingly removes from crash sites, could store videotapes as well as pilots' last words, some video tapes would look like this: a mountainside coming up at the windows from all directions, ice and snow and rock filling the screen up close and screaming by. . . . I saw the windshield fill with red rock. The mountain looked infernal, a dreary and sheer plane of lifeless rock. It was red and sharp; its gritty blades cut through the clouds at random. The mountain was quiet. It was in shade. Careening, we made sideways passes at these brittle peaks too steep for snow. Their rock was full of iron, somebody shouted at me then or later; the iron had rusted, so they were red. Later, when I was back on the ground, I recalled that, from a distance, the two jagged peaks called the Twin Sisters looked translucent against the sky; they were sharp, tapered and fragile as arrowheads. . . . I caught a snake in the salt chuck; the snake, eighteen inches long, was swimming in the green shallows. (From "The Stunt Pilot" by Annie Dillard in *Esquire*)

The soft freckled light cradles each deep shadow with brightness, illuminating the canopy of towering tree canopies, allowing breezes to accentuate dewdrops, each one reflecting a vast array of green shades and tints. A cloud moves. The light penetrates further, creating sparkling hollows around small translucent leaves laced among dripping crimson flowers. Now a cloud curtains the sun. Lavenders and plum-purples quickly veil the garden, masking the edges of the larger shadows. Every flower bends slightly in the wind as a fortune of silver-dollar eucalyptus leaves rustle, whispering a welcome. (From "Landscape Description after Monet" by Tamara TeGantvoort, freshman composition assignment)

In an even higher tone, [Castro] repeats, "*Buenos noches*," this time with a few waves to the group while hastening toward the guest of honor; and then, with his arms extended, the seventy-year-old Fidel Castro immediately obscures the lower half of [Muhammad] Ali's expressionless face with a gentle embrace and his flowing gray beard.

"I am glad to see you," Castro says to Ali, via the interpreter who followed him into the room, a comely, fair-skinned woman with a refined English accent. "I am very, very glad to see you," Castro continues, backing up to look into Ali's eyes while holding on to his trembling arms, "and I am thankful for your visit." Castro then releases his grip and awaits a possible reply. Ali says nothing. His eyes do not blink despite the flashbulbs of several surrounding photographers. As the silence persists, Castro turns toward his old friend Teofilo Stevenson, feigning a jab. The Cuban boxing champion lowers his eyes and, with widened lips and cheeks, registers a smile. Castro then notices the tiny brunette standing beside Stevenson. (From "Ali in Havana" by Gay Talese in *Esquire*)

The huddle breaks, 11 Rams amble toward the line of scrimmage, two tight ends at the left of the line. Quarterback Kurt Warner stands behind the center, and suddenly, the choreographed confusion in the St. Louis offense begins.

The tight ends might move to the right side of the line and running back Marshall Faulk changes his position behind Warner. The defensive players are pointing, shouting, some linemen moving like crabs. Warner leans down and starts calling signals, and Faulk breaks from his crouch, moves forward in a straight line and turns at a right angle to the right side of the line. There is more pointing by the defensive players, more shouting, Faulk stops, and then wide receiver Isaac Bruce sprints toward Warner, parallel to the line of scrimmage, gaining speed. The defensive players are pointing again and the ball is snapped.

(From "Rams' Organized Confusion Can Befuddle Any Defense" by Buster Olney in *The New York Times*)

Summer, ninety-five degrees. The residential unit for chronic schizophrenics sits dead and silent in the heat. I ring the bell and a fat sweating boy, his face a mash of pimples, answers. "I am here to see Dr. Siley," I say, glancing down at the job advertisement in my hand. The pimply-faced boy stares and stares at me. I can tell, from his fatness and sweat, that he is a patient. He reaches out and touches my neck. I flinch. "What's wrong?" he hisses at me, spittle foaming in the corners of his lips. "You don't like me, you don't like me, you don't like me?" He sings it more than says it, and I don't know how to answer. I want to say, "I'm sorry." I want to say, "You scare me," but instead I repeat, my voice tight, "Please, I'm here to see Dr. Siley. Could you get him for me?" The boy backs away. My very first contact with a patient has gone cold. "Dr. Siley," he wails, running down the cool hall of the institution. "Dr. Siley, some new shrink is here. Watch out for her. She's an alien. She has no bones in her neck." (From *Welcome to My Country* by Lauren Slater, psychologist)

Problem Making

Does anyone really appreciate trigonometry before being startled by an engineering problem that requires trig as a solution? Do history students sincerely appreciate the United States' system of checks-and-balances unless they have knowledge of the terror that exists in countries where that system is absent? Too often, erudite writers fail to first immerse their readers in the complexity of problems—biological, sociological, psychological, philosophical, political, historical or aesthetic design problems—instead too quickly getting to answers, stymieing suspense, and depriving readers of an appreciation of those answers, which in turn makes the answers less memorable. This fast-forwarding-to-solutions tendency in essays is about as effective as a stand-up routine where the comedian delivers the punch line before adequately setting up the joke.

Delaying. Before delivering the solution, the writer must thoroughly absorb the reader in a specific problem, delaying the delivery of the solution until the problem is so flushed out that predicament seems insurmountable. The more intriguing and seemingly insoluble the problem, the more intense and amazing will be the solution. Before giving up solutions, the writer needs to imagine a worst-case scenario, detailing all the horrible things that would happen if there were no solution.

Backgrounding. Dramatizing the problem often requires background research. But in conducting research—on Napoleon's Russian military campaign, on the amazing ability of the cheetah, on David Foster Wallace's creative use of footnotes in a short story—researchers will find sources that do not dramatize problems, that list solutions without *Punching Up* initial dilemmas. While researching, a strong writer needs to sift for problem-related material by imagining limitations one would have if Napoleon were not equipped with military strategy, the cheetah did not have specialized traits, or David Foster Wallace did not think of footnotes. What would a person do if outnumbered by a trained army and plagued by miserable weather? What would it take for a human without technology to catch a hoofed animal that runs over fifty miles an hour? What would a writer do if trying to dramatize the thin line between editorial commentary and objective reality? These are the questions that help generate details to create the problems so often taken for granted by researched writings desperate to explain with answers and solutions.

Highlighting. There are several ways to *highlight* the problem part of this essay. Research other solutions (of similar or related problems) as points of comparisons, but explain why the problem you are writing about cannot be solved in that same way. Or describe the problem by using *Anecdoting* or *Splitting the Second* to describe the problem as it unfolds in real time. Both the problem and solution parts of the essay need to employ all the *Style* techniques to breathe life into such a heavily researched essay.

Your turn. In the problem/solution paragraphs below, identify the transition point where the problem ends and the solution begins. Practice this technique by researching a bird, insect, or marine organism, noting how a particular creature solves a survival problem (excluding man-made problems). Then organize your research by first dramatizing the problem, considering all relevant factors: environment, size, and other limitations. Do not reveal the solution until you have adequately dramatized the problem.

Clinchers of Problem Making:

Poor eyesight may account for all the opossum roadkill sightings, so the opossum must rely on its others senses—a police dog sense of smell and miracle ear hearing—to negotiate its environment (Major). The North American marsupial perfumes itself in a homemade brand of *eau de saliva*, giving the animal a signature aroma; this scent enables mothers and their young to fragrance-find one another (Stewart). The opossum's cologne also whiffmarks territory and noses out neighbors, this small mammal being a loner type. But the opossum's unusual hygiene habits also open-house many small bugs around the animal as it tries to sleep: gnats, fleas and other small parasites camp inside the ear tents. While the opossum's alarm system hearing protects the animal, it also has a negative side—the opossum is nocturnal, sleeping during the day when the acoustics can reach stadium levels (Didier). Those ears, which act as vents and keep the animal cool during warm temperatures, actually work against the opossum during winter days and nights, the mammal's furry warmth escaping from these large ear holes. With annoying bugs, clamoring noise and frightful cold loitering around the opossum's ears, how does the marsupial get a good day's sleep? The opossum's amenities include Venetian blind ears which roll-up, noiseproofing the animal, do-no-disturb-signing any invaders, and keeping in the Coleman-stove warmth. (From "The Camper" by Glynis Hoffman for a freshman composition assignment)

In our closely interconnected world, sharing with those around us has long been a sign of camaraderie, the mark of a truly altruistic society, and an essential ingredient in being considered a valued member of one's own community. Yet even though we celebrate communal harmony, all too often we are guilty of behaving selfishly, greedily focusing on ourselves rather than looking at the private challenges and shameful misfortunes of others. We must pause for a moment to reflect on our responsibilities as participating members of society, and recognize the desperate need to break the egocentric cycle of only being concerned about oneself—we must make the concerns of others our own. Openness in all affairs is paramount: we must actively involve ourselves in the personal matters—intimate, sometimes even disgraceful, stuff too often unwholesomely classified as "confidential" or "none-of-our-business of our family,"—of our friends, neighbors, associates, acquaintances, passersby, and all others in our close circle of community. We must recognize our civic responsibility to bestow upon those around us any and all details (however minute, confidential, or seemingly personal) to which we are privy. One cannot underestimate the power of sharing. How it unifies. How it gives back to the community. Unselfishly, we must search outside ourselves for said details, energetically pursuing leads on interesting real-life stories that could potentially enhance dull, day-to-day conversation working towards the goal of always having some tidbit to share. If nothing titillating is available, be creative. After all, embellishments are life's artistic treasures. (From "Building Community" by Kacy Nakamura for a Devil's Advice assignment in freshman composition).

Our fear about the depiction of the Holocaust is not only that it will be trivialized, but also that it will be assimilated to the Western tradition of tragedy, that organizing it will allow us in some sense to dismiss it—to leave the theater of history, purged. But with its seemingly bizarre juxtaposition of visual and literary struggles, *Maus* [a comic book that depicts Jews as mice, Poles as pigs, and Germans as cats] manages to give dignity to the sufferers without suggesting that their suffering had any "meaning" in a sense that in some way ennobled the sufferers, or that their agony has a transcendent element because it provides some catharsis for those of us who are told about, or shown, their suffering. . . . We want an art whose stylizations are as much a declaration of inadequacy to their subject as they are of mystical transcendence. . . . The homely animal device [turning people into animals without individual faces] is able to depict the sacred by a kind of comic indirection. . . . Art Spiegelman may be rooted in a much more profound set of solutions—solutions that turn deliberately to the homely and the unpretentious, rather than to the transcendent and mystical, in order to depict the sacred. (From "Comics and Catastrophe" by Adam Gopnik in *The New Republic*)

But when the bat is nearby, three meters or less, the insect is in immediate and mortal danger, for now the bat's sonar provides an accurate localization. It is too late for swerving or veering; because of its superior speed the bat can easily track such simple evasions. What to do? . . . The answer, for a cricket or moth or lacewing that hears a bat homing in close by, is chaos. Instead of swerving away, the insect launches into wild, totally erratic, random flight patterns, as unpredictable as possible. This kind of response tends to confuse the bat and results in escape for the insect frequently enough to have been selected by evolution as the final, stereotyped, "last chance" response to the threat. It has the look of a very smart move, whether thought out or not. (From "Crickets, Bats, Cats, & Chaos" by Lewis Thomas in *Audubon*)

What happens if the work of mourning does not proceed on this detailed and stately course, if the enormous energy available for the labor of grief does not find its proper tools or associations? It can become what Freud calls "pathological mourning." Like those spirits of the dead in Greek literature who, if improperly mourned, return to cause malevolent mischief—devastating crops, destroying whole towns—the psychic energies of mourning, if repressed, can wreak grievous harm. They can turn inward into a dangerous process of self-devouring (as when we "eat our hearts out"). They can metamorphose into what we now call depression, a condition for which Freud preferred the more resonant, tradition-laden term *melancholia.*

It is not traditional, but very useful, to read Freud and Homer simultaneously. What is most striking in both texts is the sheer energy civilized folk have devoted to rituals of mourning. Here I am in books 5, 6, and 7 of *The Iliad,* looking in on the clamorous terror of Homeric battle. Lances are being driven clear through eye sockets, livers, and genitals, brains pour out of mouths and severed heads. . . . And on both sides night is spent in lamentations, in washing and anointing the treasured corpses. . . . Quite as high and treasurable as weal and fame, Homer intimates throughout the epic, is the honor of proper funeral, and life's principal terror is the disgrace of being insufficiently mourned and inadequately buried. (From "The Work of Mourning" by Francine du Plessix Gray in *The American Scholar*)

Legend has it that love is blind. And lust is blind. . . . In the vast majority of cases, erotic energy does better work when channeled and curtailed than spilled. In the vast majority of cases, students and teachers should not sleep with each other, if you ask me. Not for the reasons often cited—not because of power differentials and disillusion with authority and lifelong trauma, which occur no more or less in these than in other relationships—but because it would very quickly become dull and sap away too much energy. When a student has a crush on a teacher, it is a powerful and productive thing: she or he works much harder, listens far more voraciously, appropriates, in many cases, the teacher's intellectual enthusiasms. The student becomes a sponge for knowledge. When a teacher has a weakness for even one student in a lecture hall, the whole class benefits; she or he speaks with far greater care, switches from autopilot to real-think mode, and (with luck) even looks forward to reading papers. (From "The Higher Yearning" by Cristina Nehring in *Harper's Magazine*)

In the roadrunner's hot, dry desert environment, all this hyper-activity would seem likely to dehydrate the bird. . . . But he has adapted remarkably well to temperatures over one hundred degrees and dry winds. His biggest problem—water—is solved by careful budgeting. He rests in the shade during the hottest part of the day, and replenishes body water through his diet; he eats things like lizards, whose bodies have high water content, and then manufactures liquid by oxidation of the food into carbon dioxide. (From "With Legs Like These Who Needs Wings?" by George E. Hollister in *National Wildlife Association*)

ENCIRCLING:
Ways to Define

Thesauruscoping
Cliché Busting
Quote Sandwiching
Stress Testing
Pie Slicing

Satirist Ambrose Bierce, in *The Enlarged Devil's Dictionary*, defines a dictionary as "A malevolent literary device for cramping the growth of a language and making it hard and inelastic." Rigid English teachers limit their discussion of definition to categories of *denotation* (dictionary meaning) and *connotation* (implied associations). When defining an abstract concept, describing a familiar or strange object, or characterizing a unique group of people, elastic writers always move beyond the inflexibility of dictionary meaning, beyond categories of denotation and connotation and gravitate towards defining strategies that swing wide and penetrate deeply. This unit offers several tools for capturing complex definitions: *Thesauruscoping* makes subtle distinctions between synonyms and finds connections between antonyms. *Cliché Busting* clean-slates tired, traditional, brain-numbing definitions, preparing readers for fresh ideas. *Quote Sandwiching* borrows well-crafted prose from other writers to inspire, support, or challenge a new definition. *Stress Testing* considers a concept through different perspectives. *Pie Slicing* breaks a concept into subgroups, each segment defining and clarifying the subtype.

Thesauruscoping

Making careful distinctions between seemingly similar words or objects is one of the tasks of *Thesauruscoping*. Through the use of comparison and contrast, *Thesauruscoping* involves hunting down synonyms, not for the purpose of carelessly *replacing* an abstraction with a cheap imitation, but for *arguing* the fine distinctions in meaning between synonymous terms. For instance, a writer *Thesauruscoping* with the abstract concept "complain," first lists its word cousins: "gripe," "bitch," "whine," "protest," and "criticize." By contrasting "complain" to one of its synonyms, "whine," the writer notes a significant difference:

> A "complaint" is a formal plea, the adult way to register protest, while a "whine" is a high-pitched squeal, an adolescent gripe, where the curdling cry distracts from the actual grievance.

Accentuating the contrast between the two terms becomes a way of exploring the shades and nuances of the targeted word.

Michael Silverblatt, the host of public radio program "Bookworm," observes that writers often demonstrate how a "word means itself and its opposite." Thus another way to use *Thesauruscoping* is to make a case for how an abstract idea is more like its *antonym* or akin to a seemingly unrelated concept. For instance, complaining is often regarded as antithetical to "taking action." By looking for similarities between "complaining" and its action-taking antonym, a writer discovers interesting, overlooked facets of the word "complain":

> Conventional wisdom regarding "complaining" insists that it is a waste of time: "Doers" caution us to quit our griping and get our asses moving. However, a "complaint" can be tantamount to action; it can be proactive. Bitching is a method of preparedness, a way of campaigning for our cause, the stretching of muscles before the marathon, a mustering up of troops prior to the battle, an affidavit that declares our position for our day in court. Complaining *is* change.

Purposely flouting readers' expectations, writers generate provocative ideas and new insight into abstract concepts by contrasting *synonyms* or comparing *antonyms* with *Thesauruscoping*.

Your turn. Determine whether the *Thesauruscopings* below contrast synonyms or compare antonyms. Then, pick one of the samples and do the opposite: if the writer worked with a synonym then *Thesauruscope* with an antonym.

Tracks from Thesauruscoping:

A house: a structural arrangement of space, geometrically laid out to provide what are called rooms, these divided from one another by verticals and horizontals called walls, ceilings, floors. The house contains the home but is not identical with it. The house anticipates the home and will very likely survive it, reverting again simply to house when home (that is, life) departs. For only where there is life can there be home. (From "They All Just Went Away" by Joyce Carol Oates in *The New Yorker*)

Happiness is often misunderstood as a synonym for pleasure or as an antonym for suffering. But Aristotle associated happiness with ethics—codes of behavior that urge us toward the sensation of getting it right, a kind of work that yields the "click" of satisfaction upon solving a problem or surmounting an obstacle. (From "What's Wrong with Animal Rights" by Vicki Hearne in *Harper's Magazine*)

I had botched a great many pieces of wood before I mastered the right angle with a saw, botched even more before I learned to miter a joint. The knowledge of these things resides in my hands and eyes and the webwork of muscles, not in the tools. There are machines for sale—powered miter boxes and radial arm saws, for instance—that will enable any casual soul to cut proper angles in boards. The skill is invested in the gadget instead of the person who uses it, and this is what distinguishes a machine from a tool. If I had to earn my keep by making furniture or building houses, I suppose I would buy powered saws and pneumatic nailers; the need for speed would drive me to it. But since I carpenter only of my own pleasure or to help neighbors or to remake the house around the ears of my family, I stick with hand tools. (From "The Inheritance of Tools" by Scott Russell Sanders in *The North American Review*)

Both the *OED* and *Webster's* definitions are inattentive to the crucial distinction between envy and jealousy. . . . The real distinction is that one is jealous of what one has, envious of what other people have. Jealousy is not always pejorative; one can after all be jealous of one's dignity, civil rights, honor. Envy, except when used in the emulative sense mentioned by Aristotle, is always pejorative. If jealousy is, in cliché parlance, spoken of as the "green-eyed monster," envy is cross-, squinty-, and blearily red eyed. Never, to put it very gently, a handsome or good thing, envy. (From "The Green-Eyed Monster: Envy is Nothing to be Jealous of" by Joseph Epstein from *Washington Monthly*)

The best definition of a player derives from its antonym, though the antonym proves elusive. Several candidates come to mind. It is imprecise, I think, to say the opposite of a player is a loser. Not all players win. "Spectator" is a better antonym, but not the best.

We will get our best defining antonym by reducing the word to its root: "play." Ask any kid, "What's the opposite of play?" and you will have the word you seek: "work.". . . The opposite of the player is the worker. So said John Ruskin, who saw humanity divided into "two races, one of workers, and the other of players: one tilling the ground, manufacturing, building, and otherwise providing for the necessities of life; the other proudly idle, and continually therefore needing recreation, in which they use the productive and laborious orders partly as their cattle, and partly as their puppets or pieces in the game of death." (From "Crap Shoot" by Garret Keizer *Harper's Magazine*)

Cuteness is not an aesthetic in the ordinary sense of the word and must not be mistaken for the physically appealing, the attractive. In fact, it is closely linked to the grotesque, the malformed. The grotesque is cute because the grotesque is pitiable, and pity is the primary emotion of this seductive and manipulative aesthetic, which arouses our sympathies by creating anatomical pariahs, like E.T. or the Cabbage Patch Kids. So Shy Sherri, for instance, is an anatomical disaster: her legs are painfully swollen, her fingers are useless pink stumps that seem to have been lopped off at the knuckles, and her rosy cheeks are so bloated that her face is actually wider than it is long. (From "Cuteness" by Daniel Harris in *Salmagundi*)

Under *disorientation,* my thesaurus lists *insanity* first, followed by *lunacy, bedlam,* and that charming phrase *not all there. . . .* But my favorite options are from the dictionary, which defines *disorient* as *to turn from the east, as in the altar of a church. . . .*

To turn from the east. How curious. If I had to label a swamp's aesthetic and philosophy as primarily Eastern or Western, I'd say Eastern without a question. A swamp is receptive, ambiguous, paradoxical, unassuming. There's no logic, no duality, no hierarchy. But does immersion in a swamp have anything to do with turning a person from the altar of a church—especially an Eastern church? Try this: Buddhists say that if you meet Buddha on the road, you mustn't prostrate yourself in front of him, light incense, ring temple bells, count your breaths, or begin chanting. You should kill him—because any naming, any clinging, can too quickly become dogma. The point is to let go of everything. In a spiritual swamp, there's nothing to hold on to. (From "Refugium" by Barbara Hurd in *The Georgia Review*)

Further blurring the distinction between *reality* and *fantasy* in Faulkner's *As I Lay Dying*, Darl brings into question the existence of true reality. Speaking about emptying one's self for sleep, Darl speculates that before you empty yourself for sleep "what are you[?]" but after "you are not." And when you are filled with sleep, "you never were." In other words, before sleep you believed you existed but once asleep you cease to exist or possibly never existed. Is the existence before sleep a fantasy and the existence in the realm of sleep reality? Is either one real? Darl comments that only Jewel is sure of his existence because he doesn't know to question it. Jewel's certitude keeps him from speculating, or as Darl so eloquently puts it, "Jewel is *not* what he *is* and he is what he is not." (From "Reality Defined in *As I Lay Dying*" by Jenessa Kenway for a paper in Critical Thinking About Literature course)

Although it is frequently said that the truth shall make men free, the commandment is almost as frequently misunderstood. What is meant by the truth as a synonym for liberty doesn't emerge from a collection of facts or an assimilation of doctrine, nor does it come with a declaration of war or the blessing of Christ; it's synonymous with the courage that individuals derive from not running a con game on the unique character and specific temper of their own minds, finding a story that settles the wilderness of their experience with the fence posts of a beginning, a middle, and an end. (From "Blue Guitar" by Lewis Lapham in *Harper's Magazine*)

Cliché Busting

Even when searching for new insights into the human condition we unconsciously gravitate towards preset, worn out "truths,"comforted by a belief in simplistic or formulaic ideas: "Absence makes the heart grow fonder," "A friend is someone who is always there for you," or "Hope springs eternal." Because our attachment to these trite truisms is largely subconscious, we may reject ideas that challenge the brain's locked tabernacle of sacred clichés. In arguing for a revised definition or offering a more unsettling, ambiguous, or complex vision of a concept— absence can make one's heart vulnerable to being stolen; a friend is someone who can betray you; hope fades—a writer must first *excavate* those buried clichés with their hackneyed definitions and then *reveal* the limitations, shallowness, or fallibility of these platitudes.

Cliché Busting is usually a three-part process: It begins by identifying a generalization, a widely held assumption, or ready-made idea. After identifying the cliché, the actual bust follows— a deconstruction explaining why the stock concept is limited, worn out, or inaccurate. Once stripped of the old conception, a reader becomes more open to the writer's finely tuned and newly forged definition. A writer may be inspired to a new meaning through current events, a personal experience, or be stimulated by researching the derivation or history of a word in the *OED* (*Oxford English Dictionary*).

Your turn. In the samples below, locate the phrase used to dismiss the cliché or to transition into a new definition. After reading the samples, perform a Cliché Bust on a word, concept, or a stereotype about a group of people, and after busting it, build a new, unexpected definition.

Bursts of Cliché Busting:

The dutiful first answer seems programmed into us by our meager expectations: 'A friend is one who will be here in time of trouble.' But I believe this is a skin-deep answer to describe skin-deep friends. There is something irresistible about misfortune to human nature, and standbys for setbacks and sickness (as long as they are not too lengthy, or contagious) can usually be found. They can be *hired*. What I value is not the "friend" who, looming sympathetically above me when I have been dashed to the ground, appears gigantically generous in the hour of my reversal; more and more I desire friends who will endure my ecstasies with me, who possess wings of their own and who will fly with me. . . . It is the existence of these people that reminds me that the words "friend" and "free" grew out of each other. (OE freo, not in bondage, noble, glad; OE freo, to love; OE freond, friend). (From "To Noble Companions" by Gail Godwin in *Redbook*)

Possession of a being by another has come into more and more disrepute, so that the common understanding of one person possessing another is slavery. But the important detail about the kind of possessive pronoun I have in mind is reciprocity: If I have a friend, she has a friend. If I have a daughter, she has a mother. The possessive does not bind one of us while freeing the other; it cannot do that. Moreover, should the mother reject the daughter the word that applies is "disown." The form of disowning that most often appears in the news is domestic violence. Parents abuse children; husbands batter wives. . . .

The responsibilities and the ties signaled by reciprocal possession typically are hard to dissolve. It can be as difficult to give up an enemy as to give up a friend and often the one becomes the other, as though the logic of the possessive pronoun outlasts the forms it chanced to take at a given moment, as though we were stuck to one another. In these bindings, nearly inextricable, are found the origin of our rights. (From "What's Wrong with Animal Rights" by Vicki Hearne in *Harper's Magazine*)

There is a common superstition that "self respect" is a kind of charm against snakes, something that keeps those who have it locked in some unblighted Eden, out of strange beds, ambivalent conversations, and trouble in general. It does not at all. It has nothing to do with the face of things, but concerns instead a separate peace, a private reconciliation. (From "On Self-Respect" by Joan Didion from *Slouching Towards Bethlehem*)

The plague was not the kind of calamity that inspired mutual help. Its loathsomeness and deadliness did not herd people together in mutual distress, but only prompted their desire to escape each other. "Magistrates and notaries refused to come and make the wills of the dying[;] . . . even priests did not come to hear their confessions.". . . Cases of parents deserting children and children their parents were reported across Europe from Scotland to Russia. . . . The Pope's physician, Guy de Chauliac, was a sober, careful observer who reported the same phenomenon: "A father did not visit his son, nor the son his father. Charity was dead." (From "This is the End of the World: The Black Death" by Barbara Tuchman in *Distant Mirror: The Calamitous 14th Century*)

Pause at the word: "for-give." "for-to-give." Forgiveness is such a gift that "give" lives in the word. Christianist tradition has tried to make it a meek and passive word, turn the other cheek. But the word contains the active word "give," which reveals its truth; it involves the act of taking something of yours and handing it to another, so that from now on it is theirs. Nothing passive about it. (From *A Dance for Your Life in the Marriage Zone* by Michael Ventura)

To make love with the desire for a child between two people is to move the act out of its singularity, to make the need of the moment an eternal wish. But of all passing notions, that of a human being for a child is perhaps the purest in the abstract, and the most complicated in reality. Growing, bearing, mothering or fathering, supporting, and at last letting go of an infant are powerful and mundane creative acts that rapturously suck up whole chunks of life. . . . It is a beautiful enough shock to fall in love with another adult, to feel the possibility of unbearable sorrow at the loss of that other, essential personality, expressed just so, that particular touch. But love of an infant is of a different order. It is twinned love, all-absorbing, a blur of boundaries and messages. It is uncomfortably close to self-erasure, and in the face of it one's fat ambitions, desperations, private icons, and urges fall away with tough persistence. (From "A Woman's Work" by Louise Erdrich in *Harper's Magazine*)

The less confidence you have, the worse you do; the more confidence you have, the better you do; and so the luminous loop goes round. Based on our beliefs, we have created self-esteem programs in schools in which the main objective is, as Jennifer Coon-Wallman, a psychotherapist based in Boston, says, "to dole out huge heapings of praise, regardless of actual accomplishment." We have a National Association for Self-

Esteem with about a thousand members, and in 1986, the State Legislature of California founded the "California Task Force to Promote Self-Esteem and Personal and Social Responsibility." It was galvanized by Assemblyman John Vasconcellos, who fervently believed that by raising his citizens' self-concepts, he could divert drug abuse and all sorts of other social ills.

It didn't work.

In fact, crime rates and substance abuse rates are formidable, right along with our self-assessment scores on paper-and-pencil tests. (From "The Trouble with Self-Esteem" by Lauren Slater for *The New York Times Magazine*)

The crackdown on power differentials in student-professor (or senior colleague-junior colleague) relationships presupposes a power balance in non-pedagogic relationships that is completely fictitious. Where, one might ask, are the symmetrical relationships? If a student falls in love with a lawyer, is that more symmetrical? Should we outlaw relationships between students and nonstudents too? What about between good students and bad students? Rich students and poor students? Were we honest about our disdain for power imbalance we would have to legislate as emphatically against discrepancies in cultural, economic, and racial clout. . . . There is power in youth too—in physical attractiveness, in energy. There is power, even in yet-to-be-fulfilled promise—power in time. (From "The Higher Yearning" by Cristina Nehring in *Harper's Magazine*)

Here, I'd like to consider a word whose meaning has begun to drift like a caterpillar on a stream. The word is *margin*. Originally its meaning—the blank space around a body of type or the border of a piece of ground—had neutral connotations. . . . From the adjective *marginal* sprouted a far-fetched verb, *marginalize*, whose meaning is only bad. To be marginalized is to be a victim, and to marginalize someone else is an act of exclusion that can cost you tenure. . . .

And if the modern version of the margin is somewhere in western Nebraska, and the un-margin, the coveted red-hot center, is a site like Rodeo Drive, I wouldn't know which to choose. We need both, but especially as the world gets more jammed up, we need margins. A book without margins is impossible to read. And marginal behavior can be the most important kind. Every purpose-filled activity we pursue in the woods began as just fooling around . . . [trying] out odd ideas that you might be afraid to admit to with people looking on. Scientists have a term for research carried on with no immediate prospects of economic gain: "blue-sky" research. (From "A Lovely Sort of Lower Purpose" by Ian Frazier in *Outside* magazine)

The smooth stride of the point guard into the lane, the smooth delivery of the cue on the ball, the smooth glide of the dancing pair across the tile floor—all these things please us, they seem right, in a way we feel in our guts but would be hard-pressed to justify in rational terms. Grace is ever its own argument, is perhaps above argument altogether. Speed is the dominant trope of the age, but easy speed, unhurried velocity, is even better: it is the essence of cool.

Yet there are dangers. Aesthetic sense, too perfectly realized, becomes a form of meretricious deceit. Civil locutions are often exposed, eventually, as glib rather than polite, manipulative instead of friendly—the smooth operator is born. (From "Against Smoothness" by Mark Kingwell in his convocation address at Nova Scotia College of Art and Design)

Quote Sandwiching

Hitchhiking on the idea-bus of quotable lines from great thinkers, essayists regularly integrate passages from primary and secondary sources to define, support, or clarify their own argumentative journey. A strong writer seizes control of quoted material by sandwiching the quotation between a *lead-in* and a *follow-up*.

The *lead-in* precedes the quoted passage and may include the source and author of the quote; otherwise this information is provided in a parenthetical citation. The main purpose of the *lead-in* is to aptly characterize the tone and attitude of the upcoming quote. Effectively ushering in a quote means avoiding neutral verbs—*wrote, states,* or *says.* Instead a writer uses descriptive verbs—*exalts, laments, muses, teased*—often adding adverbs to further qualify the tone of the quote—

ironically, subtly, cleverly. Consider how the *lead-in* below sets up the quoted line from *Hamlet*:

> With a most noble and open mind which forever considers all possibilities, Shakespeare's Hamlet asserts to his provincial buddy, "There are more things in heaven and earth, Horatio/ Than are dreamt of in your philosophy" (1.5.166-67).

Another writer using the same quote might use a *lead-in* that tilts the quotation in another direction:

> Forever flip-flopping, the hesitant Hamlet unwittingly reveals his weakness as he presumptuously lectures to his more emotionally stable comrade, "There are more things in heaven and earth, Horatio/Than are dreamt of in your philosophy" (1.5.166-67).

Effective word choice in the *lead-in* provides signals for how to regard the quote and prepares the reader for the *follow-up*.

After delivering the quote, the *follow-up* explains how the passage relates to the main idea of the paragraph or essay. There are four types of *follow-ups:*

> *jumping-off:* introducing a new but related idea inspired by a quoted passage.
> *backing-up:* supporting an idea, thesis, claim, or argument with a quoted line from a primary or secondary source.
> *choosing-on:* refuting, negating, deconstructing an idea in a quoted passage.
> *digging-in:* analyzing and exploring the implications of word choice, syntax, imagery in a quoted passage.

These four types of *follow-ups* are not mutually exclusive; they can be mixed and matched.

In constructing the *follow-up*, assess the kind of language or tone used in the quote—is it general or specific, abstract or concrete, literal or metaphorical, formal or informal, philosophical or practical, personal or academic? Then distinguish your own voice by using language that contrasts with that of the quoted source.

Smooth integration of quotes also depends on management of technical aspects. When writing essays for the humanities, consult the *MLA* (Modern Language Association) guidelines for technical management of source material. Other disciplines have their own guidelines. Following is a checklist of six important tenets of *MLA* citation:

1. Use an ellipsis to designate omission of words/sentences from the original source.
2. Use brackets to surround any changes/additions for clarity to a quoted line.
3. *Block* quotes of four or more lines of text, three or more lines of poetry.
4. Avoid over-quoting; use only the portion of the quote necessary for *jumping-off, backing-up, choosing-on or digging-in.*
5. Quote verbatim only concise passages; paraphrase and summarize plain or wordy sources.
6. When quoting or paraphrasing *always* give credit for the idea by providing a citation—or else it is plagiarism, a serious academic crime.

Your turn. Mark the words and phrases used in the *lead-ins* that qualify the tone of the quote and that implicitly instruct how to interpret the quoted material. Next, decide whether the *follow-ups* are *jumping-off, backing-up, choosing-on,* or *digging-in.* Lastly, describe the difference in tone between the quoted lines and the surrounding Sandwich.

Bites of Quote Sandwiching:

And we travel, in essence, to become young fools again—to slow time down, get taken in and fall in love once more. The beauty of this whole process was perhaps best described, before people even took to frequent flying, by George Santayana in his lapidary essay, "The Philosophy of Travel"[:] "We need sometimes . . . to escape into open solitudes, into timelessness, into the moral holiday of running some pure hazard, in order to sharpen the edge of life, to taste hardship, and to be compelled to work desperately for a moment no matter what."

I like that stress on work, since never more than on the road are we shown how proportional our blessings are to the difficulty that precedes them, and I like the stress on a holiday that's "moral" since we fall into our ethical habits as easily as into our beds at night. (From "Why We Travel" by Pico Iyer in *Los Angeles Times Magazine*)

My mother had been in love for years with a friend of her youth, and remarried soon after my father's death. The suddenness of the wedding, to which I was not invited, may have made my bereavement all the more complex. "The funeral baked meats did coldly furnish forth the marriage tables," says the quintessentially melancholic griever, Hamlet, upon his mother's remarriage. As my new parents banqueted on their long-awaited happiness, I was shunted out of their lives. (From "The Work of Mourning" by Francine du Plessix Gray in *The American Scholar*)

To underscore my point, I have been making it sound as if we were all abruptly walking out of one room and into another, leaving our books to the moths while we settle ourselves in front of our state-of-the-art terminals. The truth is that we are living through a period of overlap; one way of being is pushed athwart another. Antonio Gramsci's often-cited sentence comes inevitably to mind: "The crisis consists precisely in the fact that the old is dying and the new cannot be born; in this interregnum a great variety of morbid symptoms appears." The old surely is dying, but I'm not so sure that the new is having any great difficulty being born. As for the morbid symptoms, these we have in abundance. (From "Into the Electronic Millennium" by Sven Birkerts in *The Gutenberg Elegies*)

The time has come to rethink wilderness.

This will seem a heretical claim to many environmentalists, since the idea of wilderness has for decades been a fundamental tenet—indeed a passion—of the environmental movement, especially in the United States. For many Americans wilderness stands as the last remaining place where civilization, that all too human disease, has not fully infected the earth. It is an island in the polluted sea of urban-industrial modernity, the one place we can turn for escape from our own too-muchness. Seen in this way, wilderness presents itself as the best antidote to our human selves, a refuge we must somehow recover if we hope to save the planet. As Henry David Thoreau once famously declared, "In Wildness is the preservation of the World."

But is it? The more one knows of its peculiar history, the more one realizes that wilderness is not quite what it seems. Far from being the one place on earth that stands apart from humanity, it is quite profoundly a human creation—indeed, the creation of very particular human cultures at very particular moments in human history. (From "The Trouble with Wilderness" by William Cronon in *Uncommon Ground*)

What are beginnings? A constantly melting and recomposing amalgam of images? A sentence we keep writing and revising? A messy album of meaning in which we seek patterns to explain to ourselves the mystery of personality? One of my favorite passages in Ruskin's *Praeterita* describes the soft orchestration of his family's voices:

> I never had heard my father's or mother's voice once raised in any question with each other, nor seen an angry, or even slightly hurt or offended, glance in the eyes of either. I had never heard a servant scolded; nor even suddenly, passionately, or in any severe manner blamed.

His household must have been a walled garden of mild manners. This to me is a powerful legend of childhood because it is so mysteriously remote from my own, which was charged with the electricity of blame, of real or presumed or anticipated offense. There were few mild manners in my family or in the immigrant neighborhood where I grew up. Mildness was a liability. (From "Gots Is What You Got" by W. S. Di Piero in *The Threepenny Review*)

As I understand it, and I am quick to say that I understand it only quite superficially, chaos occurs when any complex, dynamic system is perturbed by a small uncertainty in one or another of its subunits. The inevitable result is an amplification of the disturbance and then the spread of unpredictable, random behavior throughout the whole system. It is the total unpredictability and randomness that make the word "chaos" applicable as a technical term, but it is not true that the behavior of the system becomes disorderly. Indeed, as James P. Crutchfield and his associates have written, "There is order in chaos: underlying chaotic behavior there are elegant geometric forms that create randomness in the same way as a card dealer shuffles a deck of cards or a blender mixes cake batter." The random behavior of a turbulent stream of water, or of the weather, or of Brownian movement, or of the central nervous system of a cricket in flight from a bat, are all determined by the same mathematical rules. (From "Crickets, Bats, Cats, & Chaos" by Lewis Thomas in *Audubon*)

The following quote sandwich comments on a sentence by Pat Robertson that appeared in the *Wall Street Journal* editorial page. Robertson's long sentence, intended as a defense against claims that he is anti-Semitic, reads as follows:

> Intolerance in any quarter is wrong, but inasmuch as we are able, we must ensure that the trend throughout the 1990s remains in favor of a Jewish homeland in Israel and not for the elimination for the Jews.

Next in our backward journey through this remarkable sentence, consider the strange qualifying phrase, "inasmuch as we are able." Inasmuch as we are able, says Pat Robertson, we should strive to avoid the elimination of the Jews. He means, of course, insofar as we are able. "Inasmuch as we are able, read literally, would mean that since we happen to be able to, we might as well avoid the elimination of the Jews. But Robertson clearly is not saying that. He is suggesting that he is not at all sure we will be able to avoid the elimination of the Jews. Do you detect a note of noble resignation—an almost audible sigh—here? There's a sort of implied advance permission to fail, as if success is a hopeless ideal and effort is what counts. It reminds me of signs that used to be posted, many years ago, in Harrod's Department Store in London: "Please Try Not to Smoke." Do try not to eliminate the Jews, but, well, flesh is weak and we are all sinners. A body can only do so much. (From "Long Sentence" by Michael Kinsley for *The New Republic*)

Little has been written about the poet-lover's recipient in Williams' "This is Just To Say," this other, female entity, as rich and worthy of analysis as the thief who stole her plums. The existing body of criticism generally relegates her to the poem's background, a female victim of the charming and manipulative poet-thief. However, this reader argues that she is a foreground figure, who, in fact dominates the lyrical sphere of the confession poem. Critic Camille Paglia forcefully attests to the power of this neglected feminine force: "Hovering over the poem is an invisible figure[:] . . . a strong, silent female companion whose favor is begged and whose judgment is comically feared" (133). Paglia prompts readers to examine the clues that give us insight into the psyche of the poet's counterpart—an equally important player in this epistolary drama. Paglia provides insightful proof that this recipient is not, as has often been inferred, a helpless victim of a lusty betrayal, but a domestic diva, a figure of "strength" whose omnipresent "hovering" cannot be dismissed by the naughty poet nor the compassionate, though limited reader. (From a lecture for Critical Thinking About Literature by Glynis Hoffman)

Stress Testing

Abstract concepts and concrete objects do not always reveal their true worth or potential until tested by being subjected to exterior pressures. We value a building's flexible steel structure only after it survives an earthquake; we cherish a husband's courage after he stands up to a pair of bullying in-laws; we can savor the creamy unctuousness of coconut milk when it holds its own against lime, serrano chilies, and ginger in a Thai curry.

Gender, age, and culture are handy pressures available to begin any foray into *Stress Testing*. Applying the gender stress, a male writer may want to define the concept of sexiness from a female point of view. Using age as a stress, a senior citizen may find it interesting to explore how her definition of sexiness has changed since her youth. Considering "sexiness" from a generational perspective makes the word more pliable, opening up even more connotations.

Many essayists take *Stress Testing* a step further, adopting two contrasting pressures and then analyzing the similarities and differences of the dual tests. For instance, under the weight of a cultural stress, an essayist could compare and contrast the definition of "shame" from the Japanese and the American social perspective. Or a writer may press with a sub- or counterculture stress and define an abstraction from the point of view of a cowboy, lesbian, marine, Goth, or a member of the Hell's Angels. Using a "specialist" stress, a writer approaches an abstract concept like "family" and researches the differences between how a psychologist and a zoologist define this complex subject. The stress a writer chooses in order to perform the test depends largely on the concept being defined.

The discipline of literature generates other applications for *Stress Testing*. An essayist may address the subtle differences in the way two novelists define a particular human impulse within their different fictional worlds, such as the difference between how William Faulkner and Toni Morrison portray and define the abstract concept of "race." Or one could adopt a critical school of thought—a sociological, historical, deconstructionist, psychoanalytical, reader response, or formalist approach—and analyze a poem, short story, novel, drama, or any work of fiction using critical theory as a stress. (See *Deductive Analysis* under *3 HEADWORK*)

Whatever stress is used to test, one begins by listing the assumptions or worldview of that group and then applies those premises to the subject being analyzed. For instance, if defining "freedom" from a Libertarian point of view, a writer would first research the tenets and precepts of this political philosophy and use those assumptions to inform the definition. Regardless of what is used to pressure meaning out of a word (cultural, professional, or philosophical perspectives) the writers below are not satisfied with only one, but list many connotations, images, situations, and unusual associations from the group's viewpoint that would bring out different aspects of the target word. And the more the items on the list are explained and supported with details, the more the *Stress Test* moves from a dictionary-like meaning of a word to a paragraph or short essay.

Your turn. For each of the examples below, identify the "stress" being placed on the concept being explored. Then determine whether the stress test yields similarities or differences. Write about what other groups or writers would think of the same subject being stressed in the examples below.

Pressures of Stress Testing:

Do women wait more than men? I think women wait for men more than men wait for women and this despite the sisterly enjoinders that suppose that you can suppress instinct with statement. You cannot. We learn a few things as we go along, but we do not learn to love, to hate, or to quarrel very differently. Men wait, too: they wait for the promotion, they wait for the kill, they wait for the prize, and one has only to watch the antics in Parliament or in the Senate to see with what libido each is waiting for his moment to rise and strike a blow that will vanquish his opponent. . . . Men wait for women, too, once they have decided this one is the one, but they wait more busily and so little atoms of dread are likely to be diffused and tossed up and down so that they scatter. (From "Waiting" by Edna O'Brien in *Los Angeles Times Magazine*)

Young people see death as remote, aware of it but seeing it through buttered popcorn and jujubes. They selfishly see death as a superficial barrier: not going to the prom, not graduating college, never getting married or having children. They never think of it as darkening the world or being missed by family who regret they did not give more attention. They think MTV videos will never cease mourning their loss. Younger children cartoon death, band-aiding the threat of the unknown.

Elderly people see death as a Doris Day ending, an end to suffering and loneliness and of being a burden. They take comfort and pride in being part of history. Some have studied the skull icon throughout their lives, becoming spiritual, or creating a peaceful acceptance of death. (From "Death" by Jaime Vincent for a freshman composition assignment)

Everybody in the field seems to interpret [gravity-theory-is-the-same-as-field-theory] duality a little differently, depending on their own mental images of the universe. Jeff Harvey, for instance, understands it to mean that instead of having two different ways to compute what's going on with the black hole, you now need only one—the microscopic string way. . . . To Polchinski, the conjecture suggests that D-branes are somehow the atoms from which black holes are made, and gravity is just the combined effect of all these excited strings and D-branes furiously undergoing quantum fluctuations. (From "String Theorists Find a Rosetta Stone" by Gary Taubes in *Science*)

In Melville's "Bartleby the Scrivener," the soul is what we say and do; we are our souls. Bartleby's unwavering answer, "I prefer not to," created his soul more than any intangible divinity could. The soul is not apart from actions; the soul is the action. But Melville offers two contradictory ideas as to whether the soul is forged or innate. In *Billy Budd*, the narrator says, "Now something such as one was Claggart, in whom was the mania of evil nature, not engendered by vicious training or corrupting books or licentious living, but born with him and innate, in short 'a depravity according to nature.'" Here the soul is an eternal, pre-destined spirit, rather than a malleable entity that is worked by the life of the being. Thomas Paine, by contrast, asserts that "my own mind is my own church," and suggests that the purest form of the soul lies in the child, before education and fearful parents deny a child's natural doubting of the word of organized religion, Paine sarcastically adding, "as if the way to God is not open to every [soul] alike." It's the soul's choice, not God's.

(From "A Definition of Soul: American Writers Before 1900" by Angie Liggett for an American literature assignment)

Conjure in your mind a military man with an eye patch. Is there not something romantic and heroic about the injury? Doesn't it suggest a dark and complex past, a will of uncommon strength, perhaps a capability for just enough brutality to add a trace of virile unpredictability to the man?

Now replace the image of the mysterious man who wears the eye patch with the image of a 7-year-old girl who wears one. For most people, something strange happens. The romance and mystery disappear; what we see is a handicapped child. There is something sad and even pitiful about her; we fear for her future and worry about her present. (From *The Unexpected Minority: Handicapped Children in America* by John Gleeman and William Roth)

A circus is both acrobatic and elephantine, wholesome but freakish, and that is partly why we like it so—because we are two-headed. A showgirl in the center ring displays her pretty legs to daddy while his children are engrossed in watching a palomino stallion dance to the band's tempo. . . . You wouldn't necessarily trust one of the clowns or animal handlers who give such intense pleasure to tens of thousands of children with the downright raising of even a couple; they might already have abandoned a family. Like actors only more so, circus performers are expected to be manic and depressive, and we accept the paradox that a real genius at making little kids laugh . . . could verge on frightening them as a father. The funniness is vertiginous, and the hippodrome food is too sweet. (From "Circus Music" by Edward Hoagland in *Harper's Magazine*)

Jesus' crucifixion changes whenever a painter sees it. In Gruen–wald's *Isenheim Altarpiece,* done after 1510, Jesus looms upward like a broken eagle—his shoulder dislocated, his fingers curled into the black sky like spiked claws—but his feet are hammered near the ground, dispelling any notion that his spirit can ascend. He does not wear his crown of thorns; it's enmeshed into his hair like a briar. His stomach collapses even though his head tosses to the side out of air. The world is a night. Stars are dead. Blisters and sores break out where there was once lucid flesh. He is trapped on a makeshift cross, half-milled, half-chiseled. Nevertheless, he gains attention, center stage, a Semite among northerner faces and filling an eight-foot high panel. Here Golgotha is not a mere Jerusalem hillside but a mountaintop above and beyond all cities. St. John's, Mary Magdalena's, and John the Baptist's clothes are hot embers, bending flames softened by an innocent lamb that has already turned this killing into an eternal icon. John the Baptist, no longer dead, points a stringent finger linking Jesus to the word of the gospel in his other hand. The misery here is already immortal, a godly story.

But Pieter Brueghel the Elder in 1564 does not see Jesus' death as a godly story in *The Procession of Christ to Golgotha*. Jesus' death is not momentous but an eternally recurring crucifixion visiting all times and cities (here in the Netherlands) with different soldiers (here Spanish) and always unnoticed, buried by humanity. Being in the center is a tease, not an honor: Jesus is lost to gossipers, drunks falling off their horses, enemy soldiers giving alms, distant kids playing games, thieves on their way to the same killing hill but whose souls are being collected by monks who pay no heed to the present Jesus, perhaps the wife of Simon of Cyrene who has her own crucifix (again, another Jesus of another time) trying to prohibit her husband from helping with the cross, and all the while Jesus' traditional mourners are dismissed to another time and place (the foreground, away from the action) in their antiquated medieval clothes, their own sad play within a play. Who can find Jesus in this mud, this storm? He will be crucified again and again. And all for another picnic. (From a lecture for Bible as Literature by Gary Hoffman)

Pie Slicing

In attempting to define a monolithic abstraction or a seemingly homogeneous group, we may sweep the whirlwind of crisscrossing similarities and slivers of crucial differences into a heaping dust-pile of generalizations and stereotypes. A strong writer counters with *Pie Slicing*, temporarily classifying a subject by breaking up the mass into manageable portions. Ancient Chinese philosophers *Pie Sliced* all of life into two opposing but integrated principles: one called *Yang*, symbolic of activity, reason, and the celestial, and the other, *Yin*, symbolic of passivity, intuition, and earthiness. This split helps us contemplate what is otherwise an overwhelming subject.

Once the subject matter has been sliced into specific types, the slices are assigned descriptive labels to categorize the groups and subgroups. In his book *The Anatomy of Destructiveness,* psychologist Erich Fromm slices the human psyche in two, labeling personalities as either "necrophilous" or "biophilous." In its literal form, necrophilia is the desire to sexually abuse corpses, but Fromm's figurative use of the label identifies an impulse to transform liveliness into staleness; solve problems with force; a marked focus on sickness, failure, and a dark prognosis for the future; indifference towards others' enthusiasm; an obsession with the past, material things, regulations; flattened feelings that allow for self-conscious grins instead of spontaneous laughter. Biophilia, according to Fromm, is the opposite and includes a preference for the new and adventurous at the expense of retention and certainty, a belief in molding through love and reason rather than rules and force. Fromm's apt labels help to distinguish the slices from one another and begin the process of describing and defining the subtypes. The techniques in "Slang Tang" and "Break-ups" chapter will help to create pithy labels.

In his cartoon compilation of Pie-Slices, *Life in Hell*, Matt Groening also provides labels for each of "The 9 Types of Girlfrinds," among them, "the Bosser" and "Old Yeller" and "Ms. Vaguely Dissatisfied." In addition to the apt labels, Groening organizes the various girlfriend slices by listing parallel qualities: each type gets a cartoon picture complete with a balloon of what each girlfriend typically says. For instance "The Bosser" is depicted as a cartoon bunny with a lecturing finger pointed and an accompanying bubble that reads: "Stand up straight. Put on a different tie. Get a haircut. Change your job. Make some money. Don't give me that look." Below the bubble, Groening lists other aliases to help define the type. "The Bosser" is also "whipcracker," "the sarge," "ms. know-it-all," "ball and chain," "yes mom." The cartoonist finishes each slice by offering ironic pros and cons. For "The Bosser"—"Advantages: Often right. Drawbacks: Often right, but so what?" Organizing each slice with parallel structure, covering the same qualities and addressing the same concerns, Groening helps readers track distinctions between types.

After labeling and organizing the parallel qualities for each of the slices, several strategies in *Adios* help to finish the task of defining and describing the subtypes. *Anecdoting* illustrates a definition of a type by providing a short narrative. *Thesauruscoping* creates a distinction between two closely related subtypes. And *Quote Sandwiching* uses other sources for *Backing-up* a description of a subtype or as a basis for *Choosing-on* an overly generalized definition.

Your turn. For each of the excerpts below, keep track of how many different types are identified within a single subject; then note how many identifying qualities are packed within a *Pie Slice*.

Tastes of Pie Slicing:

To the untrained eye, surfers can easily egg-white into foam where it is impossible to distinguish between individuals. Most think surfers are drones, all copying one another and not showing unique characteristics. But they do. Surfers fall into one of four distinct groups: ultra-aged boarders, inland dorkets, aqua-artistes, and sub-aged pre-arts. (From "Surfers" by David Wagner for a freshman composition)

Some men are more comfortable with nakedness than others, and careful observers—please, do not stare—will note a number of towel strategies being employed. There are the matadors, who, after drying themselves in front of their lockers and laying out their change of clothes, whip off their towels in a terry cloth arabesque and dress to beat the clock. To these men, I'd just like to say, thank you.

There are the Roman senators, who leave the shower with their towels over their shoulder[s] or around their necks, and walk around air-drying and holding substantial conversations with other naked senators. I have trouble with small talk at parties at which I am fully dressed, so I can only marvel at these gentlemen's savoir-faire. . . .

And then there are the men who have at last transcended it all. Older men. Pink or brown or hairy or snowy or prolapsed but most of all oblivious, they wander cheerfully around the locker room without any towel at all, like very large babies who have slipped their diapers. There's a delightful innocence to them, or maybe it's the decadence of age. They are beyond the stolen glances, the covert locker-room comparisons of tackle that younger men, being competitive sexual animals, cannot help. (from "Towels Optional" by Dan Neil for *West Magazine*)

The women in my family divide into two general groups: those who fasten upon style, become identified with a look, and are impervious to change, weathering the years steadfastly, and those who, for a variety of reasons, are in the business of transforming themselves. In my sister's case, the quest for perfect hair originates in a need to mask her own appearance; in my mother's case, she wants to achieve a beauty of person unavailable in her own life story. Some women seek transformation, not out of dissatisfaction with themselves, but because hair change is a means of moving along in their lives. These women create portraits of themselves that won't last forever; a new hairstyle will write over the last. (From "Hair" by Marcia Aldrich in *The Northwest Review*)

The offensive [football] linemen in general are ambitious, tenacious, precise, and attentive to detail. They manifest a kind of toughness that I would call stubborn rather than explosive. They work hard. Their traits clearly suit them for their work. As blocking assignments become ever more intricate, the linemen must practice like a ballet corps to coordinate perfectly the necessary spatial and temporal movements of blocking patterns. . . . They must care only about protecting their quarterback, not about proving their masculinity in an explosive way. A sacrificial attitude toward the welfare of the team is integral to the offensive lineman. . . . The defensive team members are the renegades. They attack structure, and they feel that little is to be gained by identification with the establishment. They are basically angry and rebellious, primed to explode. The degree of inhibition controlling the trigger varies with the distance from the line of scrimmage. . . . [They are] restless, peevish, irritable, impatient, intolerant of detail, and barely under control. (From "In Pro Football They Play Best Who Play What They Are" by Arnold J. Mandell in *Saturday Review World*)

There are several categories among us. There are the tired married people with kids. There are the tired single people who work at home. There are the tired single people who are somewhat employed outside the home. And, of course, there are the tired people who have real jobs (a minority in this group).

According to the tired married people with kids, there is

no contest. They are the royalty of the tired kingdom. They are smug with exhaustion. I belong to the tired-single-people-who-work-at-home group, and in the tired race I don't have a prayer. (From "The Tired Chronicles" by Betsy Berne in *The New Yorker*)

On those remote pages it is written that animals are divided into (a) those that belong to the Emperor, (b) embalmed ones, (c) those that are trained, (d) suckling pigs, (e) mermaids, (f) fabulous ones, (g) stray dogs, (h) those that are included in this classification, (i) those that tremble as if they were mad, (j) innumerable ones, (k) those drawn with a very fine camel's hair brush, (l) other, (m) those that have just broken a flower vase, (n) those that resemble flies from a distance. (From "The Analytical Language of John Wilkins" by Jorge Luis Borges in *Other Inquisitions*)

Differences in posture, like differences in eating utensils (knife and fork, chopsticks, or fingers, for example), divide the world as profoundly as political boundaries. Regarding posture, there are two camps: the sitter-up—the so-called Western world—and the squatters—everyone else. (This bipartite division has been remarkably consistent. There is only one civilization in which sitting and squatting coexisted: ancient China.) Although there is no iron curtain separating the two sides, neither feels comfortable in the position of the other. (From *Home: A Short History of an Idea* by Witold Rybczynski)

Many suicides inflict outrageous trauma, burning permanent injuries in the minds of their children, though they may have joked beforehand only of "taking a dive." And sometimes the gesture has a peevish or cowardly aspect, or seems to have been senselessly shortsighted as far as an outside observer can tell. There are desperate suicides and crafty suicides, people who do it to cause others trouble and people who do it to save others trouble, deranged exhibitionists who yell from a building ledge and close-mouthed secretive souls who swim out into the ocean's anonymity. (From "Heaven and Nature" by Edward Hoagland in *Harper's Magazine*)

The castes of the circus [of the early 1950s] were Byzantine. The star performers—of exact balance and surpassing daring—were supreme. Then the money bosses and the performance directors. Then other, run-of-the-mill performers; the logistics bosses and department heads; the clowns, in a class of their own; the sideshow freaks and various attractions; and the longtime senior workhands. Then the come-and-go white roustabouts like me (eighty-some animal caretakers, for instance, counting the horse grooms and the "bull," or elephant department; and sixty-six men to handle the cookhouse). And finally, the black workhands, who were paid only twelve dollars a week and were limited to the one job of unrolling the big-top canvas, which would eventually seat eleven thousand spectators, sledgehammering the countless side-pole stakes into the ground for an hour or two in synchronized crews of four—chanting slave songs to keep the swings falling in perfect tandem—then getting it all up, gradually guying it all out, and tearing it all down again at eleven at night. (From "Calliope Times" by Edward Hoagland in *The New Yorker*)

Whereas Biodad couldn't care less about fatherhood in the conventional sense, Adoptodad did his damnedest to fill the void. He was more to play a dad. . . . Adoptodad tried to treat me as if I had emerged from his own loins. . . . Ultimately I resisted becoming a conventional son, because, however sincere he was, I believed he was only interested in me so long as I succeeded where his real son failed. There was incredible pressure to be a Stepford child: If I ceased to make him proud, I was over.

I was the trophy son, yet I always felt second-class around Adoptodad's family. Once at a Christmas gathering, Adopto-grandad asked me to run to the store for beverages, smack in the middle of the gift opening process. To them, I was the pitiful bastard. What a nice thing Adoptodad was doing for that poor, fatherless child. He didn't have to, you know. (From "My Three Dads" by Erik Himmelsbach in the *Los Angeles Times*)

State Secrets. "Our laws are not generally known; they are kept secret by the small group of nobles who rule us," wrote Kafka in one of his miniature stories. "We are convinced that these ancient laws are scrupulously administered; nevertheless it is an extremely painful thing to be ruled by laws that one does not know." This is the essence of state secrets. . . . State secrets range all the way from banal prohibitions on photographing customs booths and power plants to the highest levels of technical esoterica.

Atomic Secrets. "Stop me if you've heard this atomic secret," cracked William Burroughs in *Naked Lunch*. Atomic secrets may be the world's most famous class of secret, an oxymoron, surely, but for the fact that few enough people would recognize or understand an atomic secret if it landed in their mailboxes. The workaday state secret may be a matter of mere protocol or protection of resources, not unlike industries safeguarding the peculiarities of their production methods. The atomic secret, however, ascends to the level of the sacred because it manifests in concrete form the terror that mystics can only suggest: the end of the world. (From "What Secrets Tell" by Luc Sante for the *New York Times*).

BURSTING:
Ways to Disarm

Devil's Advice
Mocking
Trojan Horse
Sincerely Yours

Dismantling an opponent's viewpoint with a flat-voiced, straight-faced, gutted attitude suffocates sincere conviction. However, arguing with unbridled passion risks letting emotions overtake reason. Alternatives to both these extremes are the *Bursting* strategies, which combine elements found in traditional argument with special camouflages. *Devil's Advice* uses tongue-in-cheek satire; *Mocking* requires the knack to mimic style; *Trojan Horse* demands the ability to endow literal instructions with metaphoric subtext; and *Sincerely Yours* entails controlling passions in a personal letter. The careful modulation of voice required for maintaining each strategy's special tone prevents the writer from running amuck and overindulging his or her own emotions. However, the *Bursting* strategies are by no means staid. Their unconventional approach snaps the reader's eyes open as it kicks out the debater's podium with its comfortable rules that are simple and defined.

Devil's Advice

A traditional proposal argument employs traditional persuasive elements: It describes a problem, states a proposition, provides supporting facts, examples, statistics, cites outside sources, anticipates and responds to objections by the opposition, and predicts outcomes. The straightforward approach, however, may unwittingly "preach to the choir," reaching only the ears of those already in favor of the writer's position, while being easily dismissed by the writer's foes. The opposition can easily reject well-argued positions: Statistics bore and skeptics know "facts" can be manipulated; cited authorities may possibly be fattened with self-interest; the opposition might claim to be misunderstood; predicted outcomes may well appear to be *slippery slope* guesswork or empty threats. A still bigger obstacle—an opponent's arrogance—acts as formidable armor against any rational argument. One way to penetrate these obstacles is with *Devil's Advice*. *Devil's Advice* follows the traditional format outlined above; what makes the strategy unique, though, is that the process is completely ironic.

Earnest Introduction and Exaggerated Proposal. Use the *Problem Making* section in the *Time Warping* chapter to organize the first two paragraphs—the problem and solution or proposal. Begin by describing the "real" problem that will be addressed by the ironic proposal. For instance, in "Dating your Mom" Ian Frazier addresses the difficulty of meeting and hooking up with someone in our modern society—a real problem for young single men. The goal of the introduction is to get your audience to nod in agreement, acknowledging the existence and/or prevalence of a particular problem. In this first part, you are not yet being ironic; instead establish the *ethos* of a concerned and credible problem-solver.

After your reasonable introduction of the problem, deliver the solution: the ironic proposal that pretends to agree with and promotes a behavior or action that you are really against. Deliver the claim with a calm and staid tone, maybe using *Super-literalism* (see *Pause* in the Style unit) to bring out the horrors and augmenting with *Scrub* as a way of hiding the outrageous proposition, making your preposterous proposal sound reasonable, logical, and very important. This tongue-in-cheek proposal seduces the opponent by appearing to be agreeable. For example, if a writer wants to expose child abusers, then the bedeviler pretends to side with the abuser and advocates an exaggerated, outrageous version of the abuser's position: Children should be beaten mercilessly for minor offenses. The exaggeration does two things: it smokes out the target's most secret, repressed inclinations, and it signals to the reader that the essay is ironic, that it means the opposite of what is literally being said.

Anticipation and Dismissal of Objections. After delivering the exaggerated proposal, the essayist will anticipate a reasonable person's objection to the outrageous suggestion; in raising this objection, the essayist gives the ironic proposal its voice of reason and moral center.

However, immediately following this anticipated objection to those horrors, the writer casually dismisses the objections with the kind of slimy rationalizations, false logic, and euphemistic language typically used by those who really practice the immoral behavior being exposed. (See *Logical Fallacies* in the *Scrub* chapter of the *Headwork* unit.) This way *Devil's Advice* recovers its ironic tone, uncloaking the unethical and unreasonable justifications used by its target audience.

Conclusion. For your conclusion write a *slippery slope* prediction that explains all the proposed exaggerated benefits of implementing the proposal—explain how the problem will be solved, the perfect world or Utopia created by the plan. Or, *slippery slope* the other way—predict all the catastrophic events that will follow if the proposal is not adopted. The exaggeration and irony should increase, reaching a climax in the conclusion.

Your turn. Identify what or who the actual targets are in each piece below. What objections are being implied? Who would you like to target and what details would you bring up to ironically agree with your target?

Sulfuric Whiffs of Devil's Advice:

Did you know that in 1997 according to Howard Schultz in *Pour Your Heart Into It: How Starbucks Built a Company One Cup At a Time*, there were only about 1300 Starbucks standing in America, while according to the National Parks service, 52 national parks sat strewn and littered over this country's otherwise glorious landscape? And if nature continues to go unchecked, these park and wildlife refuges may yet spread like a cancer upon our great nation.

I, for one, as a voting, tax-paying citizen, am sick and tired of seeing my wife and two kids come home haggard and down-trodden because they were forced to walk all the way to the end of the block to the next Starbucks—by the time they get home, their double-espresso has worn off, and they need to sojourn once again, to embark upon their fifth or sixth pilgrimage of the day, for more coffee. A vicious cycle, my good, honest fellows, a vicious cycle indeed. (From "Devil's Advice" by Gary Liu for a freshman composition assignment)

Dating your mother seriously might seem difficult at first, but once you try it I'll bet you'll be surprised at how easy it is. Facing up to your intention is the main thing: you have to want it bad enough. One problem is that lots of people get hung up on feelings of guilt about their dad. They think, Oh here's this kindly old guy who taught me how to hunt and whittle and dynamite fish—I can't let him go on into his twilight years alone. Well, there are two reasons you can dismiss those thoughts from your mind. First, *every* woman, I don't care who she is, prefers her son to her husband. That is a simple fact; ask any woman who has a son, and she'll admit it. And why shouldn't she prefer someone who is so much like herself, who represents nine months of special concern and love and intense physical closeness—someone whom she actually created? As more women begin to express the need to have something all their own in the world, more women are going to start being honest about this preference. When you and your mom begin going together, you will simply become part of a natural and inevitable historical trend. Second, you must remember this about your dad: You have your mother, he has his! Let him go put the moves on his own mother and stop messing with yours. (From "Dating Your Mom" by Ian Frazier in *The New Yorker*)

Being a cocaine addict necessitates maintaining a steady diet of the drug and, as cocaine is extremely expensive, being a cocaine addict also necessitates the development of very prudent spending habits. While many people today have a very weak understanding of the value of the dollar, and in turn spend their money very foolishly, this is not true of a coke user. As the user's need for cocaine grows, he learns to trim such non-essentials items as food, medicine, and hygiene products from the budget. (From "Miracle Drug" by Gregory Bedford for a student assignment)

**The Crack Cocaine Dealers
of Capitol Hill want to
Rock Your World.
We operate convenient, full-service outlets and
Guarantee no police hassles or interference.**
Stop by and talk to our sales associates at:
1300 block of D Street SE
(Convenient for Safeway shoppers)
1600 block C street SE
(Right behind a Metropolitan Boys and Girls Club.)
16th & D Street
(Just pull over, roll down your window.)
16th & E Street
(New Locale! Excellent for late-night needs)
300 block 14thStreet
(Conveniently located behind a liquor store. Always a party!)
WE ACCEPT CASH OR STOLEN GOODS.

(From a flyer posted by Washington, D.C., residents who felt their complaints about lack of police patrol were being ignored)

Always obey your parents, when they are present. This is the best policy in the long run, because if you don't they will make you. Most parents think they know better than you do, and you can generally make more by humoring that superstition than you can by acting on your own better judgment. . . .

You want to be very careful about lying; otherwise you are nearly sure to get caught. Once caught, you can never again be, in the eyes of the good and pure, what you were before. Many a young person has injured himself permanently through a single clumsy and ill-finished lie, the result of carelessness born of in-complete training . . . . The young ought to be temperate in the use of this great art until practice and experience shall give them that confidence, elegance, and precision which alone can make the accomplishment graceful and profitable. (From "Advice to Youth" by Mark Twain delivered to a graduating class)

Having spent the better part of a week eating dog food, I'm sorry to say that I now know the answers to [advertising claims made for dog food]. While my dachshund, Shortie, watched in agonies of yearning, I gagged my way through can after can of stinky, fat-drenched nuggets. And now I understand exactly why Shortie's breath is so bad. . . .

Well, I may be a sucker, but advertising *this* emphatic just doesn't convince me. I lined up all seven flavors of Milk-Bone Flavor Snacks on the floor. Unless my dog's palate is a lot more sensitive than mine—and considering that she steals dirty diapers out of the trash and eats them, I'm loath to think it is— she doesn't detect any more difference in the seven flavors that I did when I tried them. (From "No Wonder They Call Me a Bitch" by Ann Hodgman in *Spy*)

I have been assured by a very knowing American of my acquaintance in London, that a young healthy child well nursed is at a year old a most delicious, nourishing, and wholesome food, whether stewed, roasted, baked, or boiled; and I make no doubt that it will equally serve in a fricassee or a ragout. . . .

Infant's flesh will be in season throughout the year, but more plentiful in March, and little before and after. . . . There are more children born in Roman Catholic countries about nine months after Lent than at any other season; therefore, reckoning a year after Lent, the markets will be more glutted than usual, because of the number of popish infants is at least three to one in this kingdom; and therefore it will have one other collateral advantage, by lessening the number of Papists among us. (From "A Modest Proposal For Preventing the Children of Poor People in Ireland From Being a Burden to Their Parents or Country, and For Making Them Beneficial to the Public" by Jonathan Swift)

It has long been theorized that the week prior to an exam is an extremely dangerous time for the relatives of college students. Ever since I began my teaching career, I've heard vague comments, incomplete references and unfinished remarks, all alluding to the "Dead Grandmother Problem.". . . As can be seen in Table 1, when no exam is imminent the family death rate per 100 students (FDR) is low and is not related to the student's grade in class. The effect of an upcoming exam is ambiguous. The mean FDR jumps from 0.054 with no exam, to 0.574 with a mid-term, and to 1.042 with a final, representing increases of 10 fold and 19 fold respectively. . . . Only one conclusion can be drawn from these data. Family members literally worry themselves to death over the outcome of their relatives' performance on each exam. . . . Three possible solutions come to mind: 1. Stop giving exams. . . . 2. Allow only orphans to enroll at universities. . . . 3. Have students lie to their families. (From "The Dead Grandmother/Exam Syndrome and the Potential Downfall of American Society" by Mike Adams in *The Connecticut Review*)

Mocking

Principled writers find themselves in the predicament of having to face off with the foolish premises and specious arguments of a self-righteous group. A traditional, academic refutation requires the writer to identify an opposing faction's central claim, seriously consider and even concede some of the group's minor points, issue a counter claim, and provide facts to support the rebuttal. (See *Refutation Claim* in the *Claim Cast* chapter of the *Headwork* unit.) But these customary persuasive devices might prove ineffective for undercutting the pomposity, certitude, and verbosity of academicians, lawyers, politicians and religious leaders and others who consider themselves above criticism. And these traditional strategies may have limited potential for countering the literal-mindedness of groups who have unbending faith in simplistic beliefs. A conventional approach may prove disproportionately weighty for those twisted targets: Instead of succinctly revealing the flaws of the opponent, a writer employing a traditional academic refutation risks appearing as pretentious and self-important as the writer's targeted group. *Mocking* breaks this cycle by using humor.

Mode. *Mocking* allows the writer to expose the hidden agendas and silly premises of a group by purposely forcing that group's ideas into a formulaic genre or conventional mode of communication—a local newspaper, business newsletter, personal ad page, legal brief, restaurant review, travel book—any genre of writing that has become stale. In preparation, the writer studies the sentence structures, stock phrases, typical imagery, and word choice or jargon of a type of writing. For instance, a legal brief uses legal *War Paint* (see *Scrub* in the *Headwork* unit) and the passive voice.

Subject. Next, the writer fills this hackneyed format with subject matter that is either too monumental, too exaggerated, or too trivial for that chosen format: The personal injuries of a cartoon character are too frivolous for the loftiness of a legal brief; the death of God is too significant for a local newspaper format. The content gets its wind punched out by being pressed into the cliché restrictions of the format and the artificial seams of the writing format are magnified trying to contain the content. Structure and subject become magnified, rendering each other ridiculous. *Mocking* is a symbiotic satire, killing two cocks with one rock.

Your turn. Identify which parts of the passages below *Burst* a standard writing format and which parts attack a specific subject or attitude.

Decibels of Mocking:

One lovely touch at Fabrizio's is Spinelli's boneless chicken Parmigiana. The title is ironic, for he has filled the chicken with extra bones, as if to say life must not be ingested too quickly or without caution. The constant removal of bones from the mouth and the depositing of them on the plate gives the meal an eerie sound. One is reminded at once of Webern, who seems to crop up all the time in Spinelli's cooking. (From "Fabrizio's: Criticism and Response" by Woody Allen in *The New Yorker*)

[Regarding strategy for Jesus' public relations at His second coming.] Day Three. *Theme:* Distancing from Father. Your Father, our numbers indicate, has very high positives and that causes you some problems. He's considered more of a doer, you more of a talker. He's a deity's deity—wrath, compassion, says what He means, first week in office created cosmos, oceans, continents. Next to that, your program of forgiveness, repentance, love—albeit widely admired—brings up "wimp factor.". . . We suggest the phrase "mistakes were made." It associates You with the good of His programs, while allowing You to show strength and autonomy by criticizing certain acts of the past. *Media Strategy*: heavy buys in top markets; ads deal with current array of urban problems (fitting with the theme of "mistakes") and end with presumption that You can lead mankind from the darkness. (From "Advance Memo" by Ron Suskind in "He's Back" in *Harper's Magazine*)

Opening Statement of Mr. Harold Schoff, attorney for Mr. Coyote . . . Mr. Coyote states that on eighty-five separate occasions he has purchased of the Acme Company (hereinafter, "Defendant"), through that company's mail-order department, certain products which did cause him bodily injury due to defects in manufacture or improper cautionary labeling. . . . The premature detonation of Defendant's product resulted in the following disfigurements to Mr. Coyote: 1. Severe singeing of the hair on the head, neck, and muzzle . . . 3. Fracture of the left ear at the stem, causing the ear to dangle in the aftershock with a creaking noise . . . 5. Radical widening of the eyes, due to brow and lid charring. (From "Coyote v. Acme" by Ian Frazier in *The New Yorker*)

Addressing the assemblage of teachers, NEA president Cheryl Brodhagen described an "alarming erosion of grammar skills" among America's teens, in whose suicide notes can be found double negatives, split infinitives, improper word usage and, in the worst cases, unnecessary use of the passive voice. . . . Teacher Ed Salmons: "I'm seeing overwrought, melodramatic, bathetic writing that demonstrates no grasp of subtlety or style. It's really hard for me to take pretentious, self-indulgent suicide notes like these seriously as pieces of writing.". . . Therapist Eli Wasserbaum said, "One Florida boy who recently shot himself in the head wrote, 'I cant talk to anyone about my problems.' 'Cant'? Is he referring to the noun defined as 'the wining, sing-song speech of beggars and thieves'? Somehow, I don't think so." (From "Nation's Educators Alarmed By Poorly Written Teen Suicide Notes" in *The Onion*, Volume 32, Issue 3)

On December 20 there flitted past us, absolutely without public notice, one of the most important profane anniversaries in American history—to wit: the seventy-fifth anniversary of the introduction of the bathtub in these states. . . . On the one hand it was denounced as an epicurean and obnoxious toy from England, designed to corrupt the democratic simplicity of the republic, and on the other hand it was attacked by the medical faculty as dangerous to health and a certain inviter of "phthisic, rheumatic fevers, inflammation of the lungs, and the whole category of zymotic diseases." (I quote from the Western Medical Repository of April 23, 1843.) (From the *Bathtub Hoax and Other Blasts and Bravos from The Chicago Tribune* by H. L. Mencken)

[Regarding a Taco Bell commercial starring Willie Nelson, Western singer] The battle for sexual hegemony illustrated in the burrito incident is plainly mirrored by a larger context, i.e., the European domination and desecration of the native peoples and landscapes of the New World. Is there a more powerful symbol of rapacious imperialism than the taco? In the empty shell of corn we see the sad defeat of the maize culture that once flourished in the American Eden. Within the taco resides ground beef, representing the speciesistic carnage perpetrated upon the bovine community and, by extension, all non-human life forms. (From "Deconstructing Willie" by Stephen Harrigan in *Texas Monthly*)

History: Describe the history of the Papacy from it origins to the present day, concentrating especially, but not exclusively, on its social, political, economic, religious, and philosophical impact upon Europe, Asia, Africa, and the Americas. Be brief, concise, and specific. *Music*: Write a piano concerto. Orchestrate and perform it with flute and violin. You will find a piano under your seat. In the interest of time, you may omit the coda. (From "General Examination for the Doctor of Philosophy Degree" by Woody Allen in *Chronicle of Higher Education*)

I have recently written two biographies of the same famous politician. One is intentionally filled with disgusting lies; the other is based solely on truth. The problem is, they are identical. Which one should I publish?

The key word in your question is that the lies are "intentional." Your admitted intention makes the first biography wholly honest, whereas there might be errors in the one based on fact. Publish the one with the disgusting lies. (From "Shouts & Murmurs: The Ethicist" by Steve Martin in *The New Yorker*)

If you happened to stand over four feet tall, the agony awaiting you at Sacred Heart Elementary began the moment you took your seat. There were mean little chairs corralled into a "theater" haunted by the lingering stench of industrial strength lasagna. . . . "The Story of the First Christmas" is an overrated clunker of a holiday pageant. . . . In the role of Mary, six-year-old Shannon Burke just barely manages to pass herself of as a virgin. A cloying, preening stage presence, her performance seemed based on nothing but an annoying proclivity toward lifting her skirt and, on rare occasions, opening her eyes. . . .

Once again, the sadists at the Jane Snow-Hernandez Middle School have taken up their burning pokers in at attempt to prod A Christmas Carol into some form of submission. . . . A strong proponent of trendy, racially mixed casting, Michaels [an eleven-year-old] gives us a black tiny Tim, leaving the audience to wonder, "What, is this kid supposed to be adopted?" It's a distracting move, wrongheaded and pointless. . . . The program notes that he recently lost his right foot to diabetes, but was that reason enough to cast him? (From "Front Row Center with Thaddeus Bristol" by David Sedaris in *Holidays on Ice*)

Trojan Horse

Although readers may willingly read and follow instructions (what English teachers call process essays) for practical matters— making sound investments, baking a cake, growing hybrid roses, "whispering" to a horse, building strong abdominal muscles— when it comes to more sensitive matters—sexual technique, personal hygiene, morality—readers become resistant to advice. One way to slip through the gates of this obstinacy is to hide suggestions and criticism inside a *Trojan Horse*, metaphorically camouflaging serious guidance behind seemingly practical, innocuous advice. With the writer's serious advice hidden as subtext, the target reader lets down his or her guard.

As with all instructions, *Trojan Horse* uses the second person "you," which is often implied through the use of *imperative* form verbs. (See the *Humbling Lens* in the *Opt* chapter.) The in-your-face nature of the second person disarms the reader because he or she is being told to act instead of being allowed to passively observe, which in turn minimizes the distance between the writer, reader, and the task to be performed. The reader's resistance is unlocked. The impulse to learn a new task is locked on.

Directions. Before creating this subtext, the writer details step-by-step directions. Then the writer glances back and notices any details that he or she will definitely want to embellish because, even in their literal form, they have metaphorical possibilities: programming a cell phone suggests having more intimate communication with someone; rewiring a lamp parallels becoming enlightened; abdominal instructions to strengthen the back lead to having more political backbone. Some writers like W. S. Merwin (see below) might even consider *un* doing their process: unmaking a cake, unlearning to swim, unpreparing a will.

Ripen. After constructing rough-draft directions using second-person point of view, the writer infuses with ripened words (sensory details, feelings, and unexpected thesaurus replacements), all contributing to developing that subtext. Consider the passage below: Merwin's tree-trimming instructions refer to the tree's structure as "skeleton of the resurrection" and expands its suggestiveness by including unexpected directions, going beyond handbook techniques, and adding tips on preparing for the emotional process: "you will wonder," "you will sleep badly," "you will hope," "entertain yourself." Confronting these unusual intrusions guides the reader to the subtext's meaning. What appeared to be about tree pruning actually hints at rebuilding one's spiritual life; instructions remind the reader that it is possible to start life over with different values but with emotional costs.

Often writers title the subtext in parentheses under the literal title as a way of keeping the focus while ripening and then drop it by the final draft.

Finally, once the essay is ripened, then the writer adds metaphors to clarify the subtext. (See *Fusion* in the *Style* unit.)

Your turn. Explain the different subtexts below before writing your own instructions and infusing them with a subtext.

Camouflages of Trojan Horses:

At this point, all the careful contact will distract the horse, but be cautious. You will feel your spurs at your own heart when you notice the horse's muscle mass, the gleam of the velvet coat, the rich brown hue of his eyes. Now you must fasten the strap of the love bridle under the horse's jaw. You are ready to lead the horse to the hitching post. Gently wrap the reins of commitment over the post so if the equine spooks, he will not be aggravated by the love reins tightening on the ego post. He will feel free to step away even if it's not too far. Don't worry. It's the horse's illusion. (From "How to Control Your Boyfriend" by Kristin Showalter for freshman composition)

Bark sawdust in particular the earth lays claim to very quickly. You must find your own ways of coping with this problem. There is a certain beauty, you will notice at moments, in the pattern of the chips as they are fitted back into place. You will wonder to what extent it should be described as natural, to what extent man-made. It will lead you on to speculations about the parentage of beauty itself, to which you will return. . . . The day comes when it is all restored, even to the moss (now dead) over the wound. You will sleep badly, thinking of the removal of the scaffolding that must begin the next morning. How you will hope for sun and a still day!

The removal of the scaffolding or tackle is not so dangerous, perhaps, to the surroundings, as its installation, but it presents problems. (From "Unchopping a Tree" in *The Miner's Pale Children* by M.S. Merwin)

I was hoping to see Tony's father, Emmett, a retired mechanic, in order to settle a question that had been nagging me: Is it possible to get out of a locked car trunk?. . .

The trunk was shallow and hot. . . . This one was a little suffocating. I imagined being trapped for hours, and even before he had got it closed I regretted the decision with a slightly nauseous feeling. I thought of Edgar Allan Poe's live burials, and then about something my fiancée had said more than a year and a half before. I had been on her case to get married. She was divorced, and at every opportunity I would reissue my proposal—even during a commercial. She'd interrupted one of these chirps to tell me, in a cold, throaty voice, that she had no intention of ever going through another divorce: "This time, it's death out" I'd carried those words around like a lump of wet clay. (From "How to Get Out of a Locked Trunk," in *Harper's Magazine* by Philip Weiss)

Next, testing the "certainty of the reality and immortality of things," roll a leaf of paper in half lengthwise and press on the bowed-out curve; it resists your touch. Alternately, you now roll the paper in half widthwise and press; the bowed area "exhales from . . . head to foot." You have now discovered "that what the preaching could not accomplish is accomplished," what only your convincing hand could tell you—the direction of the grain of the paper. The grain manifests the direction you should travel "to know the universe itself as a road" while corrupted papers that fold against the grain "do not conceal themselves, and cannot conceal themselves." Now determine the book's magnitude and cut the text paper to the height and twice the width of your determined size. Sawing away at the manly stack, you realize cutting single sheets is easier and you need not worry because "some divine rapport has equalized" them. (From "How to Make a Soft Cover Booklet: How to understand Walt Whitman" by Erin Barrow for a literature assignment)

Like folk songs and aphorisms and the grainy bits of language, these tools have been pared down to essentials. I look at my claw hammer, the distillation of a hundred generations of carpenters, and consider that it holds up well beside those other classics—Greek vases, Gregorian chants, *Don Quixote*, barbed fishhooks, candles, spoons. (From "The Inheritance of Tools" by Scott Russell Sanders in *The North American Review*)

Take one gruff, vulgar, immature brute and marinate in the daily, desperate, overpopulated scramble for survival among the drunk gypsy thieves and carnival con artists praying upon the road of life; sauté in a cheap Chianti flavored with false madonnas and forgotten virtues; roast until rigid with hostility in the oven of rejection and disapproval; and finally sprinkle with the salt of retribution born of self-hatred too long asimmer. (From *La Strada* a la Fellini" by Richard Rawe for a film as literature assignment)

Sincerely Yours

Writing an effective letter that demands a redress for being wronged is one of the most common and daunting compositional tasks a writer will face. Feeling mistreated (or witnessing the mistreatment of another) by family members, close friends, business associates, or even public entities, our impulse is to strike back by beginning our letter of retribution on a fervent pitch, dispensing *ad hominems* (see *Logical Fallacies*) to insult the recipient proportionately to our own sense of injury. Although venting provides the writer with temporary, cathartic relief, inflammatory words will freeze the reader, sending careful consideration of grievances into the shredder. Pelted by personal attack, the accused reader will seek shelter by dismissing or denying the writer's charges. Also, a writer beginning at full battle cry leaves no space for any escalation in tone necessary to stress more sober criticisms. For the writer's message to be given serious consideration, the writer must avoid these obstacles that make the reader less receptive.

Facting. Thus, the writer must start the letter by *Fact-spraying* objectively and dispassionately, recounting the events, documenting the facts—those verifiable, indisputable actions and words—thus delaying the discharge of a passionate proposal, stern recommendation, or wicked cussing-out. In addition, the writer must avoid the temptation to characterize or describe how something was said or done: "You maliciously refused to return my phone calls" must be "You did not return my phone calls." By sticking to the facts while maintaining a neutral, reasonable tone, the plaintiff induces the offender, to continue reading.

Interpreting. With no cause to turn away, the recipient moves on, often intrigued. Now the writer begins *Interpreting* the facts. Too many writers assume that once facts are presented their significance is self-evident. Not so. Even if the recipient cannot deny the events in the first part of the letter, he or she will rationalize, minimize, revise, or deny any harm done by the injustice of the events. Therefore, the writer—maintaining a rational tone—must explain the effect of the reader's actions, not only on the writer but also in terms of the reader's future life.

For instance, a dishonest manager hurts not only customers or employees but also himself in terms of wasted energy covering up with lies or forcing employees to use each other as scapegoats, resulting in an unproductive workplace.

Delivering. At this point, any readers, not just the recipient, but outside observers too, are trapped, intellectually and emotionally primed to accept a final pitch. *Delivering* can mean a resignation notice, a formal assertion of independence, a pronouncement of forgiveness, a proclamation of one's release of responsibility, a request for compensation or an apology, a harsh admonishment, a disclosure of the terms of any future transactions. It can be bitching the reader out.

Voices of Sincerely Yours:

Facting:
Dear Mike [Michael Ovitz, CEO of Creative Arts Agency (CAA)], . . . I knew when I walked in that you wouldn't be happy [with my leaving to have my old friend be my agent]—no other writer at CAA makes $1.25 million a screenplay—but I was unprepared for the crudity and severity of your response. You told me that if I left, "my foot soldiers who go up and down Wilshire Boulevard each day will blow your brains out.". . . You said that you would sue me. . . . Rand Holston [another CAA agent] was friendly, too, but he described the situation more specifically. . . . "Mike's going to put you into the fucking ground," Rand said. "There's no telling what Mike will say when he's angry," Rand said. "When I saw him after the meeting with you, the veins were bulging out of his neck." Even worse, Rand said, was that you would make sure the studio people knew that I was on your "shit list."

Interpreting:
As I thought about what had happened, I continued, increasingly, to be horrified by it. You are agents. Your role is to help and encourage my career and my creativity. Your role is not to place me in emotional turmoil and threaten to destroy my family's livelihood if I don't do your bidding. . . . I think the biggest reason I can't stay with you has to do with my children. I have taught them to fight for what's right. What you did is wrong. I can't teach my children one thing and then, on the most elemental level, do another. . . .

Delivering:
So do whatever you want to do, Mike, and fuck you. I have my family and I have my old imperfect manual typewriter, and they have always been the things I've treasured the most. (From a letter sent to Ovitz and the Writers Guild by Joe Eszterhas, film screenwriter, printed in *Harper's Magazine*)

Facting:
It was only necessary to be happy about something or other, to be filled with the thought of it, to come home and speak of it, and the answer was an ironical sigh, a shaking of the head, a tapping of the table with one finger: "Is that all you're so worked up about?" or "I wish I had your worries!". . . The main thing was that the bread should be cut straight. But it didn't matter that you did it with a knife dripping with gravy. One had to take care that no scraps fell on the floor. In the end it was under your chair that there were most scraps. At table one wasn't allowed to do anything but eat, but you cleaned and cut your fingernails, sharpened pencils, cleaned your ears with the toothpick.

Interpreting:
Please, Father, understand me rightly: these would in themselves have been utterly insignificant details; they only became depressing for me because you, the man who was tremendously the measure of all things for me, yourself did not keep the commandments you imposed on me.
(From a letter to his father by Franz Kafka)

Facting & Interpreting:
Dearest Peter, Apostle of the Son of Man,

My immediate recollection of your deeds always begins with your denial of Jesus, first denying your allegiance to Jesus when a servant-girl recognizes you, then upon being recognized as a Galilean like Jesus and the rest of his disciples. And despite the way you "broke down and wept," you still turned your back on your leader no matter how "vehemently" you swore not to deny him. But this kind of inconsistency of action—not being strong enough to stick to your principles and ideas when beatings are being handed down—is quite characteristic of you and the rest of the disciples: "do you not understand this parable" is Jesus' way of showing that he still loves you enough to let you in on the "secret of the kingdom of God," all the while, you and the disciples do not really understand Jesus' parables—and you are his disciples, for Christ's sake; you and your ilk are quick to rebuke men "casting out demons in [Jesus'] name" while Jesus himself is ecstatic to have people passing on his message in his name. . . .

Delivering:
So if having Jesus around was not inspiring enough, then I recommend another
form of inspiration, *Don Quixote, the man and the work,* which embodies the very facets of loyalty and belief that give meaning to life, Quixote himself so wrapped up in the love of his beliefs (chivalry) that he would attack windmills and call a halt to his march at the sound of felling hammers, suspecting both to be giants ripe for knight-erranting into oblivion. In one light this kind of insanity, brought about by stories that "Aristotle himself" could never "decipher or understand," appears grotesque and perverse, modeling one's life after mere stories; but from this insane devotion Don Quixote is willing "to serve you" and give "consolation in affliction to find someone who mourns with you." Here Don Quixote is opening his services to a complete stranger, even though it stems from the insanity of chivalry, one minute using this code to console Cardenio, the next allowing chivalry's accouterments involving Queen Madasima's personal affairs to arouse fighting between himself and Cardenio. And Don Quixote takes the beating. (From "Dear Peter" by Andy Stuart for World Literature Before the Renaissance)

M

Facting:
Dear Fellow School Board Members,

You have raised several objections against reading grotesque literature, especially concerning the potential of such mature content to harm young minds still in their formative stages. You speculated that excessive amounts of "gray area" created by characters lost in confusion and pain may imbue students with depression and a loss of hope in humanity for a bright future. You complained that Nathanael West's novel, *Miss Lonelyhearts,* is primarily gray area, leaving the reader somewhere between hard-boiled and heartbroken, not knowing which way to turn. You point to such comically grotesque scenes as the male character, Miss Lonelyhearts, bringing the considerably large and troubled Mrs. Doyle to his apartment where she precedes to tidal-wave him into bed. Furthermore, you were bothered that Miss Lonelyhearts is depicted in the beginning with a fairly lucid frame of mind; however, through a series of increasingly grotesque situations, progresses towards obsession and denial, ending by dying a sudden and seemingly pointless death when he rushes to embrace a cripple and gets shot, while even denied a final moment of clarity to justify his existence. Such depressing and pessimistic content, unaccompanied by an uplifting message, may seem an advocacy of despair and suicide.

Interpreting:
While such objections against the novel seem valid, there are enormous benefits and insights into humanity to be gained by reading such grotesque literature that cannot be obtained in other types of literature. Grotesque literature challenges our know-it-all attitude and forces us to question commonly held beliefs. For instance, West confronts society's hypocritical piety by deconstructing common responses to tragedy such as our inclination to feel sorry for the downtrodden but then immediately have frustration and anger at our inability to fix the problem, a dynamic West dramatically illustrates with an anecdote where Miss Lonelyhearts, who accidentally steps on a small frog and sees its spilled guts, is filled with pity "but when its suffering had become real to his senses, his pity [turns] to rage and he [beats] it frantically until it [is] dead" (West 17).

All the time we hear about people dying in wars overseas, starving to death, youth getting shot in gang wars, and women getting raped, and we feel sorry for them but, if we are honest, we admit being angry: "Why can't those people stop fighting and grow food?" or "Why can't men not rape or those women not walk alone at night?" West picks right up with this angry, the-world-is-hopeless feeling and leads right in to the next common response, "the rock," which is emotional detachment. . . . West ends the novel with Miss Lonelyhearts giving in to the "coiled snake" of hysteria and transforming into a self-deluded magical-Christ figure, which in the beginning he had despised so much. . . .

Delivering:
By your denying grotesque literature in the classroom, you allow students to delude themselves. Not allowing grotesque literature into the classroom gives students confidence that they can disassociate from the grotesque, which in turn gives the perverse the ability to insidiously penetrate their consciousness, whereas bringing to light the subtle inner perversities and hypocrisies we

harbor within ourselves brings them out into the open where all of us can confront our darkness with an honest understanding and acceptance of who we are and challenge ourselves to become better. (From "Proposal Letter" by Jenessa Kenway for a Critical Thinking About Literature essay)

Facting:
I have selected this day on which to address you, because it is the anniversary of my emancipation; and knowing of no better way I am led to this as the best mode of celebrating that truly important event. Just ten years ago this beautiful September morning, yon bright sun beheld me a slave—a poor, degraded chattel—trembling at the sound of your voice, lamenting that I was a man, and wishing myself a brute. The hopes which I had treasured up for weeks of a safe and successful escape from your grasp were powerfully confronted at this hour by dark clouds of doubt and fear, making my person shake and my bosom to heave with the heavy contest between hope and fear. . . . I was making a leap in the dark. . . .

Since I left you, I have had a rich experience. I have occupied stations which I never dreamed of when a slave. Three out of the ten years since I left you, I spent as a common laborer on the wharves of New Bedford, Massachusetts. It was there I earned my first free dollar. It was mine. I could spend it as I pleased. . . . I soon, however, learned to count money, as well as to make it, and got on swimmingly. . . .

Interpreting:
I met Wm. Lloyd Garrison [who] put it into my head that I might make myself serviceable to the cause of the slave by devoting a portion of my time to telling my own sorrows, and those of other slaves which had come under my observation. . . . I was thrown into society the most pure, enlightened and benevolent that the country affords. Among these I have never forgotten you, but have invariably made you the topic of conversation— thus giving you all the notoriety I could do. I need not tell you that the opinion formed of you in these circles, is far from being favorable. They have little respect for your honesty, and less for your religion. . . . I had not long enjoyed the excellent society to which I have referred, before the light of its excellence exerted a beneficial influence on my mind and heart. Much of my early dislike of white persons was removed. . . . I therefore made an

effort so to improve my mind and deportment as to be somewhat fitted to the station to which I seemed almost providently called. To transition from degradation to respectability was indeed great. . . .

At this moment, you are probably the guilty holder of at least three of my own dear sisters, and my only brother in bondage. . . . You have kept them in utter ignorance, and have therefore robbed them of the sweet enjoyments of writing or receiving letters. . . . Your wickedness and cruelty committed in this respect on your fellow-creatures, are greater than all the stripes you have laid upon my back, or theirs. It is an outrage upon the soul—a war upon the immortal spirit, and one for which you must give account at the bar of our common Father and Creator. . . .

Delivering:
I will now bring this letter to a close;] you shall hear from me again unless you let me hear from you. I intend to make use of you as a weapon with which to assail the system of slavery—as a means of concentrating public attention on the system, and deepening their horror of trafficking in the souls and bodies of men. I shall make use of you as a means of exposing the character of the American church, and clergy—and as a means of bringing this guilty nation with yourself to repentance. In doing this I entertain no malice towards you personally. There is no roof under which you would be more safe than mine, and there is nothing my house, which you might need for your comfort, which I would not readily grant. Indeed, I should esteem it a privilege, to set you an example as to how mankind ought to treat each other.

I am your fellow man, but not your slave. (From "Letter to His Master" by Frederick Douglass)

Facting:
To the editor:
All right, call me a dumbfuck, but I just found out the other day that Washington, D.C., isn't in the state of Washington.
Interpreting:
The sad thing is that I am eighteen and never knew this. I passed government and geography—how I made it through without knowing this, I don't know. I've read stories in *Thrasher* on D.C. skaters and skate spots too. I found out where it was by looking for it on this U.S. map.

Delivering:
I just want to say fuck everyone for never telling me, and I think you should print this because I don't want this to happen to anyone else. D.C. Dumbass, Westminster, CA (From "Letter to the Editor" in *Thrasher,* a skateboarding monthly)

☑

Facting:
Dear Mom,
[The first part of this letter is loaded with specific examples where B___ betrays the writer.]

Interpreting:
Mom, those flowery compliments on your hair ("It makes you so young, Mrs. ___!"), your cooking ("You didn't get this recipe out of a cookbook? No!"), and your daughter ("I love her, Mrs. ___. I will do anything to make her happy") have been just worthless babble. Each was merely a ploy to win your heart as he had won mine. He knew that if he was in good with you, nothing could stand in his way of gaining my trust, that I would have to believe in him if you did, and as he grew to realize that both of us were on his side, he became treasonous to our credence of his character. He fooled us. He tricked us. He took advantage of every don't-be-silly-B___'s-a-good-kid reply that came out of your mouth.

Delivering:
I have had my head up my ass for the past year with this guy, as have you, Mom. One of us needed to open her eyes, and I don't feel that you will be doing that any time soon. I know this won't be easy for you to take, but B___ is an asshole. If you love him so much, you go be with him. I, on the other hand, have already begun to look for an apartment and a roommate. I think that if my relationships are the pinnacle of your existence, neither of us is going to carry on a healthy life. I have had a lot of changes take place in a short amount of time, and I think that by moving out, I can continue to become the woman that I want to be. Mother, I know you mean well and want the very best for me; however, I think that it's time for me to get out on my own. It's time for both of us to grow up.
(From "Dear Mom" by an anonymous student for a freshman composition assignment)

PUNCHING UP:
Ways to Intensify

Echoing
Netting
Q&A-ing
Masquerading
Raising the Dead

When writers need to make key sections of an essay pop they turn to some less conventional strategies to get readers' attention. The pounding and thumping rhythm of *Echoing* delivers an emphatic proposal. The sweeping, energetic vibration of *Netting* replicates the unrelenting rhythm of a shocking omnipresence. If sections of an essay fade because ideas become abstract, a paragraph can benefit from the jolt of *Q&A-ing* or the coyness of *Masquerading*. *Raising the Dead* revives writing that might be perceived as antiquated material.

Echoing

When delivering a stirring sermon, presenting a significant scientific discovery, orating a political call to action, or providing provocative testimony about environmental abuse, a speaker's passionate message is emphasized by tone of voice, gestures and pace. In contrast to speaking, writing foils our ability to gesture and inflect our words. A writer may try to desperately recover the lost emphasis by overwhelming a composition with empty superlatives—*It's magnificent!*—or by using high-flown phrases: *This is an urgent matter; we must act now!* Choking on overwrought language, an essay's strong points dissipate instead of gaining momentum.

To remedy the problem of creating emphasis without coming off as manic, a writer needs to break one of those what-not-to-do commandments of academic writing—*Thou shall not repeat thyself*—choosing instead to purposefully *Be fruitful and multiply.* The intentional repetition of phrases, key words, syllables or even sounds within words can weld together hot items, building towards a searing conclusion. *Echoing* prevents important sections of an essay from becoming flat notes or a whole essay from becoming anti-climactic. While repetition is often associated with poetry or sacred texts, *Echoing* offers a melodic fusion, pushing an idea or argument towards a secular crescendo.

In crafting and refining *Echoing*, a writer must sustain the reverberation over several sentences. *Echoing* is referred to in classical rhetoric by several terms, depending on how the technique is used: *alliteration*, the repetition of consonants in two or more adjacent words (searched, seized, sunk); *assonance*, the repetition of similar vowel sounds, proceeded and followed by different consonant sounds (came, bake, take); *anaphora*, the repetition of the same word or groups of words at the beginning of successive clauses (see most of the examples below); *epistrophe*, the repetition of the same word or group of words at the ends of successive clauses (life is sacred, sex is sacred, cats are sacred); *anadiplosis*, repetition of the last word of one clause at the beginning of the following clause (happiness makes one think of sadness, sadness makes one think of despair); *antimetabole*, repetition of words, in successive clauses, in reverse grammatical order (you like it, it likes you); *polyptoton*, repetition of words derived from the same root (useless by overuse). Even though passionate writers do not necessarily know these techniques' names, they often *Echo* them in their writing.

Your turn. In the samples below identify what kind of tone the *Echoings* create; then explain the relationship between the content and the repetition. Next, review a past essay, memo, or letter that was flat. Revise one section with *Echoing* to create important emphasis.

Tones of Echoing:

He was moving to Santa Monica, of course: of course, because Santa Monica is where all of the amazing young, aspiring people in Los Angeles end up. Because it's *amazing*. And sometimes, while these amazing young, aspiring people are living there, amazing developments occur in their lives or in their careers, and sometimes in both. The first amazing development in the career of my amazing roommate occurred before he had even moved to Santa Monica, when he was selected to play a small but important supporting part in a movie that was being produced. By his father. (From "Life is Amazing I Hate You" by Eli S. Evans in *The Dublin Quarterly*)

It's time to stop actively supporting and passively allowing hunting and time to stigmatize it. It's time to stop being conned and cowed by hunters, time to stop pampering and coddling them, time to get them off the government's duck-and-deer dole, time to stop thinking of wild animals as "resources" and "game," and start thinking of them as sentient beings that deserve our wonder and respect, time to stop allowing hunting to be creditable by calling it "sport" and "recreation." Hunters make wildlife *dead, dead, dead*. It's time to wake up to this indisputable fact. As for the hunters, it's long past checkout time. (From "The Killing Game" by Joy Williams in *Esquire*)

I want a wife who is sensitive to my sexual needs, a wife who makes love passionately and eagerly when I feel like it, a wife who makes sure that I am satisfied. And, of course, I want a wife who will not demand sexual attention from me when I am not in the mood for it. I want a wife who assumes the complete responsibility for birth control, because I do not want more children. I want a wife who will remain sexually faithful to me so that I don't have to clutter up my intellectual life with jealousies. And I want a wife who understands that *my* sexual needs may entail more than strict adherence to monogamy. I must, after all, be able to relate to people as fully as possible. (From "I Want a Wife" by Judy Brady in *Ms. Magazine*)

The space between the idea of something and its reality is always wide and deep and dark. The longer they are kept apart—idea of thing, reality of thing—the wider the width, the deeper the depth, the thicker and darker the darkness. This space starts out empty, there is nothing in it, but it rapidly becomes filled up with obsession or desire or hatred or love—sometimes all of these things, sometimes some of these things, sometimes only one of these things. (From "On Seeing England for the First Time" by Jamaica Kincaid in *Transition*)

This one always had been working. This one was always having something that was coming out of this one that was a solid thing, a charming thing, a lovely thing, a perplexing thing, a disconcerting thing, a simple thing, a clear thing, a complicated thing, an interesting thing, a disturbing thing, a repellent thing, a very pretty thing. This one was one certainly being one having something coming out of him. This one was one whom some were following. . . . This one was one who was almost always working. This one was not one completely working. This one was one not ever completely working. (From "Picasso" by Gertrude Stein in *Selected Writings of Gertrude Stein*)

On the first day, then, [Bombay] seemed a city of terror, of despair. But I was wrong—or, at any rate, only partly right. It takes time to read Bombay. It takes time to understand that those moss-blackened apartment blocks are not slums, that they very probably are the homes of middle-class people and that the outer neglect is deceptive. It takes time to understand that those squatter huts occupying the pavement outside the stadium may contain transistor radios and gas cookers, that the men who live in them may have regular clerkly jobs. . . . It takes time to penetrate the veil of apparently hopeless dereliction and to see that the city still works reasonably well: buses run; trains run; electricity lights the roads and skyscrapers; water (more or less) flows; telephones (more or less) work. Bombay lives. (From "The City by the Sea" by Shiva Naipaul in *Beyond the Dragon's Mouth*)

Someone asked me why a surgeon would write. . . . A surgeon should abstain. A surgeon, whose fingers are more at home in the steamy gulleys of the body than they are tapping the dry keys of a typewriter. A surgeon, who feels the slow slide of intestines against the back of his hand and is no more alarmed than were it a family of snakes taking their comfort from such an indolent rubbing. A surgeon, who palms the human heart as though it were some captured bird.

Why should he write? . . . It is to search for some meaning in the ritual of surgery, which is at once murderous, painful, healing, and full of love. (From *The Art of Surgery: A Variation on the Art of Writing* by Richard Selzer)

Go back to Mississippi, go back to Alabama, go back to Georgia, go back to Louisiana, go back to the slums and ghettos of our northern cities, knowing that somehow this situation can and will be changed. . . . I have a dream that one day this nation will rise up and live out the true meaning of its creed: "We hold these truths to be self-evident: that all men are created equal." I have a dream that one day on the red hills of Georgia the sons of former slaves and the sons of former slave owners will be able to sit down together at a table of brotherhood. I have a dream that one day even the state of Mississippi, a desert state, sweltering with the heat of injustice and oppression, will be transformed into an oasis of freedom and justice. I have a dream that my four children will one day live in a nation where they will not be judged by the color of their skin but by the content of their character. I have a dream today. (From a speech delivered at the Lincoln Memorial in Washington, D.C., on August 28, 1963, by Martin Luther King, Jr.)

Netting

In our everyday lives we use simple lists to capture and organize our thoughts—grocery lists, guest lists, things-to-do lists, pro-con lists. Great essayists use arranged lists that we call *Nettings* to communicate meaning through the quantity and tight arrangement of the entries on the list. *Nettings* catch those omnipresent forces that flow undefined and undetected, hidden below the skin of life's normal hustle and bustle: many people are addicted to more than just drugs; gluttony manifests itself in myriad ways besides just overeating; rare things appear everywhere; straight lines permeate our lives. Identifying a robust abstract concept or seizing a hidden but omnipresent force requires convincing the reader of the existence and/or prevalence of that clandestine impulse.

To capture the power and magnitude of these overwhelming, all-encompassing worlds, a writer bombards readers with an unrelenting stream of related facts, a litany of complaints or commands, an intriguing collage of images or products, an inventory of startling names or foods, or a glossary of paradoxes or unusual places—any outpouring of details that will encapsulate. But before this outpouring can be deemed a *Netting,* a writer uses three crucial design strategies—*Specifying, Sizing,* and *Sorting.*

Specifying. A typical first attempt at *Netting* begins with a brainstorm of all the associations a writer has with the subject. Vanessa Schueler generated the following list for her rough draft on the abstraction gluttony:

> Gluttony: gobble, gulping, gorging, gross, greedy, hefty, hungry, indulge, feasting, fat, large, obese, piggy, rapacious, stuffed, surplus, saturation, voracious.

Though the list is short, it is onerous to read—predictable and boring. Using all general terms to define gluttony prevents any expansion of meaning and limits the reader's careful consideration of the subject. In revising, the writer adds specific examples—particular descriptions of the effects of gluttony (*praying to the porcelain god*), certain holidays associated with overindulgence (*Thanksgiving, New Year's Eve*), unusual kinds of gluttony beyond overeating (*shopping, having sex*), and people associated with the deadly sin (*Robert Downey Jr., Vampires*). By varying the level of particularity—keeping some items general while making others extremely specific—the list traps a wider, more startling range of examples resulting in a more appealing texture that encourages the audience to keep reading to discover surprise gluttonies.

Sizing. But *Specifying* alone is not enough to give readability to and establish definition in a list. Attention must be given to rhythm and pace. In Vanessa Schueler's first attempt, the single-word *sizes* of those entries create a monotonous rhythm. In revising,

Schueler retains some single word entries: "oversexed, lush, lust, nymphomaniac, wild," but in *Specifying*, she also begins *Sizing* or lengthening entries into descriptive clauses: "preferring shots to mixed drinks" and "wolfish appetite for destruction." By varying the *Sizing* of each item on the list, having some entries pared down to a single word, while developing others into longer clauses, a more expressive rhythm begins to beat. A *Netting* can even contain *Freighting* or *Telescoping* sentences (see the *Flow* section) that add mega-*Sizing* to the list. Generally, complete sentences (independent clauses) should be used sparingly so as not to undercut the listing rhythm of the *Netting*.

Sorting. The last step in converting a list into a polished *Netting* is *Sorting*—the positioning of items on the list to establish intriguing associations or clashes. For instance, in *Specifying*, Schueler identified two holidays associated with overindulgence—New Year's Eve and Thanksgiving. The writer underscores the connection by *Sorting* the two celebrations, placing them next to one another in the *Netting*. Next, the two different kinds of gluttony these holidays provoke are *Sorted*: "belly worship" and "praying to the porcelain god." The common denominator of the religious references "worship" and "praying," link the two examples and suggest an irreverent aspect of this deadly sin. Other times the *Sorting* achieves a clash by juxtaposing contrasting details, giving the *Netting* a paradoxical punch. Schueler may consider adding some items that are the opposite of gluttony: "sparseness" and "sobriety." The subliminal organization achieved through *Sorting* helps readers effortlessly move from item to item in the *Netting*.

Once items of varying *Size* and *Specificity* have been *Sorted* into interesting relationships, the writer begins micro-*Sorting* by connecting entries using commas, semicolons, and single dashes. Some entries can be interrupted with parenthetical statements and with dash skewers (see the *Pause* section). Other items can be disconnected with definitive pauses by inserting some *Very Short Sentences* and adding an occasional period or colon. While colons often introduce a list, consider using colons in unexpected ways, creating a mini-*Netting* inside of a *Netting*. Using *Hieroglyphics* not only unifies all the disparate parts of the list, but also creates variety of tone, the punctuation guiding the reader as to what kind of pause and emphasis to give the entries.

After revising her list using the principles of *Specifying, Sizing,* and *Sorting,* Vanessa Schueler created this *Netting.*

> New Year's Eve party and Thanksgiving dinner: overindulging, guzzling, swinish belly-worship, binge drinking—praying to the porcelain god. Preferring shots to mixed drinks; intoxication, inebriation, unrestrained addiction a la Robert Downey, Jr. and Timothy Leary, the summer of love, oversexed, lush, lust, nymphomaniacal, wild, wolfish appetite for destruction, the Vampire Lestat, omnivorous, wasteful, intemperate, shopoholic, sin. Gluttony is an emotional escape, a sign something is eating you: depression, austerity, sparseness, and sobriety.

Your turn. Analyze and identify examples of *Sizing, Specifying,* and *Sorting* in the examples below, but also articulate the larger schemes organizing the sample *Nettings.* Then create your own *Netting* to suggest the prevalence or omnipresence of a word, force, concept, or impulse.

Weavings of Nettings:

Blue pencils, blue noses, blue movies, blue laws, blue legs and stockings, the langue of birds, bees, and flowers as sung by longshoremen, that lead-like look the skin has when affected by cold, contusion, sickness, fear; the rotten rum or gin they call blue ruin and the blue devils of its delirium; Russian cats and oysters, a withheld or imprisoned breath, the blue they say that diamonds have, deep holes in the ocean and the blazers which English athletes earn that gentlemen may wear; afflictions of the spirit—dumps, mopes, Mondays—all that's dismal, low-down gloomy music, Nova Scotians, cyanosis, hair rinse, bluing. Bleach; the rare blue dahlia like that blue moon shrewd things happen only once in, . . . the constantly increasing absentness of Heaven (*ins Blaue hinein,* the Germans say), consequently the color of everything that's empty, . . . social registers, examination booklets, blue bloods, balls, and bonnets, beards, coats, collars, chips and cheese, . . . (From *On Being Blue* by W. H. Gass)

Of course, we do not just wait for love; we wait for money, we wait for the weather to get warmer, colder, we wait for the plumber to come and fix the washing machine (he doesn't), we wait for a friend to give us the name of another plumber (she doesn't), we wait for our hair to grow, we wait for our children outside of school, we wait for their exam results, we wait for the letter that will undo desolation, we wait for Sunday, when we sleep in or have the extra piece of toast, we wait for the crocuses to come up, then the daffodils, we wait for the estranged friend to ring or write and say, "I have forgiven you," we wait for our parents to love us though they may be long since dead, we wait for the result of this or that medical test, we wait for the pain in the shoulder to ease, we wait for that sense of excitement that has gone underground but is not quite quenched, we wait for the novel that enthralls the way it happened when we first read *Jane Eyre or War and Peace,* we wait for the invitation to the country, and often when we are there, we wait for the bus or the car that will ferry us home to the city and our props, our own chairs, our own bed, our own habits. We wait (at least I do) for new potatoes, failing to concede that there are new potatoes all the time, but the ones I am waiting for were the ones dug on the twenty-ninth of June in Ireland that tasted (or was it my imagination?) like no others. We wait to go to sleep and maybe fog ourselves with pills or soothing tapes to lull us thither. We wait for dawn, the postman, tea, coffee, the first ring of the telephone, the advancing day. (From "Waiting" by Edna O'Brien in the *Los Angeles Times Magazine*)

[A *Netting* on what it means to be alive:]To see the golden sun and the azure sky, the out-stretched ocean, to walk upon the green earth, and to be lord of a thousand creatures, to look down giddy precipices or over distant flowery vales, to see the world spread out under one's finger on a map, to bring the stars near, to view the smallest insects under a microscope, to read history, and witness the revolutions of the empires and the succession of generations . . . as of a faded pageant, and to say all these were, and are now nothing, to think that we exist in such a point of time, and in such a corner of space, to be at once spectators and a part of the moving scene, . . . to traverse desert wilderness, to listen to the midnight choir, to visit light halls, or plunge into the dungeon's gloom, or sit in the crowded theaters and see life itself mocked, to feel heat and cold, pleasure and pain, right and wrong, truth and falsehood, to study works of art and refine the sense of beauty to agony, to worship fame and to dream of immortality, to have read Shakespeare and belong to the same species as Sir Isaac Newton; to be and to do all this, and then in a moment to be nothing, to have it all snatched from one like a juggler's ball, . . . (From "On the Feeling of Immortality in Youth" by William Hazlitt)

You stand at one end of an aisle and look down the length of a Wal-Mart Super Center, and you've got affordable plenty as far as the eye can see. There are glitter lava lamps, "the Prayer of Jabez" inspirational books, Inca-design polyester place mats, Secret Treasures see-through panties, schools of blue gourami in the fish department and DripMoist Vegetable Garden soaker systems in the garden department. . . . Then you go over to one of those Price Club stores and you enter abundance on steroids. Here you can get laundry detergent in 40-pound tubs, 30-pound bags of frozen Tater Tots, frozen waffles in 60-serving boxes and packages with 1,500 Q-Tips—which is 3,000 actual swabs since there's cotton on both ends. (From "Why the U.S. Will Always Be Rich" by David Brooks in *The New York Times Magazine*)

Rarity, then, is an emotion as much as it is a statistical truth. Just say the word over to yourself: *Rare. O rarer than rare.* A long, piercing curve of light appears and fades in one's darkened memory. It's like the diminishing cry of cartoon characters when they are tricked into running off a cliff. *The rare book room. A rare disease. Rarefied air. A miracle of rare device.* Comprehended in the notion are all sorts of contributory pangs: brevity, chances barely missed, awe, the passing of great men and glorious eras. Frequency is a sudden movement of many wings, a riffle through a worn paperback; rarity holds the single hushing index finger raised. And yet the absolute number of "raremes" is enormous—too large in fact for us to give each one of them the rapt monocular attention it deserves. Not only are there priceless misstamped nickels, oddball aurora borealises hanging their ball-gowns over unpopulated areas, fraternal bananas enclosed in a single skin, holes-in-one, and authentic Georges de La Tours; there are also all the varied sorts of human talent and permutations of character: the master mimic of frog sounds, the memory of prodigy, the man who can mix wit with sympathy. The universe of rares is surprisingly crowded, and yet it is somehow capable of holding its inmates in seeming isolation, each of them floating in a radiantly placental, fluid-filled sphere of amazement, miles from any neighbor. (From "Rarity" by Nicholson Baker in *The Size of Thoughts*)

And with every dime you've got tied up in your new place, suddenly the drains in your prep kitchen are backing up with raw sewage, pushing hundreds of gallons of impacted crap into your dining room; your coke-addled chef just called that Asian waitress who's working her way through law school a chink, which ensures your presence in court for the next six months; your bartender is giving away the bar to underage girls from Wantagh, any one of whom could then crash Daddy's Buick into a busload of divinity students, putting your liquor license in peril, to say the least; the Ansel System could go off, shutting down your kitchen in the middle of a ten-thousand-dollar night; there's the ongoing struggle with rodents and cockroaches, any one of which could crawl across the Tina Brown four-top in the middle of the dessert course; you just bought the thousand dollars' worth of shrimp when the market was low, but the walk-in freezer just went on the fritz, and naturally it's a holiday weekend, so good luck getting a service call in time; the dishwasher just walked out after arguing with the busboy, and they need glasses *now* on table seven; immigration is at the door for a surprise inspection of your kitchen's green cards; the produce guy wants a certified check or he's taking back the delivery; you didn't order enough napkins for the weekend—and is that the *New York Times* reviewer waiting for your hostess to stop flirting and notice her? (From "Owner's Syndrome and Other Medical Anomalies" by Anthony Bourdain in *Kitchen Confidential*)

At any given moment, there must be thousands of people sighing. A man in Milwaukee heaves and shivers and blesses the head of the second wife who's not too shy to lick his toes. A judge in Munich groans with pleasure after tasting again the silky bratwurst she ate as a child. Every day, meaningful sighs are expelled from schoolchildren, driving instructors, forensics experts, certified public accountants, and dental hygienists, just to name a few. The sighs of widows and widowers alone must account for a significant portion of the carbon dioxide released into the atmosphere. Every time a girdle is removed, a foot is submerged in a tub of warm water, or a restroom is reached on a desolate road . . . you'd think the sheer velocity of it would create mistrals, siroccos, hurricanes; arrows should be swarming over satellite maps, weathermen talking a mile a minute, ties flapping from their necks like flags. (From "The Fine Art of Sighing" by Bernard Cooper in *Paris Review*)

Americans have an obsession with lines. From the time we're very small we're taught to line up, stay in line, toe the line, and for heaven's sake don't get out of line. If we step over the line there'll be hell to pay, and forget about a refrigerator exhibition if we color outside the lines. We anxiously await the headlines each morning, sign on the dotted line when we make a deal, and cheer for line drives. We love our by-lines, protect our property lines and can't wait to get online. And finally, after we've lived out our lives, we reach the end of the line. All this suggests a sort of single, right organization to things; a healthy delineation between one activity and another in order to keep moving in our chosen directions, step-by-step, one foot after the other, left, right, eyes forward, hemmed in, stubborn and methodical, boring and predictable: science fair kids with pocket protectors, thick black plastic eyeglasses and sensible shoes, always whining that they have another earache and need to be excused from PE class, to go home to their Minute Maid moms and *Reader's Digest* dads, for hello-honey-and-how-was-your-day, eat a properly balanced meal featuring the five basic food groups, then it's homework first before the National Geographic special. Orderly thinking produces orderly lives: go to bed at a reasonable hour so it can be done again tomorrow and next year, organized, obedient, never defiant, never random or serendipitous. Undisciplined thinking prohibited: keep out! (From "Linear" by Terry Snyder for a freshman composition assignment)

Q&A-ing

Writers devote themselves to posing important and, at times, *impertinent* questions about the human condition—Is our destiny the result of fate or our own free will? Is a woman's charm more powerful than a man's CEO position? Can love transform us into better people? When essayists too readily gush answers, soaking their audiences in pontification or wise guyisms, they deprive readers of the invigorating, tough questions that writers depend on for powering essays. Readers will more seriously consider answers when the essayist includes the audience in the development of any conjecture.

In a colloquium, a lecturer uses leading questions:
Q. "Why use a short dialogue as an example in an essay?"
A. "To fire up your audience and generate discussion."

Even without a live audience, a writer can make use of a lecturer's questions by creating a virtual dialogue or recreating part of an actual dialogue. Although frequently associated with fictional or dramatic works, scripted question-and-answer dialogue in an essay can turn didactic chatter into organized claims and support. More importantly, the questions anticipate and stand in for the reader's own inquiries, doubts, or ignorance. The questions modulate the answers' loudness. The reader listens.

The use of a mock dialogue has been around for centuries, from Plato's *The Republic* to the cartoon of Garry Trudeau, who in his strip, *Doonesbury*, focuses on philosophical discourse. Trudeau's strip contains very little movement of body positions between frames, little dramatic lighting or shadow, and virtually no shifts in perspectives common to superhero and romance strips. Instead the emphasis is on dialogue, often being bounced off a "fall" person. In an essay, a writer can create a question-and-answer dialogue by using a substitute or mock interrogator to extend the exchange, inventing a fall person, a foil, a naïf or a devil's advocate who prods the writer or another created character; or the essayist might adopt famous personas who chat with one another in the present moment.

Your turn. Have Einstein correct a present-day scientist's use of physics; have Oprah host-referee a panel of philosophers from different periods; have Woody Allen ask advice on Comedy from Shakespeare; have a historian get spit at by Henry VIII. To prepare, research a character's or historical figure's background and writings, analyzing his or her style to create dialogue, and come up with questions that will allow you to capture substantial details to bring the characters' positions quickly into focus. Don't banter or waste time.

Sounds of Q&A-ing:

[In this essay, an imaginary "fiftyish fellow with fine teeth and a foolproof pension plan" wants to kill himself, prompting the writer to ask questions on our behalf.]
What about your marriage?
"She's become more mannish than me. I loved women. I don't believe in marriage between men."
Remarry, then!

"I've gone impotent, and besides, when I see somebody young and pretty I guess I feel like dandling her on my knee."
Marriage is friendship. You can find someone your own age.
"I'm tired of it."
But how about your company?—a widows-and-orphans stock that's on the cutting edge? . . .
"I know what wins. It's less and less appetizing." (From "Heaven and Nature" by Edward Hoagland in *Harper's Magazine*)

[The following "Q&A" is narrated by another character so has single within double quotes. Following is the "Q" who is the Grand Inquisitor of Seville, busy torching heretics, questioning Jesus in a dream, who responds only at the end of the chapter.]
"'Instead of taking men's freedom from them, Thou didst make it greater than ever! Didst Thou forget that man prefers peace, and even death, to freedom of choice in the knowledge of good and evil? . . . Thou didst choose all that is exceptional, vague and enigmatic, what was utterly beyond the strength of men. . . . So that, in truth, Thou didst Thyself lay the foundation for the destruction of Thy kingdom, and no one is more to blame for it. Yet what was offered Thee? There are three powers alone able to conquer and to hold captive for ever the conscience of these impotent rebels for their happiness—those forces are miracle, mystery and authority. Thou hast rejected all three and hast set the example for doing so.'" (From "The Grand Inquisitor" by Fyodor Dostoyevsky in *The Brothers Karamozov)*

[A young writer drags his best friend, Johnson, on an arduous journey, arranging for him to dine and socialize with notorious people and then asks him a range of questions having to do with the sacred and the profane.]
Boswell: I asked him what he thought was best to teach children first.
Johnson: Sir, it is no matter what you teach them first, any more than what leg you shall put into your breeches first. Sir, you may stand disputing which is best to put in first, but in the
 meantime your breech is bare. Sir, while you are considering which of two things you should teach your child first, another boy has learnt them both. (From *The Life of Samuel Johnson* by James Boswell)

Hawthorne: The title character of my work "Young Goodman Brown" is placed in a similar position. Like Winterbourne in James's story "Daisy Miller," he sees the world only in black or white, without shades of gray, and also ultimately wastes his life. Therefore when Faith, his wife, falters he cries out, "My Faith is gone! There is no good on earth; and sin is but a name. Come, Devil; for to thee is thus the world given" (30).

Dickinson: Things might have been so different for your young Goodman Brown had he caught Faith in his embrace—accepting her for who she was—and kissed her in the street as she wanted. The same is true of Winterbourne—yes cold, but more than that, prideful and self-important; he could not go against his polite society that treated Daisy so cruelly.

James: You do sound so much as I am sure that Daisy would if she spoke on the matter.

Dickinson: Well, if I do, then let me say this for her: "I'm nobody! Who are you? Are you nobody, too? Then there's a pair of us—don't tell! They'd banish us, you know. How dreary to be somebody! How public, like a frog, to tell your name the live-long day to an admiring bog!"

James: She very well may be thinking something similar when she says, speaking of the society that rejects her: "They are only pretending to be shocked. They don't really care a straw what I do" (316), perhaps hoping that Winterbourne would conspire to be her fellow nobody. (From "Raising James, Hawthorne, and Dickinson" by Crystal Colwell for an American literature assignment)

I'm 82, and I'll Conduct My Own Interview, Thanks. . . .
Aren't you nervous about your own, er, mortality?
No. When I was 16, I was nervous about everything—boys, pimples, holding up my stockings with a garter belt. I absolutely never thought of myself as departing this world. Why start now?. . .
But don't you secretly wish you were younger?
Wouldn't wish being younger on anyone. When you're young, you panic. You want everything, and when you get something, you wonder how to get rid of it.
Like love?
Especially love, Oh, the agony, the distress. It's not until you're older that—
Like 82? Don't tell me that—
Yes. At 82, even older, love can and does bloom.
(From "Of Age and Attitude" by Lucille deView in *Los Angeles Times Magazine*)

[Part of a memo written after September 11, 2001, by an admin-
istrator at a high school located near the World Trade Center]
Q: We don't look like terrorists. Why do we have to wear ID
cards in school?
A: All terrorists do not look like Osama bin Laden. Let me repeat,
every nut and fanatic has heard of Stuyvesant [High School].
Everyone who didn't make the cutoff on the test, everyone who
is angry with his teacher, everyone who hates. Everyone. There
are a quarter of a billion people in this country alone.
Q: You fascist pigs with your Big Brother mentality are just trying
to scare us. There's no real danger.
A: Are you for real?. . . There are bad people out there who
believe that they will spend all eternity in heaven with seventy-
two virgins if they can kill some of us while killing themselves.
They really believe that. There are nuts that see Satan, there is
an infinite variety of other kinds of nuts and wackos, and you
think that you are above wearing an ID card while in school.
(From "Readings" in *Harper's Magazine*)

[Q does not respond in the following, perhaps because Q's
response is implied in the answer.]
'The whole thing is incredibly confusing, and it's one reason I'm
so hesitant to bring it up with you, out of fear that I won't be able
to be clear about it and that you'll misunderstand and be hurt,
but I decided that if I care about you I have to have the courage
to really act as if I care about you, to put caring about you before
my own petty worries and confusions.'
Q.
'Sweetie, you're welcome. I pray you're not being sarcastic.
I'm so mixed up and terrified right now I probably couldn't even
tell.'
Q.
'I know I should have told you some of all this about me sooner,
and the pattern. . . . Especially because I know your moving
out here was something I lobbied so hard for. School, your
apartment, having to get rid of your cat—just please don't
misunderstand.' (From *Brief Interviews with Hideous Men* by
David Foster Wallace)

"How is it going to look for me when I tell them you want to
pay back the loan already?"
"But can't you use the money?"
"Our business is to make loans," he said. "What kind of
institution do you think we'd have if everybody came in here and

said they would like to pay back their notes before they were due? We're just lucky everyone is not as venal as you are."

"I'm sorry," I said. 'I didn't think I was doing anything wrong."

"I'll have to talk to the president about this." The vice-president called over two of the bank guards and said to them, "Watch him closely. He wants to pay back a loan." (From "The Credit Risk" by Art Buchwald in *And Then I Told the President*)

It is both comical and sad to watch silent dancing [in a silent family film]. Since there is no justification for the absurd movements that music provides for some of us, people appear frantic, their faces embarrassingly intense. It's as if you were watching sex. Yet for years, I've had dreams in the form of this home movie. In a recurring scene, familiar faces push themselves forward into my mind's eye, plastering their features into distorted close-ups. And I'm asking them: "Who is she? Who is the old woman I don't recognize? Is she an aunt? Somebody's wife? Tell me who she is."

> "See the beauty mark on her cheek as big as a hill on the lunar landscape of her face—well, that runs in the family. . . . The young girl with the green stain on her wedding dress is *La Novia*—just up from the Island. See, she lowers her eyes. . . a girl should express humility in all her actions. She will make a good wife for your cousin. . . . If he marries her quickly, she will make him a good Puerto Rican-style wife; but if he waits too long, she will be corrupted by the city—just like your cousin there.". . .
>
> "Your *prima* is pregnant by that man she's been sneaking around with. Would I lie to you? I'm your *Tia Politica*, your great-uncle's common-law wife—the one he abandoned on the Island to go marry your cousin's mother. I was not invited to this party, of course, but I came anyway. I came to tell you that story about your cousin that you've always wanted to hear. Do you remember the comment your mother made to a neighbor that has always haunted you? The only thing you heard was your cousin's name, and then you saw your mother pick up your doll from the couch and say: 'It was as big as this doll when they flushed it down the toilet.'. . . Your cousin was growing an *Americanito* in her belly when this movie was made." (From "Silent Dancing" by Judith Ortiz Cofer in the *Georgia Review*)

Masquerading

Specific details are key to any good writing, but particularities marching ant-like across the page—instead of dancing in a Mardi Gras parade—tire readers. Scientific, technical, and documentary writers who present loads of specific facts and data can become drill sergeants of flatness, clipping the wings of their passion for their subject because they fear losing "objectivity." Much of the modern world assumes that when language has mathematical flatness (a simplistic view of math in the first place) it is objective, and all details must have equal significance, as opposed to prioritizing, emphasizing, and dramatizing key, defining details.

A case in point of scientific flatness is Roger Peterson's bird-manual description from *A Field Guide to Birds.* He describes a bird that

> runs on the ground (tracks show 2 toes forward, 2 aft.) Large, slender, streaked; with a long white-tipped tail, shaggy crest, strong legs. White crescent on open wing. (Song 6-8 dovelike coos descending in pitch.)

While the description may be objective, any birder could expect to have field-trouble matching this description to the actual bird because many of the listed characteristics are shared with other birds. Because Peterson does not punch up the details, the reader's consciousness sinks into a swamp of information bits before finally recognizing that the guide is describing a roadrunner. Compare Peterson's flat description to that of George Hollister:

> He's half tail and half feet. The rest of him is head and beak. When he runs, he moves on blurring wheels. He can turn on a dime and leave change. He doesn't need to fly because he can run faster. He kicks dirt in a snake's face, and then eats the snake.

While one could argue that Hollister's description is not literally accurate, the sharpness of the description, based on scientific research and observation, captures a reality of the roadrunner that Peterson's "objective" details totally lack. A writer who wants to sharpen and showcase specifics—leaving no opportunity for the reader to alpha-wave them—can *Masquerade* the data using

Riddling and *Personifying* or combining the two techniques.

Riddling. A riddle eliminates clutter that could sidetrack the reader and showcases predominant details so they attain a life of their own; yet the riddle also *Masquerades* the subject so that the reader has to pay close attention, uncluttered by the self-satisfaction of knowing what the subject is until the very end of the section. By highlighting important details while at the same time playing coy with information, *Riddling* helps a reader to see the subject in a fresh light. *Riddling* can be performed on anything—insects, high-profile personalities, scientific concepts, feature films, historical incidents, a personality trait, and a ubiquitous object.

To begin *Riddling*, list at least ten of the most unique, definitive, and predominant details of the subject. Be selective. In Peterson's description, the fact that the roadrunner makes dove-like coos might be omitted from the riddle if there are other birds, including doves, which also make that coo. Or a writer could use a trait shared by other subjects as a smoke screen clue, for example: "She coos like a dove, but is not known for her flying grace."

Next present these selected details in third person (he, she, it, they), using short compound sentences (sentences that combine with a connecting word such as "and" or "but"), juxtaposing clue pairs to create memorable paradoxes or ironies. For instance, "He can smell microscopic-sized food, but you can smell him from fifty feet away" or "It always barks but never meows. . . ." or "He will tolerate the snow; however, he thoroughly enjoys the water." The *Riddling* quality of these clue pairs can be intensified if the writer contrasts the short compound sentences with a few single clues wrapped in a long sentence.

Clues that are "giveaways" should be pushed towards the end of the riddle or masked. For instance, if given the clue that "she has a long neck" a reader too easily guesses that "she" is a giraffe. By masking the details with lively language (see *Fusion* and *Superliteralism*), one might describe the giraffe's most prominent feature as "she dons a soaring necklace" or "he wears a high collar of vertebrae"; the reader then begins to paint a picture in the mind in order to decode the clue before solving the riddle. Using playful language will help to engage the reader's imagination and make the riddle more playful. The game is complete when, at the end of the list of clues, the writer invites the reader to guess the identity of he, she, it, or they.

Personifying. Personified analogies, a second form of *Masquerading*, work best when writing on abstractions (love, hate, humor, anger) and inanimate objects (famous landmarks, innovative machines, cities, cuisines). Personified analogies are also a way to punch up a list of specifics that could repel readers. Note the example on concrete below. Using this approach, the specifics associated with the subject come alive by becoming the subject's costume, friends, diversions, enemies, and other lifestyle items. Note the examples below on "Boredom" and "Silence," which merge both *Masquerading* techniques— personified analogy and the riddle.

To begin *Personifying* create a biographical profile for the abstraction or the object you are describing. First build a framework by assigning very general human characteristics— select gender, age, and race will bring life to this non-human entity. Then begin using specific details—hobbies, personality quirks, pet peeves, favorite music, occupation, physical attributes including clothing style—to fill out the whole profile. The characteristics you assign should not be random; instead, use the *Personified* characteristics to uncover subtle but fitting attributes of the subject.

Your turn. How much do you know about a famous person, insect, or city? Do a little more research, pick one of the masquerades below as a model to dress up in, and then read your *Masquerade* to a seven-year-old or at an adult party.

Teases of Masquerading:

I am a sturdy statue of mud and have been given more nicknames than a childhood bud. Regulars sit with me for hours a day, while reading, thinking, or muscling through the fray. With a push on my arm, a whoosh, and a counterclockwise spin, I still sit on my spot and bear the torment of being aimed at or not. Technology has improved me since my original day, from plastic, to cushion, to heated seats in Green Bay. I may not be associated with respect or repute, but I must be important if found all the way to Beirut. I am the toilet. (From "Privy to Antiquity" by Robert Hulliger for freshman composition assignment)

They've got the most fabulous personal trainer in town, the best lawyer, the top BMW mechanic, and make sure the world knows it. They're charming enough to attract friends, associates, and lovers—only to drop them as soon as better prospects show up. They need the best table in the house, the lion's share of the conversation and, above all, top billing, whether on the marquee or in the mailroom. . . . [Their] behavior can be entertaining, even encouraged, and it's usually relatively harmless.

Yet some of these seemingly overconfident people are actually in considerable psychological trouble, suffering what psychiatrists call narcissistic personality disorder, one of the most self-destructive and difficult-to-treat conditions in the lexicon of mental illness. (From "The Narcissist, Unmasked" by Benedict Carey in *The Los Angeles Times*)

She went to Harvard Law School, works at a tony boutique law firm in Boston, and still manages to get to her sculpting class the night before a big day in court. She has captivated a jury with her closing arguments, but she appalled a cathedral full of people with an impromptu Henny Youngman-esque eulogy at the funeral of one of her law professors.

With the precision of a surgical strike, she once tripped a woman in a supermarket who was rude to her; and with the wobbliness of a toddler, she once rose from her seat and tumbled to the floor in front of one of her law firm colleagues who happens to be her ex-boyfriend (still loves him) and his lawyer bombshell wife (hates her but kind of likes her too).

She's been known to enjoy a sexual fling with a great-looking guy (most memorably, the well-endowed bimbo model in the sculpting class) but hallucinates a dancing baby, the apparent manifestation of her 27-year-old biological clock. She has committed the transgression of sleeping with a married man, but she has never, judging by the reed-thin look of her, sinfully overeaten so much as one fat-free Entenmann's coffee cake.

She is real and not even close. But mostly, she is the centerpiece of her eponymous television show, "Ally McBeal."
(From "The Woman Is: 1. A '90s Heroine 2. A Retro Ditz/Choose One. (If You Can.)" by Carla Hall in *The Los Angeles Times*)

Does anyone really know what Boredom is like? He rarely goes anywhere without at least one of his friends. He can't stand to be alone. On Sunday afternoons he goes to the bar on the corner and drinks beer with Futility, Rage, and Anxiety. They all have such strong personalities. In conversations with that bunch boredom tends to get lost. It's not that he doesn't say anything. It is just that what he says never sounds as interesting or vivid or memorable. If you listen carefully, you will see that he actually has some very good ideas. He simply lacks the energy to carry them out. (From "Boredom" by J. Ruth Gendler in *The Book of Qualities*)

Life wasn't black or white, he knew; Implication was a friend of all the colors.

As he grew up, Implication found himself running with a not very fast crowd—Irony, Irreverence, Adoration, Poetry. They all got together though they came from different worlds, in unlit places away from the main streets. . . .

And then one day Implication heard he was on a blacklist. The word came from Rumor, and it said there was no room for either of them in the new dispensation. . . .

In the past he'd been employed by the Department of Education; Implication was how people began to learn understanding. But now a sentence was running by, no time for him, and seconds later, the sentence had crashed into another and they were both lying lifeless on the road. (From "It's All in the Implications" by Pico Iyer for *The Los Angeles Times*)

The daunting mistress to wealthy politicians, she is used by men of great political power to rid their extramarital affairs. Local law enforcement, prosecutors, witnesses, jurors, even judges have been paid huge sums of filthy lucre just to keep her. . . . You thought she was good, entrusting her with intimate secrets. When you were violated at age five by a family friend, it was she, who was voiceless, who brought you childhood ulcers to alert others that you needed help. Later, if it had not been for her, everyone would have been left in the dark about your late-night excursions to fast- food establishments. Longing to be noticed, she now had killer status. She has left you exposed, open-heart-ed with clogged arteries and then triple bypassed. She is the opposite of noise. I present to you, Silence. (From "Silence" by Donna Roberts for a freshman composition assignment)

Promiscuous, doing what everyone wants if the person is strong enough to hold it, concrete is the slut, gigolo of materials. . . . Once it has set, what a difference! Concrete becomes adamant, fanatical, a Puritan, a rock, Robespierre. It declares like no oth-er material the inevitability, the immorality—the divinity—of the shape it comprises, be the shape a glopped heap on the ground or a concert hall, ridiculous or sublime. (From "Concrete and Burton" by Peter Schjeldahl as the catalogue essay for a show of Burton's furniture sculpture)

Hope pities us and lies. It pities our terrors and invites us to tell ourselves that the things we fear happen only to other people. We are a special case. When it comes to us, says hope, calamity will turn aside.

Hope pities our dowdiness. It promises that we will find the treasure, marry the prince, and inherit the kingdom. Hope has it that it is our birthright to win the lottery and write a classic novel. If we are American it will be a bestseller. We will make the NBA, be a rock star, become president.

And hope pities our disappointment with the world. It tells us to look forward to the time of the messiah to come, or backward to the paradise that must surely have been. The heart rebels at the truth that what is, is. (From "My Grandfather's Walking Stick, or the Pink Lie" by Lore Segal in *Social Research*)

Raising the Dead

Referencing ideas and writings from the past—encumbered by dated social customs, unfamiliar settings, archaic language, unusual storytelling techniques—can distract the reader's interest in an essay. Imaginative directors and caring literature professors often transform a scene in an older work of literature into a relevant, present-day experience or into modern vernacular to capture the spirit of the writing, then quickly bring the students back to the unique use of language in the original work.

In *Raising the Dead*, the writer must carefully study the style of a modern English vernacular. This lively and, at times, irreverent language style acts as a muse, giving the seemingly remote or inaccessible work from the past new life, restoring its power to create curiosity and interest in contemporary audiences. In addition to renovating the language, a writer must have new ideas in mind, updating or modernizing themes to be relevant or address pertinent political or social issues. This Raised work not only enlivens new issues, but also sometimes helps the reader appreciate the issues of the original work. Sometimes the updating is done to connect old purposes with new purposes, as with the "Declaration of Sentiments"; sometimes more details are added to help take the old passage in a slightly new direction, as in "The Eleven Commandments." The new version immediately recalls the weight of the past piece and borrows its importance for its own nourishment.

Your turn. Look up a famous passage in Shakespeare or the Bible or any historical or political document. Revise the document by relating the details to some aspect or issue in your own life—your family, friends, work, or school colleagues.

Sightings of Raising the Dead:

We hold these truths to be self-evident: that all men and women are created equal; that they are endowed by their creator with certain inalienable rights. . . .

The history of mankind is a history of repeated injuries and usurpations on the part of man toward woman, having in direct object the establishment of an absolute tyranny over her. To prove this, let facts be submitted to a candid world.

He has never permitted her to exercise her inalienable right to elective franchise.

He has compelled her to submit to laws, in the formation of which she had no voice. . . .

He has made her, morally, an irresponsible being, as she can commit many crimes with impunity, provided they are done in the presence of her husband. . . .

He allows her in Church, as well as State, but a subordinate position, claiming Apostolic authority for her exclusion from the ministry, and, with some exceptions, from any public participation in the affairs of the Church.

He has created a false public sentiment by giving the world a different code of morals for men and women by which moral delinquencies that exclude women from society are not only tolerated, but deemed of little account in man. (From "Declaration of Sentiments" by Elizabeth Cady Stanton and others of the National Woman Suffrage Association)

1. In argument or court or the market, do not use my name for

influence. I am a private god. I intervene when I wish, but you are not me. Do not stand in the pulpit babbling as if you are God. If you pass for me, I will erase you like an idol. . . .

7. Do not sleep with the spouse of another. There are many to sleep with, including your solicitude, which may delight you with never imagined feasts. The world has a mountain of partners. Why look for trouble? If your heart is beating with desire, remember me, your Lord, who has everyone and no one. I stand alone in the sky. (From "The Eleven Commandments" by Willis Barnstone in *Southwest Review*)

(See Hamlet, Act I, scene v)

Ghost: I don't have much time before I must make like a duck and get the flock out of here, but listen up cuz I got some serious shit to lay on you.

Hamlet: It's cool. Spill your guts.

Ghost: You're going to kick some heavy-duty ass when you comprehend, man.

Hamlet: Say what?

Ghost: I'm your blood bro and old man's ectoplasm, the leader of the sharks. I'm supposed to cruise this ditch at night; in the day I barbecue in the Big Man's basement, and I can't get upstairs until the motherfucker who did these badass crimes eats shit. What I'm about to say will make you crap your insides out.

Hamlet: Holy shit!

Ghost: Your old man was dusted, and you must splatter the sleaze's brains for my unnatural biting of the big one.

Hamlet: Waste him?

Ghost: You got it. We're talking about putting his asshole where his mouth is now.

Hamlet: Just tell me who the geek is, and it will be signed, sealed, and delivered.

Ghost: Now you're talking. Some say a snake in the orchard dusted me, but this is a crock of shit. My own bro offed me.

Hamlet: I can't take it. Our main man, Bubba?

Ghost: You got that shit right. Now he's plugging my bitch every night. I can't believe she'd hang out with a freak that'd snuff a guy just 'cause he was born first. I was the perfect stud to my main squeeze but now that a-hole has her. Oh well, Christ. I can catch a whiff of the morning air. Short but sweet, I'll lay it out for you: Like, I was crashing in the orchard one day, burned-out as usual, and my brother slides up and pours this poison shit in my ear. This stuff courses through me like Montezuma's revenge of the blood, man. I break out in blisters all over like I had a bad case of syph or something. Then he starts stabbing me as if I was Mr. Bill. This guy cuts me short before I can get off even one Hail Mary for all the bad karma I bought before. This is bunk, man. Bunk! Whatever you do to this guy, don't mess with your old lady. Her guilt trip will do her righteously anyhow. The damn firebug is pooping out so morning is almost here. Stay tuned to my vibes. Later days!

(From "Hamlet Redux" compiled by Gary Hoffman from introductory literature student assignments)

Ghost: Pity me not, nor eat mold, but hear the story I shall unfold.
Hamlet: Talk to me, talk with me, with me you will talk,
      and I will listen as we walk.
Ghost: Avenge must you when I tell who.
Hamlet: Well apples and cheese and a jellybean,
      tell me Mr. Ghost what do you mean?
Ghost: A spirit am I, but please don't be shy
      as I'm your father's spirit, and yes I can fly.
Hamlet: Oh heavens me, oh heavens my,
      I did not know that spirits could fly.
Ghost: Yes I can fly, but never mind that.
      You must avenge a murther, and take off that hat.
Hamlet: Murther or murder, which did you say?
      I have never seen murder spelled that way.

(From "Green Eggs and Hamlet" by Joe Jacob for a introductory literature assignment)

For the Wasteful

    O God, in Your benevolence look with kindness upon those who travel first class in high season, on those who spend whole afternoons in cafes, those who replay songs on jukeboxes, who engage in trivial conversations, who memorize jokes and card tricks, those who tear open their gifts and will not save the wrapping, who hate leftovers and love room service, who do not wait for sales. For all foolish virgins, for those who knowingly give their hearts to worthless charmers . . . (From "Prayers" by Mary Gordon in *The Paris Review*)

    1 Corinthians (13:1-8) If I start, like, talking like some plainly normal commoner or like an angelic-looking rock singer, but I don't have love, I'll sound like some air-headed chatterbox or horrible garage band. If I'm like, *psychic*, and I like, totally understand everything (at like, an Einstein level) and figure out all that brainy stuff that can change the Earth, and if I totally believe in my talents of messing with the Earth, but don't have love, I'm like, nothing, some random loser with a big forehead. If I give away ALL the stuff daddy bought me, even my Tiffany

bracelet, and even let go of my perfectly tanned and tone body, and like, announce it over the PA system at school that I did that, but don't have love, I won't get a kick out of having a giving heart.

Hey! Ready? Gimme an L-O-V-E, love! They're patient, it's patient, oh yes, it's patient! When I say "love," you say, "It's kind": Love! It's kind! Love! It's kind! Yay!

Love isn't like some jealous bitch; it doesn't brag like a totally cute MVP jock; it's not some stuck-up know-it-all with a library card, and it's not cranky like some girl on a no-carb diet. It's not grouchy like my mom who keeps muttering she regrets giving birth and this and that. But love does get all high off of the truth. It believes in, like, *everything*, has hope in all things, you know, like a cheerleader who still looks happy even when the team is down by fifty points and everyone is booing us. Love is here forever and ever and ever! (From "Paul as an Air-Headed Cheerleader: 1 Corinthians 13:1-8" by Rosy Torres for The Bible as Literature class)

O Lord our Father, our young patriots, idols of our hearts, go forth to battle—be Thou near them! With them—in spirit—we also go forth from the sweet pace of our beloved firesides to smite the foe. O Lord our God, help us to tear their soldiers to bloody shreds with our shells; help us to cover their smiling fields with the pale forms of their patriot dead; help us to drown the thunder of the guns with the shrieks of their wounded, writhing in pain; help us to lay waste their humble homes with a hurricane of ire; help us to wring the hearts of their unoffending widows with unavailing grief; help us to turn them out roofless with their little children to wander unfriended the wastes of their desolated land in rags and hunger and thirst, sports of the sun flames of summer and the icy winds of winter, broken in spirit, worn with travail, imploring Thee for the refuge of the grave and denied it—for our sakes who adore Thee, Lord, blast their hopes, blight their lives, protract their bitter pilgrimage, make heavy their steps, water their way with their tears, stain the white snow with the blood of their wounded feet! We ask it, in the spirit of love, of Him Who is the Source of Love, and Who is the ever-faithful refuge and friend of all that are sore beset and seek His aid with humble and contrite hearts. Amen.

(From "The War Prayer" by Mark Twain)

TRANSITIONING:
Ways to Connect

Twist Ties
Captions
Double Exposures
Thirteen Ways

Any of the previous strategies from the *Form* unit can be expanded over several paragraphs into a larger essay. The *Form* strategies can also be combined and connected in different ways. For instance, in her essay "On Waiting," Edna O'Brien merges many different strategies—*Stress Testing, Netting,* and *Anecdoting*—to explore and define the concept of waiting. In shifting from one strategy to the next, O'Brien arranges the disparate sections with *Transitions* to build a cohesive essay, and it's these *Transitions* that provide the essay with its overall structure or organizational pattern. The purpose and content of an essay determine what kinds of *Transitions* a writer will select for welding purposes: Some essays require seamless connectors (*Twist Ties*); others demand suspense-creating or time-marking shifts (*Captions*); and still others insist on abrupt or jarring transitions (*Double Exposures* and *Thirteen Ways*).

Twist Ties

A seamless and sophisticated way to connect different strategies for a structural flow in an essay is with *Twist Ties*. To *Twist Tie*, the writer takes a key word or concept in the last line of a paragraph and Ties the word to a *synonym, antonym* (see *Thesauruscoping*), *metaphor* (see the *Fusion* chapter), or a theme in the first line in the following paragraph.

A key word is defined as any noun (person, place, or thing), verb (an action word), or an adjective or adverb (words that describe). These parts of speech tend to communicate.

Suppose the last line of a paragraph reads: "I began to have a sharp vision."

Following are a few possibilities for the opening of the next paragraph:

A synonym for "vision": *Clarity* was not something I expected.
An antonym for "vision": *Obscurity* dominated on the next day.
A metaphor that extends "sharp": My vision *needled* me to . . .
A theme that extends "vision": Visions were always important to aboriginal groups.
A theme that reverses "vision": Sometimes *confusion* trumps.

Twist Ties can connect any of the different strategies listed in the *Form* unit: By isolating a significant word or theme and then reiterating it with a closely related noun or verb in the next sentence, *Twist Ties* provide a conceptual connection, carrying vital ideas from one strategy to the next—a seamless solder imparting tight flow in the structure of an essay. *Twist Ties* operate on the same premise as *juxtaposing* (see *Netting* in the *Punching Up* chapter), connecting ideas between two paragraphs by situating words with similar connotations or analogous terms in close proximity to one another.

In more subtle uses of *Twist Ties*, the *Transition* does not always happen in the first and last sentence of *juxtaposed* paragraphs but can be embedded a few sentences away from this junction point. For instance, note that the word "evolution" in the Stephen

J. Gould example below, mentioned in the first part of the first paragraph, stays dormant at the end of that first section and is not explored again until at the beginning of the last paragraph. The reemergence of the *Twist Tie* establishes a link between two ordinarily unrelated themes or topics—the evolution of the game of baseball and Darwin's theory of evolution.

Your turn. Read the sample sets below and identify the key word or concept that *Ties* together the two paragraphs. Then decide whether the *Twist Tie* is a synonym, antonym, metaphor, or thematic transition. Lastly, using a key word or concept in the last lines of each of the last sentences, create *Twist Tie* transitions connecting your newly created topic sentence.

Weaves of Twist Ties:

Twist Tie of Sliced Pie and Netting on a theme:
Some of these [abandoned] houses had been inhabited as homes fairly recently—they had not yet reverted to the wild. Others, abandoned during the Depression, had long since begun to rot and collapse, engulfed by vegetation (trumpet vine, wisteria, rose of Sharon, willow) that elsewhere, on our property for instance, was kept neatly trimmed. I was drawn to both kinds of houses, though the more recently inhabited were more forbidding and therefore more inviting.

   To push open a door into such silence: the absolute emptiness of a house whose occupants have departed. Often, the crack of broken glass underfoot. A startling buzzing of flies, hornets. The slithering, ticklish sensation of a garter snake crawling across floorboards. (From "They All Just Went Away" by Joyce Carol Oates in *The New Yorker*)

Twist Tie of two contexts of a word:
Evolution is continual change. . . . In particular, Cartwright introduced two key innovations that shaped the disparate forms of town ball into a semblance of modern baseball. . . . [He] introduced foul lines, again in the modern sense, as the batter stood at home plate and had to hit the ball within lines defined from home through first and third bases. . . . The New York Game may be the highlight of a continuum, but it provides no origin myth for baseball. . . . Balls had to be caught on the fly in Boston, and pitchers threw overhand, not underhand as in the New York Game (and in professional baseball until the 1880s).

Scientists often lament that so few people understand Darwin and the principles of biological evolution. But the problem goes deeper. Too few people are comfortable with evolutionary modes of explanation in any form. . . . [One] reason must reside in our social and psychic attraction to creation myths in preference to evolutionary stories—for creation myths, as noted before, identify heroes and sacred places, while evolutionary stories provide no palpable, particular thing as a symbol for reverence, worship, or patriotism. Still, we must remember—and an intellectual's most persistent and nagging responsibility lies in making this simple point over and over again, however noxious and bothersome we render ourselves thereby—that truth and desire, fact and comfort, have no necessary, or even preferred, correlation (so rejoice when they do coincide). (From "The Creation Myths of Cooperstown" by Stephen Jay Gould in *Natural History*)

Twist Tie of the past and present on a theme:
I was fifteen when I started my romance with Indians, and I only knew that I was in love with life outside the constricting white mainstream, and with all the energy that vibrates on the outer reaches of cultural stability. My heart and what would later become my politics were definitely in the right place, and I have never regretted where I went or what I came to know. But for twenty years that knowledge spoiled me for another kind of knowing.

Whatever my romantic notions were about the ideal forms of American Indian wisdom—closeness to the land, respect for other living creatures, a sense of harmony with natural cycles, a way of walking lightly in the world, a manner of living that could make the ordinary and profane into the sacred—I learned that on the reservation I was inhabiting a world that was contrary to all these values. (From "Wounded Chevy at Wounded Knee" by Diana Hume George in *The Missouri Review*)

Twist Tie of a Netting to a Stress Test to an Anecdoting on a theme:
Jealous lovers, black garters with silk stockings, crotchless panties, edible underwear, strawberries and champagne, warm almond oil, late-night phone calls, honey dust, dinner after 10 PM, hotel suites, eating a pint of Godiva ice cream alone, caviar, decadence.

Whether decadent or not, the ideas of lust differ for the sexes. Women tend to romanticize lust with love, rather than sex: the rich color of a rose bright in bloom, with thick sweet fleshy petals; the musky rich scent of night jasmine, a remembrance of a grandfather's story about a Turkish whorehouse with velvet pillows and silk sheets; the crystal cut sparkle of a diamond, rainbow-ing hopes and tragedies; the insatiable appetite for shoes—closed toe or open, strappy or slutty. Women fantasize lust; the smallest details are what they will remember. What men remember is flesh: they lust after lips, tits, and ass; Playboy, strip club; and fantasize about what a first date will look like naked, wonder if she wears a bra and what size. They wonder about the feminine pink parts, sexual gratification first.

But first things first. Lust can bring pleasure and pain. I recall first meeting him. I immediately drew to attention, despite the horror of being in my boyfriend's pajamas in his house. I hustled back to my boyfriend's bedroom, interrogating him for details of this new stranger who was now beyond the door. . . . (From "Lust: A Definition" by Aaerielle Nisson for a freshman composition)

Twist Tie with a synonym:
Love is powerfully helpful when the roof falls in—loving other people with a high and hopeful heart and as a kind of prayer. . . . Love is an elixir, changing the life of the lover like no other. And many of us have experienced this—temporary lightening of our leery, prickly disapproval of much of the rest of the world when at a wedding or a funeral of shared emotion, or when we have fallen in love.

Yet the zest for life of those unusual men and women who make a great zealous success of living is due more often in good part to the craftiness and pertinacity with which they manage to overlook the misery of others. You can watch them watch life beat the stuffing out of the faces of their friends and acquaintances, yet they . . . [accept] loss and age and change and disappointment without suffering punctures in their stomach lining. (From "Heaven and Nature" by Edward Hoagland in *Harper's Magazine*)

Twist Tie of contrasting views of a theme:
In my calendar, that year of drought will always be one of the best years of my childhood, because it was then, in a dusty clearing by a trickling mountain spring, I got my first glimpses of the wonders, the mysteries, and the promises hidden beneath the folds of a woman's dress. Fish and oranges from heaven . . . you can get over that.
But, in another way, the year of the drought was also one of the

worst of my life, because that was the year that Abu Raja, the retired cook who used to entertain us kids by cracking walnuts on his forehead, decided it was time Magdaluna got its own telephone. (From "The Telephone" by Anwar F. Accawi in *The Sun*)

Twist Tie of Stress Tests on a theme:
ATLANTA, GA, Nov. 9—God, creator of the universe, principal deity of the world's Jews, ultimate reality of Christians, and most eminent of all divinities, died late yesterday during major surgery undertaken to correct a massive diminishing influence. . . . [Here the piece includes a long list of surgeons present, the names all being well-known academic theologians, and representatives from different faiths.]

Unable to be in Atlanta owing to the pressure of business at the second Vatican Council, now in session, the Pope, in Rome, said, in part: "We are deeply distressed for we have suffered an incalculable loss. The contributions of God to the Church cannot be measured, and it is difficult to imagine how we shall proceed without Him.". . . [The piece includes reactions from politicians including a plea that "this is not a time for partisan politics."]

(In New York, meanwhile, the stock market dropped sharply in early trading. . . . The market rallied in late trading, after reports were received that Jesus—see "Man in the News"—plans to assume a larger role in the management of the universe.) [After reactions from the world's great and from the man in the street, finally there are] unconfirmed reports that Jesus of Nazareth, 33, a carpenter and reputed son of God, who survives, will assume the authority, if not the title, for the deceased deity. Jesus, sometimes called the Christ, was himself a victim of death. . . . The case is complicated by the fact that Jesus, although he died, returned to life, and so may not have died at all [and] . . . will occupy the power vacuum created by the sudden passing of God. (From "God is Dead in Georgia," excerpts from the "Diaries of the Late God" by Anthony Towne in *motive* magazine)

Twist Tie with a word in different contexts:
That the idea of something and its reality are often two completely different things is something no one ever remembers; and so when they meet and find that they are not compatible, the weaker of the two, idea or reality, dies. That idea Christopher Columbus had was more powerful than the reality he met, and so the reality he met contin died.

And so finally, when I was a grown-up woman, the mother of two children, the wife of someone, a person who resides in a powerful country that takes up more than its fair share of a continent . . . I saw England, the real England, not a picture, not a painting, not through a story in a book, but England, for the first time. In me, the space between the idea of it and its reality had become filled with hatred . . . so I could only indulge in not-favorable opinions.

There were monuments everywhere; they commemorated victories, battles fought between them and the people who lived across the sea from them, all vile people, fought over which of them would have dominion over the people who looked like me. The monuments were useless to them now. People sat on them and ate their lunch. They were like markers on an old useless trail, like a piece of old string tied to a finger to jog the memory . . . . (From "On Seeing England for the First Time" by Jamaica Kincaid in *Transition*)

Twist Tie of Cliché Busting with Anecdoting:
Hope is the lie that we tell others, a fib that separates us from reality and from the feelings that go along with reality and ourselves—despair, sadness, loss, anger or pain. Hope, ironically, removes us from the despair of real life and takes us to the desperation of hoping for the impossible, improbably. A vicious cycle created by us to keep us from dealing in the here and now where we have some control, some power and puts us into the future and a constant state of powerlessness. There is no present in hope.

I have or had (I'm not sure which exactly) a friend. For over six years we did everything together, including growing up. Ten years ago this month she moved from California to Maryland. I have not heard from her. She was my best friend. I still "hope" that someday she will call and be my best friend again. My expectation is unreasonable and if I were willing to admit that to the universe, and myself, I would have to grieve the loss of my dear friend. I would have to let her go out of my life and free all that space in my heart and my head for other people to be my new best friends. So instead of just facing the truth—that my friend is gone from my life forever—experiencing the feelings of hurt and anger brought on by my loss, and getting on with the business of living, I drag out the pain so that, if allowed, it could go on forever. A scab that never heals. (From "Hope is a Many-Splendored Thing" by Debbie Wicken for freshman composition)

Captions

Good storytelling depends on suspense, the storyteller constantly positioning the audience in a mental state of anticipation and uncertainty, momentarily resolving anxiety with mini-climaxes, and then restarting with new issues. This dynamic is life's seismic pattern: Just as we resolve one problem, we are confronted by our next challenge. Sometimes essayists take advantage of this crest-and-valley rhythm to transition from one part of an essay to another, each part bringing material to a mini-climax, forcing the reader to believe no more on the subject could be told, only to open the next section of the essay with a headline or *Caption*. These *Captions* suggest there is not only more, but also that the details are either intensifying, as denoted by *strip tease Transtions*, or shifting to a new time and location, marked with *flashback Transitions*.

Strip Tease. The secret power of an essay with *strip tease Transitions* rests in the delivery of a series of credible mini-resolutions, each section's conclusion seeming like the dramatic finale for the entire essay. These mini-conclusions tease the reader, creating a gasp of disbelief when the writer reveals the next *Captioning*, a *Transition* that either denotes an *escalation* or *intensification*. Typical *strip tease Captioning* might resemble the following *Transition Captions*:

"The situation became even more horrible."

"Revelation number three."

"But an even greater irony followed."

"The idea was handled with even superior subtle wit."

"Shock number five."

Each new *Captioning* that reveals an unexpected section allows the reader to savor each one—the same way one relishes the subplots in a novel or film—each new *Captioning* permitting the writer to leapfrog over minutia towards the next intriguing section of the essay.

All researched material is ripe for *strip tease Captioning*: an historical occasion, the rise towards fame, the invention and marketing of a product, a comparison of three comedies with each having a more foolish protagonist than the last, five psychological studies that become increasingly convincing in developing a hypothesis. Also, each new *Captioning* can bond different strategies from the *Form* section to create a new intensity: For instance, a writer can start with *Anecdoting*, shift to a surprising *Thesauruscoping*, and finish with a shocking *Devil's Advice*, or start with *Splitting the Second*, surprise with *Cliché Busting*, and finish with an unexpected *Trojan Horse*.

Flashback. Instead of organizing an essay with a *strip tease Transition*, a writer can also hopscotch through material with time or place markers, or *flashback Transtions:*

"Let us jump ahead now to fifty-one years ago this past November."

"Senior Year at La Mirada High School."

"The scene shifts twenty minutes later to Los Angeles."

"Now it is spring."

"Two years after, the Peace Accord is signed"

"The Coliseum in Rome, 300 A.D."

In outlining events to be joined with *time Transitions*, sometimes a writer drafts the conclusion of the essay first: a personal revelation about marriage, the downfall of a general, the outcome of an important trial, the discovery of a new vaccine. After the conclusion, the essay is written backwards so that, next, the writer *flashbacks* to the incident that led to that conclusion, composing what will be the second-to-last section in the essay. Then, the writer moves further back to the most crucial incident that set up the second-to-last incident. The writer keeps working back in time, recovering key episodes that lead to the one just composed. The rough draft is developed by flashing back through a chronology of events; however, the final essay will present the episodes in chronological order, flashing forward using the *time Transitions* to open each section. Using the present tense throughout the essay (see *Pulsing the Tense* in *Time Warping*) will help accentuate the *time Transitions*, making the flashing forward of events more intense. *Time Transitions* can be used with any of the strategies in the *Form* unit or *Critical Analysis* sections of *Peel*.

Your turn. Describe what aspects of the topics below are being escalated by either *flashback* or *strip tease* transitions. Write down several incidents that, with further research, would be subjects for strong *strip tease* or *flashback* essays.

Captures of Captions:

Years later, after he shot a grandmother in the face, prosecutors say, he cooked himself noodles in her kitchen and poured himself a glass of milk while she died. He would say later that he made just two mistakes: not getting out of the house sooner, and not trying to shoot his way past the cops once he was caught.

That's half the story.

Stephen Wayne Anderson, 48, scheduled to die by lethal injection Tuesday morning at San Quentin State Prison, also has an IQ of 136. Beaten as a boy, disowned at 17 and forced to live outdoors and alone in the hills of New Mexico, he has become an accomplished poet, writing behind bars about the smell of honeysuckle and the wind ticking the trees in the fall. (From "Conflicting Portraits of Killer Emerge" by Scott Gold in *The Los Angeles Times*)

I arrived at the Prehistoric Museum of Aarhus, in mid-Denmark, to find a dead body on the floor of my office. On an iron sheet stood a large block of peat, and at one end of it the head and a right arm of a man protruded, while one leg and foot stuck out from the other end. His skin was dark brown, almost chocolate colored, and his hair was a brownish red. . . . At this point we turned for help to the professor of forensic medicine. . . . "This most unusually well-preserved body has . . . undergone a process of conservation which appears to resemble most closely a tanning. . . . On the front of the throat was found a large wound stretching from ear to ear. . . ."

So the man from Grauballe had had his throat cut, and we had a murder mystery on our hands. [Other transitions in this essay include the following: "The investigation went on," "But they could tell more," "Tollund Man was found to be naked, . . . " "It is clear, I think, that we have a case of mass murder," "These are not ordinary burials," "We are entering a dark region."] (From "The Body in the Bog" by Geoffrey Bibby in *Horizon*)

Below us, on a floodlit tennis court, an international tennis tournament was in progress. Pretty Indian girls in T-shirts and fashionably patched jeans dotted the wooden terraces erected for the occasion. The warm night was scented with a smell of dust. Lit-up skyscrapers loomed like mountain ranges. The match ended, the victorious Indian player shaking hands with his American opponent. Without warning, the spell was broken.

Out of nowhere, as if born of the musty night itself, a small army of sweepers invaded the court, meager, stick-limbed men wielding short, soft brooms. Crouched on their haunches, their gaze anchored to the ground, they began brushing the playing surface. The middle-class lady did not look at this dwarfish, less-than-human crew. They were not supposed to be looked at. . . . [Other transitions in this essay include the following: "On that first day, then it seemed a city of terror, of despair. But I was wrong," "Much of the life of the city is invisible," "Bombay deceives at every level," "The statistics numb—as they always do in India. Every night one and a half million people sleep out on the city's streets," "The migrants, despite everything, keep coming," "The variety, the color, of Bombay street life disguise its terrors."] (From "The City by the Sea" by Shiva Naipaul in *Beyond the Dragon's Mouth*)

PARIS
The French study group . . . in early 1982, hadn't set out to discover the cause of the mysterious and still-unchristened epidemic. At first, they simply wanted to track the new diseases as they made their splashy entrances in various hospitals. Rozenbaum already had approached Parisian gay doctors but found that they simply did not believe that the new maladies were anything but some new plot to drive them underground.

What they had to offer, they figured, was a perspective unencumbered by America's preoccupation with divining who was homosexual and who wasn't. American scientists thought it odd to view the new epidemic as an African disease, but the French thought it unusual to view it as a homosexual disease. This was a disease that simply struck people, and it had to come from somewhere. . . .

January 12
2 FIFTH AVENUE, NEW YORK CITY
In the meeting at Larry Kramer's apartment, everybody agreed that Paul Popham would be the ideal president of the new organization, Gay Men's Health Crisis, which was geared to raising money for gay cancer research. Some of the more salient reasons were left unspoken. Paul personified the successful Fire Island A-list gays who had never become involved in Manhattan's scruffy gay political scene. . . .

March 2, 1985
IRWIN MEMORIAL BLOOD BANK,
SAN FRANCISCO
The future of the AIDS epidemic arrived in a black Chevrolet as night fell in San Francisco. Abbott Laboratories had airfreighted

. . . the first AIDS antibody tests to be publicly released any-where in the United States. . . . (From *And the Band Played On: Politics, People, and the Aids Epidemic* by Randy Shilts)

John Donne's poem "The Ecstasy" begins with an overtly erotic tone which becomes evident after deciphering Donne's euphemistic metaphors for parts of the body such as "a pregnant bank" referring to a stomach and "the violet's reclining head" referring to a man's not-aroused "unit." Donne's choice of the violet for his sexual metaphor is significant because in Renaissance times the violet symbolized faithful love and so by violet-ing sex he directly links it with fidelity. From his "violet" being on her stomach we can ascertain that the two lovers are in an extremely amorous position. To express his contentment in their current bodily position or perhaps about the overall state of the relationship, Donne states, "Sat we two, one another's best." Further embellishing on this intimate scene, Donne informs us that he and his lover's "hands were firmly cemented," and that their "eye-beams twisted . . . upon one double thread," these two details serving to transform the feeling of the poem from one of relaxed cuddling to sweaty-palmed, rapt-gazing intensity.

Things intensify even more in the next verse. Transposing the setting from the bedroom onto a metaphysical battlefield, Donne poetically illustrates and dramatizes the conflict and compromise that goes on in relationships by likening his soul and that of his lady to "two equal armies." [Other transitions in this essay include the following: "Donne feels he can take their love still higher yet," "As if his claim that their love was quite beyond the physical were not clear enough already," "Abruptly, Donne drags his lover and the reader back down to the lustful present," "Donne has still more celestial excuses to pull from his bag."] (From "The Ecstasy" by Jenessa Kenway for a Critical Thinking About Literature assignment)

Large-scale uranium mining in the United States started in the '40s. . . . Many of the miners who were doing this work inhaled the radon gas, which attaches itself to tiny dust particles and lodges in the terminal air passages in the lungs.

Now what had happened? Well, here are the cells in the lung and here is the radon, which has been continuously emitting its radioactive alpha particles . . . and what happened . . . was that one of the alpha particles in the gas by chance hit the regulatory genes in one of the cells and damaged it. And the cell sat very quietly for many years until one day, instead of dividing to produce daughter cells as it should, it went berserk and produced millions and trillions of daughter cells—a clone of abnormal cells—and that is cancer. . . .

The next step in the nuclear cycle is enrichment. It takes a full ton of uranium ore to make four pounds of pure uranium, and about 99 percent of this pure uranium is unfissionable—not usable for making energy. [This section explains all the dangers of this process and the vulnerability of nuclear plant meltdown that could easily result in the illnesses and deaths of 10,000 to 100,000 people.]

That would happen in a relatively short time, but there are long-term effects too. . . . [This section explains how hundreds of thousands of people would become sterile, "develop hypothy-roidism, lose their appetites and at the same time become fat," and how thousands of babies would be born as "pinheads" or "cretins," with ablated thyroids and neurological damage.]

Now let's talk about plutonium. . . . If you took just ten pounds of plutonium and put a speck of it in every human lung, that would be enough to kill every single person on earth. Ten pounds! And each nuclear reactor makes 500 pounds of it every year. (From "What You Must Know about Radiation" by Helen Caldicott in *Redbook*)

It started by mistake in a New Haven laboratory, and turned into a bonanza by sheer chance on New York's Fifth Avenue. There has never been a more accidental toy.

Maybe it had to be. Who could have sat down and deliberately designed a piece of pink goo that stretches like taffy, shatters when struck sharply with a hammer, picks up newsprint and photos in color, molds like clay, flows like molasses, and—when rolled in a ball—bounces like mad? . . . The prodigy is Silly Putty. . . . One day, a Scottish engineer named James Wright dropped some boric acid into a test tube containing silicone oil. When he examined the resultant compound, he found, to his amazement, that it bounced when thrown on the floor.

Accident number one: Silly Putty is born.

Meanwhile, Peter Hodgson . . . was exploring the infant marketing profession. [The essay explains Hodgson's learning marketing techniques but then losing his job in New Haven, and having his marriage dissolve.]

Accident number two: A New Haven toyshop hires Hodgson to publish its catalog. [The essay now explains how toys before WWII were sold in department stores and not toy stores, the rise of toy stores for baby boomers, the beginning of adults playing with the accidental goo at General Electric, the catalog makers' rejection of the goo, Hodgson's decision to sell it on the shelf, its outselling all other shelf toys except crayons.]

Accident number three: Economic necessity forces Hodgson to encase his product in plastic "eggs," which would be cheap and easy to ship in inexpensive cartons. . . . [Other accidents include a writer from the *New Yorker* getting involved with the goo and writing about it, the lack of chemical materials for the Korean War, starting all over on marketing, the toy having to survive quality controls for kids so it would not stick to hair, renewed success.] (From "The Toy with One Moving Part" by Marvin Kaye in *The Story of Monopoly, Silly Putty, Bingo, Twister, Frisbee, Scrabble,* Etcetera)

Body-marring event number one. My love of skateboarding begins with the ever-present trade winds and whizzing-on-wind-currents skating. . . . The infrequently used fresh-tar-smooth road was free of rocks, but edged by sand, sided by the vast, off-limits airport runway; flanking the other side were fierce ocean trades and roaring reef waves. The perfect setup. Until the smash-up. . . .

Body-marring event number two. One late afternoon, Mark Emerald, my down-the-street neighbor, and I were having a fine time skating, Mark ripping air in the steep and deep bowls #1 and #2, while I was unsatisfactorily ripping in wide, curvy, bowl #4. Watching Mark really spurred me, my body blasting down the lean run of hardened, head-high waves, with Mark speeding towards the wall of the bowl, gliding up it effortlessly and then spitting out four feet into the air. Holding onto his board he would turn and slip right back into the bowl. With this image in my head, I decided to rip bowl #3 like it had never been ripped before, completing a scarring top slide. My body, heated and craving speed, angled for the bowl: It was air or nothing. Air I got. [The essay describes other marring events, including one that results in a skull fracture and finally fate sending a message when his board is stolen.] (From "Strip Tease" by Steve Kessler for a freshman composition)

Up until January 1978, I was never involved in politics in any way. My husband was working for the Izalco Sugar Company and I was taking care of our four children. . . . [The piece explains how the workers go on strike, her husband is active in this, and how she begins work with CoMadres, a human rights group that called press conferences when people disappeared.]

In May 1980, I moved with my husband and children to Sonsonate. My husband had gotten a job there building houses. Barely a month later he was assassinated. . . .

From June 1980 until August 1982, I lived with my children in San Salvador. I continued to be very active in CoMadres, which was under intense pressure from right-wing death squads and security forces. In 1980 the CoMadres office—which we shared with the governmental Human Rights Commission—was bombed twice. Several unidentified decapitated bodies were left in the front of the office.

In 1982 Archbishop Rivera y Damas recognized the work that we at CoMadres were doing and he gave us office space in the archdiocese. [The piece describes continuing police surveillance of her, fleeing for her life to Mexico, recognition in 1984 from the Robert F. Kennedy Foundation for human rights, her return to El Salvador and request for visas to the U.S. that were denied, international travel hoping the recognition for human rights would protect her, protection from European parliamentarians who ended up assassinated in El Salvador in 1986 on return.]

On May 6, 1986, I was grabbed suddenly by a man at a bus top. I was pushed into a white car. . . . I was held for three days. During this time I was beaten and brutally raped by the three men, all while blindfolded. I was seven months pregnant. They gave me no food and only a little water. Later they started carving my belly with a sharp object. Then they questioned me more about CoMadres. . . . [After being dropped off she is arrested again and tortured for four days, held as a terrorist, never tried, released in a public ceremony by President Duarte where she points out a torturer, invited to the U.S. as a speaker, and now requests political asylum.] (From an affidavit by Maria Teresa Tula viuda de Canales. According to *Harper's Magazine* her request was denied, the Immigration and Naturalization Service claiming she was a "prominent guerrilla activist.")

Double Exposures

Looking at old family photos or videotapes gives us an eerie feeling because we are reminded of the dual nature of reality. First, there is the reality of the visual image: Parents holding their infant at a baptism; Grandpa blowing out candles on the cake for his eightieth birthday; newlyweds embracing in front of the Coliseum in Rome. Then, there is the reality off camera: embarrassed parents whose infant urine-soaked the priest; the grandfather not recognizing anyone at his birthday party due to Alzheimer's disease; the frustrated couple's inability to conceive a child on their honeymoon. The world is saturated by *Double Exposures*: the personal layered on the historical, the legal woven into the moral, the professional camouflaging the sexual, the scientific glazing the artistic, or the philosophical superimposed on the practical.

To capture any double-pronged reality, a writer begins by composing two essays (maybe one longer than the other) on a single subject, but each one addressing a different aspect of the topic and each written in a distinct style appropriate to that particular reality. By having two different points of view (see the *Opt* chapter) those stylistic differences will be further enhanced. In presenting divergent but complementary realities on a single topic in one essay, a writer braids together the two versions using the *Double Exposure Transitions*.

Like *Twist Ties*, *Double Exposure Transitions* rely on the *juxtaposition* of related concepts. However, instead of tightly connecting sections by reiterating key words in the concluding and topic sentences between two paragraphs, a *Double Exposure* positions parallel paragraphs next to one another, omitting taut transitions. In their place, the writer uses visual format clues: a switch between italics and non-italics or a change in font size for each *Exposure*—any technique that announces a shift. Jumping back and forth between *Exposures* can be confusing (notice the hectic jumps skillfully managed by Joy Williams below), so a writer usually limits the number of shifts to three per 8x11-inch manuscript page. *Double Exposures* are an effective way of combining any of the strategies in the *Form* unit or argumentative claims in the *Critical Analysis* sections of *Peel*. For instance, a writer can use *Anecdoting* for one *Exposure* with *Netting* for the other, or braid *Mocking* into an academic *Inductive Analysis* for the other strand. The combinations are endless.

Your turn. With each passage below, articulate the emotional tone and intellectual position of each *Exposure*. Write a second *Exposure* for a piece you have written in the past.

Splices of Double Exposures

Since her creation by a Los Angeles couple who originally set up shop in their garage, over 135 million Barbies . . . have been sold. The first doll with a "fully mature figure" (i.e. breasts, an adult-proportioned head, and permanently arched feet), Barbie's enormous success catapulted her maker, Mattel, Inc., to the top of the fiercely competitive toy industry. . . . In the process, she has revolutionized the definition of play and taught an entire generation of girls how to be women. . . .

I resented that Barbie always looked just right, no matter what I did to her, and I was always a mess. And it was so irritating to look at those blank bumps that were her breasts. There was nothing to identify with. First I drew in nipples. Then I bashed them on my night side table. Paula, 23, secretary. . . .

Barbie also provided a certain outlet for her owner's sexual curiosity. Many doll owners encouraged sex or unnatural acts between Ken and Barbie despite the lack of genitalia or technical expertise that meant that intercourse was still a matter of imagination.

I wasn't sure who was on top and who was on bottom, so instead Ken and Barbie had sex flying through the air. Once I used Ken to masturbate, but then I felt guilty. I was afraid he'd remember. Delores, 29, artist. (From "Boobs in Toyland" by Gwenda Blair in *The Village Voice*)

We have a home movie of this party. Several times my mother and I have watched it together, and I have asked questions about the silent revelers coming in and out of focus. It is grainy and of short duration, but it's a great visual aid to my memory of life at that time. And it is in color—the only complete scene in color I can recall from those years.

We lived in Puerto Rico until my brother was born in 1954. Soon after, because of economic pressures on our growing family, my father joined the United States Navy. . . . It seems that Father had learned some painful lessons about prejudice while searching for an apartment in Paterson. Not until years later did I hear how much resistance he had encountered with landlords who were panicking at the influx of Latinos into a neighborhood that had been Jewish for a couple of generations. . . . Not many years later that area too would be mainly Puerto Rican. It was as if the heart of the city map were being gradually colored brown—*café con leche* brown. Our color.

The movie opens with a sweep of the living room. It is "typical" immigrant Puerto Rican décor for the time: the sofa and chairs are square and hard-looking, upholstered in bright colors (blue and yellow in this instance), and covered with the transparent plastic that furniture salesman then were so adept at convincing women to buy. . . . When I ask my mother why most of the women are in red that night, she has shrugged, "I don't remember. Just a coincidence." She doesn' have my obsession for assigning symbolism to everything.

The three women in red sitting on the couch are my mother, my eighteen-year-old cousin, and her brother's girlfriend. The novia *is just up from the Island, which is apparent in her body language. She sits up formally, her dress pulled over her knees.* . . . (From "Silent Dancing" by Judith Ortiz Cofer in the *Georgia Review*)

Death and suffering are a big part of hunting. A big part. Not that you'd ever know it by hearing hunters talk. They tend to downplay the killing part. To kill is to put to death, extinguish, nullify, cancel, destroy. But from the hunter's point of view, it's just a tiny part of the experience. *The kill is the least important part of the hunt*, they often say, or, *Killing involves only a split second of the innumerable hours we spend surrounded by and observing nature.* . . . For the animal, of course, the killing part is of considerable more importance. . . . Hunters kill for play, for entertainment. They kill for the thrill of it, to make an animal "theirs.". . . Alive, the beast belongs only to itself. This is unacceptable to the hunter. *He's yours.* . . . *He's mine.* . . . *I decided to.* . . . *I decided not to.* . . . *I debated shooting it, then I decided to let it live.* . . . It's virtually impossible to miss a moose, a conspicuous and placid animal of steady habits. . . . *I took a deep breath and pulled the trigger. The bull dropped. I looked at my watch: 8:22. The big guy was early. . . .* They use sex lures . . . . *The big buck raised its nose to the air, curled back its lips, and tested the scent of the doe's urine. I held my breath, fought back the shivers, and jerked off a shot.* (From "The Killing Game" by Joy Williams in *Esquire*)

Over in a corner of the shop is the apartment he carved out of the vast cavern of the old factory, and sketched on his door is an arrow pointing down to the floor and a message to slide the mail under. It has the look of something a twelve-year-old would do. And enjoy doing. . . . I'm in the past, a place Paul picked to find the future. There is a feeling of grime everywhere, and oil-based grime that has come off machines as they inhaled and exhaled in the clangor of their work. I stand over a worktable and open a cigar box of crayons and carefully pluck two for myself, a blue and a red. . . . I come back to the factory room and see a piece of black doormat that Paul had nailed to the wall. It says quietly, GET HOME.

I think, well, shit, so this is where he hung himself.

King Solomon's palace was probably one warm home. He lived with seven hundred wives and three hundred girlfriends and somehow everybody tore through ten oxen a day, plus chunks of gazelles and hartebeests. The Bible said the wise old kin had twelve thousand horsemen charging around the countryside scaring up chow for the meals back home.

Money does not replace the lust for food. (From "The Bone Garden of Desire" by Charles Bowden in *Esquire*)

Sanseviaeria trifasciata "Lauarentii," mother-in-law's tongue or snake plant, is a member of the bowstring hemp plants from tropical Africa. Their rosettes of leaves, usually dark green and fleshy, differ in size an shape, often variegated, and die after flowering like the *Agave.* . . . The family grows well in sun or shade if sparingly watered. They are also good in mesh hanging baskets, where their underground stems push through and form a cascade of rosettes.

Three years ago, our male neighbor gave us a nice-looking plant, which is commonly known as "tiger tongue." Its leaves had strange light yellow border stripes running up to form tapered triangular, zigzagging bolts of deep green—a Frankenstein production. The plant was certainly healthy: the pastel blue plastic container bulged. I was joyous about this gift. Soon I remembered better. The neighbor had an ugly black mole with one long hair sticking out of his face, a common symbol in Vietnamese culture for an unusual infatuation of sex and girls—lasciviousness—that was true as he often spied on me when I, forgetting my keys, had to climb in the window of my bedroom. His nutty daughter, my former friend, who was schizophrenic, had glued some bird stickers and yin-yang symbols on three leaves to keep the plant in safe company. For all these reasons, I resented the tiger's tongue.
(From "Plants" by My Tong for a freshman composition)

With greater distance from Ground Zero [of an imaginary atomic bomb blast in Chicago], the effects diminished. About ten miles from the Loop, in the area around the Brookfield Zoo, the fireball was merely brighter than a thousand suns. Glass did not melt, but shattered window fragments flew through the air at about 135 miles per hour. All the trees were burning even before the shock wave uprooted most of them.

The enormous temperatures associated with all nuclear weapons, regardless of yield, result from fission—the process in which certain atomic nuclei become unstable and disintegrate. . . . As the nuclei break up and form new atoms, they yield neutrons and immense amounts of energy. The atoms created by fission are so radioactive that if one could collect two ounces of them one minute after their creation, they would match the activity of 30,000 tons of radium. . . .

In the pleasant western suburb of Hinsdale, some sixteen miles from the Loop, . . . paint evaporated off house exteriors. Children on bicycles screamed as the flash of the fireball blinded them. An instant later, their skin was charred. . . . At Argonne [laboratories instrumental in developing the bomb and twenty-one miles from Ground Zero] researchers who happened to be looking out a window on that Friday morning . . . towards the Sears Tower . . . were blinded. . . . Their clothing ignited on their bodies. . . .

The density and activity of the particles is such that a belt four to five miles wide quickly develops radiation levels of more than 3,000 roentgens per hour. . . . In a particularly strategic concentrated metropolitan area subject to direct strike . . . virtually the entire population cold be expected to perish. (From "The Day the Bomb Went Off" by Erwin Knoll and Theodore Postol in *The Progressive*)

Teen magazines today are shameless. They target young girls by focusing on their interests and ways of life in order to secure a cult-like following. The forty-something writers adopt the typical problems of youth so that naïve teen readers will feel like *someone understands.* The magazines stress a sickening importance of perfection from a pampering point of view throughout the entire read. *Get gorgeous from tresses to tootsies with this ultimate spa guide.* They are obsessed with euphoric makeovers: *We made sure we changed up her looks with designer make-up. We also included step-by-step instructions so you can try to achieve her glamness at home. We're helpful like that.* They gleefully suggest odd-but-supposedly-important "secret" methods of fixing oneself up in dismal advice and beauty remedy columns. *Mash a ripe banana and mix it with a few drops of almond oil. Rinse thoroughly with warm water and you'll look delicious.*

They try dearly to be cool—like a father *hangin'* with his distant teenage step-daughter—or they are setting out to blend every possible known teenage lingo together into one compact, messy, confused dialect. At some point they use sounds incredibly moronic in an air-headed way (*-ish, thingees, farty people*), then they dab a pinch of ebonics (*peace, our bad, straight up, thang*), mixed with three-quarters cup of hip diva (*what a fox, hot babe, 'do, scoop, girlie, go disco diva, parents dig, these pants rule*), all thrown into a well-boiled pot of the nerdishly tame (*ninny, yacker, schlimo, c'mon*). Oh, and don't forget to add some surfer/skater lingo for seasoning (*'cause it sounds pretty rad, studette*). I find it amusing when adults try to sound my age, but that's only in consideration of their furry motives. (From "Teen Magazine—Double Exposure" by Payvand Abghari for a freshman composition)

It's my brother, and he's calling to say he is now my sister. I feel something fry a little, deep behind my eyes. Knowing how dreams get mixed up with not-dreams, I decide to do a reality test at once, "Let me get a cigarette," I say, knowing that if I reach for a Marlboro and it turns into a trombone or a snake or anything else on the way to my lips that I'm still out in the large world of dreams.

The cigarette stays a cigarette. I light it. I ask my brother to run that stuff by me again.

> It is the Texas Zephyr at midnight—the woman in a white suit, the man in a blue uniform; she carries flowers—I know they are flowers. The petals spill and spill into the aisle, and a child goes past this couple who have just come from their own wedding. . . . My mother. My father. I am conceived near Dallas in the dark while a child passes, a young girl . . . who feels an odd hurt as her own mother, fat and empty, snores with her mouth open, her false teeth slipping down, snores and snores just two seats behind the creators.

News can make a person stupid. It can make you think you can do something. So I ask The Blade question, thinking that if he hasn't had the operation yet that I can fly to him. . . . That we can talk. That I can get him to touch base with reality. (From "Oranges and Sweet Sister Boy" by Judy Ruiz in *Iowa Woman*)

Thirteen Ways

In his poem "Thirteen Ways of Looking at a Blackbird," the well-known American poet Wallace Stevens looks at blackbirds through thirteen short stanzas, each one embodying its own meaning for the blackbird (from one with the bird symbolizing strength to one with it signifying irrational fear), emphasized by thirteen different situations (including one where the bird's eye is the most dynamic item in a large landscape to one where the bird is part of a sexual trinity), underscored by thirteen different styles (from one stanza written like a mathematical problem to one that is a mini-fable). Framing the blackbird *Thirteen Ways*, each stanza shock cutting against the other without tight transitions, a more complete reality emerges than would be possible with one thesis, one situation, and one style.

Cubism. *Thirteen Ways* is an attempt to transcend the reality of our limited-to-a-single-point-of-view eye by including several points of view taken at different times, culminating in a fragmented unity. Energizing the truth, but the concept is ancient. Art historian E.H. Gombrich reminds us that ancient Egyptians combined different points of view by simultaneously presenting in one image the most identifiable traits of a person—frontal eyes, a profile nose, anterior torsos, and profile legs both with insteps. This accuracy for soul-identification was more important than an illusion of reality dependent on the "authenticity" of a single perspective. Similarly, m by combining several shifts in focus and styles may seem radical or even postmodern odern criminologists believe eyewitnesses are more reliable when their reality portfolio is built by considering the crime from not only their own, but the criminal's and victim's points of view and from different time sequences, not merely from the beginning to the end.

Abruptness. In the spirit of this cubistic, *Thirteen Ways* world, many contemporary essayists rely on abrupt shifts to disparate parts in an essay. Whereas *Double Exposure Transitions* back and forth between two realities, *Thirteen Ways* keeps constantly cutting to the next reality without returning to a former one. Defying the tight bonding quality of the *Twist Ties*, the cubistic transitions purposely exploit the natural breaks, gaps, and leaps between sections of an essay. The lack of overt connectors results in a pastiche effect where the central subject of an essay stays constant, but where focus, content, format, and style keep shifting. While the cubistic *Transitions* might be described as "transition-*less,*" a writer can still signal these sharp shifts: Each section can be numbered or demarked with a decorative symbol or icon; or mini-titles can be applied. With *Thirteen Ways* a writer can combine any of the strategies in the *Style* or *Form* units, each providing ideas for a new angle: The writer could shift from a heavily *Fused*, metaphoric section, to an academic one that almost needs *Scrubbing*, to *Devil's Advice*, to *Anecdoting*, to *Q&A-ing*.

Your turn. Identify the *Thirteen Ways* strategies used in the passages below. Explain what each angle offers on the subject that is missing from the other angles.

Angles of Thirteen Ways:

Tuxedos in the daytime and sunglasses at night. Earning off the books and learning on the job. Being invited to a party you can't get into and getting into a party you weren't invited to. . . . A limo to the airport and a budget flight to Rome. . . . Make-up on boys and crew cuts on girls. Nine to 5 P.M. and 9 to 5 A.M. New York. —Annie Flanders, editor and publisher, *Details* magazine

•

New York is a city of port and sport. Its style is both portly and sportly. A port in that it is a city that thinks of itself as being on the water. And at the same time, it is a city of the good sport where you get along and don't complain. . . . —Jerzy Kosinsky

•

For the holidays, we the Cathedral of St. John the Divine put up a 40-foot Christmas tree. . . . The decorations, however, are not the usual ones. They are 2,000 origami paper cranes folded by New York schoolchildren as part of a tradition started in Hiroshima by an eleven-year-old girl who was dying from radiation and made the first such cranes on her deathbed. . . . —James Parks Morton, Dean,
Cathedral Church of St. John the Divine

•

The avenues in my neighborhood are Pride, Covetousness, and Lust; the cross streets are Anger, Gluttony, Envy, and Sloth. I live on Sloth, and the style on our street is to avoid the other thoroughfares. . . . —John Chancellor

•

I was down in the village recently on a very rainy day when a cab pulled up at a light. A young man and a young woman started to get out with their baby as the light turned green, and a second car pulled up behind them. The man in the second car got out and started yelling, "Are you out of your f------ mind? Are you out of your f------ mind?" That is New York style.—David Mamet (From "Setting the Style" compiled by Peter Blaunder in *New York* magazine)

2.

Eleven years ago, at the famous PEN congress . . . the world's writers discussed "The Imagination of the writer and the imagination of the State," a subject of Maileresque grandeur, dreamed up, of course, by Norman Mailer. Striking how many ways there were to read that little "and." For many of us, it meant "versus.". . .

3.

The nation either co-opts its greatest . . . or else seeks to destroy them. . . . Both fates are problematic. The hush of reverence is inappropriate for literature; great writing makes a great noise in the mind, the heart. . . .

4.

Beware the writer who sets himself or herself up as the voice of a nation. This includes nations of race, gender, sexual orientation, elective affinity. This is the New Behalfism. Beware behalfies! . . . [The New Behalfism] abhors the tragic sense of life. Seeing literature as inescapably political, it replaces literary values with political ones.

It is the murderer of thought. Beware! . . .

9.

Much great writing has no need of the public dimension. Its agony comes from within. The public sphere is as nothing to Elizabeth Bishop. Her prison—her freedom—her subject is elsewhere.

Lullaby.

Let nations rage,

Let nations fall,

The shadow of the crib makes an enormous cage upon the wall.

(From "Notes on Writing and the Nation" by Salman Rushdie in *Index on Censorship*)

::::

(1)

If you live in Eugene, Oregon, you are one of four groups. . . . The Yuptowers are the royalty of the valley. . . . Each morning they dance into their Volvo, Benz, and Lexus in their Nike workout gear. . . . After the abs-are-us rehearsal, they head over to the 5th Street Market Juice Club for lunch. As the sunless sky gets darker, they bolt back up the hill to prepare for the evening performance at the Hult Center. Take your time. The performance is a repeat classical dancer from the Eugene Ballet Company . . . .

The Earthtranqs live in close to the Willamette River, the University and the library. Their yards are crawling with vegetables, herbs, and gobs of colorful flowers. They are found every weekend manufacturing their goods at the Saturday Market downtown: diversion soaps, spirited incense, moody candles, cranky tie-dyed shirts, and perky beads. They have time to work on city issues such as where there needs to be a new footbridge . . . . On occasion you will find them eating a tofu omelet and carrot juice. . . .

(3)

John Stewart Mill (1806-1873) was a strong utilitarian and a secular humanist. He was very optimistic about human nature and our ability to solve our problems without recourse to providential grace (Pojman 108). In addition, he was an empiricist— one who believed that all knowledge-justified belief was based in experience (111). John Stewart would have felt that Eugene would be an experience for everyone and a great place to grow up because of the variety of pleasure in a closed environment . . . . He would have chased [all his food] down with every imaginable local beer. . . .

(5)

Today, much to [the police's] horror, they have found that the freedom is spilling out as oppression. . . . They are now engaged in a bloodthirsty new-wave crusade, with a young bad, boastful, hostile Black Army Faction. Anarchists. A Mr.-Rogers-versus-the-devil scene. . . . Their hopes are to tear down the over-merchandized, over-commercialized city and return it to the primitive Ozzie-and-Harriet way of life (Gwartney 16). . . . In climbs Chief Jim Hill from the woodlands. Jim, the city's WD-40 knight in armor, who works behind a tidy, memo-filled, coffee-ringed desk, . . . is attempting to organize a peaceful Pow-Wow . . . .

(7)

Free money built it, but it's expensive to maintain. Admission used to be a piece of wood, but today it's only willingness to succeed. The outside remains strong, but the inside creaks . . . . It co-starred in a movie with Donald Sutherland and John Belushi. What is it? It's the University of Oregon's Deadly Hall, Department of Mathematics. (From "Eight Ways of Looking at Eugene, Oregon" by Sharron Perez for a freshman research assignment)

Take an object. Do something with it. Do something else with it. (Jasper Johns) . . .

Do your own work but use someone else's clothes. (Cindy Sherman) . . .

Be ready to admit that jealousy moves you more than art. They say action is painting. Well, it isn't and we all know abstract expressionism and pop art have moved to the suburbs. (Larry Rivers and Frank O'Hara) . . .

Make a painting in which every part of the painting is of equal importance. (Chuck Close) . . .

Use the worst color you can find in each place—it usually is the best. (Roy Lichtenstein) . . .

In the morning make long lists of things to do. In the afternoon write down whose ideas they were. (Jennifer Bartlett)

(From *Sketchbook with Voices* edited by Eric Fischl with Jerry Saltz)

∷∷

Legally blind, I know the eternal Freudian slip of misread signs
. . . .
A friend calls me to say she'll meet me in half an hour. She drives a red Chrysler. I walk down to the street and approach the car. I reach for the door on the passenger's side and give it a tug, but it's locked. . . . I see at last the face of a genuinely terrified Chinese woman. . . . I try to explain my mistake in sign language—pointing to my eyes, telling her loudly that I've mistaken her car for that of a friend. I begin backing away from her into the street like an ungainly kid on roller skates. . . .

•

Today I ran six miles and collided with a pair of shopping carts in the tricky shade of several trees. I ran from sunlight into dark. A big crash of cymbals. . . . I nearly gelded myself. . . .

•

In the great Prado museum in Madrid, I find that I cannot see the famous paintings of Velasquez and Goya because they are hanging behind ropes that prohibit the insane from drawing too near. So I see the ocean of mud. . . . Then I turn a corner into a great, vaulted darkness of nonbeing where an important painting hangs behind a veil, black as an abandoned lighthouse. . . .

•

Last night I heard a woman on the radio talking about her experiences with menopause—she'd had to put her head in the freezer, she felt her body betraying her, etc. It was the unfairness of it: her body was doing this to her too soon; she was old already, in her early forties. "Me too," I said to the radio. "Me too!" I'm already a very old man. (From *The Planet of the Blind* by Stephen Kuusisto)

⠿

1. Friday, in the Jerusalem neighborhood of Baka, there are not braided challahs [rich white bread for the Jewish Sabbath] for sale at the corner bakery. . . . Earlier in the week, a block away, three neighbors were stabbed to death by a single Palestinian. For the next few days all Palestinians are barred from entering Jerusalem. Only they know how to bake the braided challahs. . . .

5. I am in the Ministry of Interior. . . . The overworked clerk is beside herself, the scores of people congregating around her desk and spilling over in the hallways. Most of the Russians do not speak Hebrew; she knows no Russian . . . . Finally, completely losing her cool, she begins to scream at the new immigrant standing before her: "I hate Russians, you Russians are all shit, why don't you go back to where you came from and leave us in peace?". . .

6. On the first wintry night in Jerusalem, my wife and I go to the reunion of the Lamaze class . . . together with the other "graduates.". . . Justin tells us that he has found a surefire remedy for calming his crying baby when all else fails. He lifts up his pant leg to reveal the revolver tucked in its ankle holster. . . . He explains that Israel's policy of house demolition [of Palestinians] is no more severe than forms of collective punishment found in the United States. There, too, a family can lose their house through foreclosure when their breadwinner is sent to jail. Justin works in the Human Rights Office of the Ministry of Justice. (From "Jerusalem—Fall 1990" by Aaron Back in *Tikkun: A Bimonthly Jewish Critique of Politics, Culture & Society*)

⠿

For a while, it seemed like most of them were named John, tall blonds with moustaches. Then I noticed that several of my boyfriends had grown up without their fathers. But the instant G. took off his glasses to kiss me, it became perfectly clear. I knew that gesture so well it made me shudder. The real common denominator was bad eyesight. . . .

Our arguments—especially those endless, circular debates about the possible intentions behind a remark—leave me, usually a rapid-moving person, feeling like a stagnant pool. Time inches by with him; that's why I stay with him, my foul fountain of youth . . . .

My last boyfriend and I were together for five years. He taught me to be celibate. . . .

Joe learned to be a slob by living with me.
Joe was deeply disturbed by modern dance.
Joe adored home tours.
Joe was the kind of man you take home to your parents and leave there. (From *The 100ᵗʰ Boyfriend* by Bridget Daly and Janet Skeels)

:::

I am not a New Man. I am a Man. Imagine that one fine morning you discover that rhinoceroses have taken power. They have a rhinoceros ethic, a rhinoceros philosophy, a rhinoceros universe. The new master of the city is a rhinoceros who uses the same words as you and yet it is not the same language. . . . (*No. In fact, rhinoceroses have deliberately distorted, deliberately diverted the meaning of words, which are the same for them, which they understand but which they corrupted for propaganda purposes. . . .*)

For centuries humanity lived either amid tyranny or amid disorder. I prefer disorder to tyranny. The [French] Revolution managed to combine disorder and tyranny. . . .

A headache after having drunk too much. Life is not a flower. Shit is. The ragout of orangutan of Rangoon. Rangoon makes the taste of orangutan ragout distasteful. I have burning regrets when, sometimes, I realize that I have tied myself down, that I have bound by hands, put leaden chains on my feet. To be free, to walk, to run, not to crawl anymore. . . .

In the history of humanity there are not civilizations or cultures which fail to manifest . . . this need for an absolute that is called heaven, freedom, a miracle, a lost paradise to be regained, peace, the going beyond History . . . for the Ideal City, that is to say the desire to purify the world, to change it, to save it, to reintegrate it metaphysically. There is no religion in which everyday life is not considered a prison;

there is no philosophy or ideology that does not think we live in alienation. . . .

I have the key to happiness: remember, be profoundly, profoundly, totally conscious that you are.
I myself, sorry to say, hardly ever use this key. I keep losing it. (From *Present Past, Past Present* by Eugene Ionesco, translated by Helen Lane)

3
Headwork

PEEL

SCRUB

BASTE

Strong and Weak Noodling

Headwork gives an essay muscle. English teachers too often separate critical thinking from the *Style* and *Form* concerns earlier in this book—a fatal mistake that bleeds the life out of good arguments and makes them unreadable. Writers give strength to ideas and details with *Style* and *Form*, but deciding which details to consider in the first place and what to think about them has to do with critical thinking or analysis. Whatever an essayist writes about—a business proposal, literature, history, engineering—the essayist must discover the truth of the subject under examination. This unit looks at ways to discover truth (*Peel*), ways to purge weak thinking that deceives and obscures the truth (*Scrub*), and ways to test thinking with research (*Baste*). Being open to discovery and being honest about findings takes intellectual endurance and emotional strength. Too many writers lack the discipline to do this and when they lack that discipline, they turn their backs on writing as discovery and force old biases on readers.

PEEL:
Ways to Seek Meaning

Inductive Analysis
Deductive Analysis
Claim Cast
Infer-styling

"Nay, it is. I know not 'seems'" is one of Hamlet's knife-like lines in Shakespeare's *Hamlet, Prince of Denmark*. Using both reason and intuition, Hamlet tries desperately to cut through the appearance of what *seems* to be true, to reach what *is* true. His struggle is every good writer's struggle. If truths were transparent, most of the need to write would disappear: Everyone would agree on which economic policy to follow, artistic works would be immediately understood, legal issues would move quickly to conclusions, history would not leave mysteries, and there would be no personal discord. Life is more complex. Strong writers use two general ways of thinking to understand it, *Inductive* and *Deductive Analysis*. In transforming an *Analysis* into an essay, the writer makes different *claims* and then uses *Style* to link all the details in the argument to inferences and the thesis.

Inductive Analysis

Examining any experience in its entirety (a personal relationship, business deal, philosophical film, political candidate) increases the risk of ignoring crucial details that might change the subject's value. With a complex subject, details or facts can play peek-a-boo. We observe them; then we lose them. One can easily panic when experiencing the onslaught of details from a Shakespeare play, a painting by Salvador Dali, a proposal to invest in a Mars landing, the dynamics of a political conflict, or other *primary sources*. *Primary sources* are the ones we directly observe (the play *Hamlet*) while *secondary sources* are *Analytical* sources that help us understand the *primary sources* (a critical analysis of *Hamlet*). A *secondary source* can be *Analyzed* by a *tertiary source* (another critic's reaction or refutation to the analysis of *Hamlet*).

Also, when subjects are gulp-sized, dazzling surface deceptions (see *Logical Fallacies*) can be tempting diversions from the truth. To avoid these problems, writer-thinkers *Peel* the experience apart, isolating its details to carefully consider the worth of each detail on its own terms, separate from the whole. This is the first stage of *Inductive Analysis*.

Withheld Judgment. While considering the value of each detail of the *primary* or even a *secondary source*, the critical thinker withholds any prejudgment, or hunch (called an *hypothesis*), or assumption (called a *warrant*) about the final truth of the subject being analyzed. The *Inductive* thinker makes only one assumption, called a *generalization warrant*, that it is possible to *eventually* derive a general conclusion from an ample number of particular examples or details. By not ignoring any important details and examining each detail's implications, the writer will eventually be in position to bring all those implications together to form a final conclusion, known also as a *thesis* or *claim*.

Juicing. Every detail has literal, *denotative* significance as well as implied, *connotative* meaning. For instance, examining a garden on the literal, *denotative* level, one might think "green plants and walkways." On a *connotative*, or implied-meaning level, a writer examining the garden would juice the green plant's characteristics—green, shade, oxygen, freshness—and from these come up with a connotative meaning such as "peaceful respite from work." The more a writer considers other particulars of the garden—like the plant arrangements and curves of walkways that work together, forcing the eye to wander before coming to places of rest—the more complicated the implications of the garden will grow, until ultimately, the garden design becomes a metaphor for existence: Life's journey and one's place in the universe.

One can get through life without being so aware; however, strong essayists know that the more carefully details are considered, the more refined meaning becomes. When confronted by a picture of a baby in a bath, an American might see the image as representing "cleanliness," baby and water both implying rejuvenation. However, as Edward Hall points out in "The Anthropology of Manners," women in India are offended by the image. They take one more detail and its implications into consideration: The water is still, so they wonder, "How could people bathe a child in stagnant water?"

Thesis. After days, weeks, or maybe years, when every detail has been listed with its unique connotations, finally the thinker can start pulling all those connotations or implications together to arrive at a *thesis, hypothesis, warrant, general statement,* or *claim.* This thesis statement must be general or complex enough to connect to all the details' connotations. Strong writers do not oversimplify the thesis and, in fact, find that their essay becomes richer when implications contradict each other.

To resolve and articulate a thesis that can accommodate contradiction, the writer might use *ambiguity* (a statement that is not cloudy, but intentionally uses rich, suggestive language to convey more than one meaning, such as to write that images in a surreal painting "buckle" to imply both coming apart and coming together). Or a writer employs *paradox* (a statement that seems contradictory or absurd but which is well founded, such as Paul in Corinthians writing "For when I am weak, then I am strong"). *Irony* (a statement that means the opposite of what is said, or in a larger sense, that describes the incongruity of two realities, such as a story being about "beauty that is grotesque inside") is yet another tool for capturing contradictions.

Because a thesis gradually forms after carefully considering a large sampling of details, *Inductive Analysis* has the power to yield original and insightful conclusions. However, in logicians' terms, an induced thesis is *probable* and not *certain* because of the potential to gather new or unobserved details with new implications that could, in turn, cause a writer to revise or further qualify the original thesis. When a writer starts building an essay to express and support a thesis, the thesis can be either *implied* or *stated* throughout the entire piece, or stated only once at the beginning, end, or even middle of the piece. Some stodgy English teachers require students to state the thesis in the introductory paragraph; however, a sampling of essays from the yearly *Best American Essays*, shows that the thesis statements can be found in a variety of places, or else implied and never overtly articulated.

Intentions. Beginning critical thinkers are plagued by doubts as to whether the creator of a *primary source*, such as either the designer of the garden or the baby-bath photographer mentioned above, intends the viewer to come away with a specific thesis. Strong thinkers avoid this concern. They know that an *Inductively*-arrived-at thesis is strong enough to contradict those intentions. *Inductive* thinkers know that there is always the possibility that the creator of the *primary source*—a business person drawing up a proposal, a church architect, a film maker— did not end up with what he or she intended to create. Often intuition or the subconscious overrides a creator's intentions. If the creator voices any intentions, he or she could be pulling the critical thinker's leg. In fact, for a critical thinker to avoid thinking *Inductively* and instead to decide the worth of a *primary source* based on its creator's expressed or implied intentions, is called the *intentional fallacy*, an avoidance of thinking. (See *Logical Fallacies*.)

Focusing on intentions has other pitfalls: A creator of a *primary source* can be a fraud, creating a *primary source* that moves a thinker even further away from the creator's true intentions. In his book *The Armada*, Garrett Mattingly analyzes a "drama" Mary Queen of Scots creates at her execution. She turns her own death chop into an artistic drama with herself in the lead- ing role so that the implications of the event will establish her as a martyr instead of a criminal. She designs and paints the day of her own execution by arranging every detail: Wearing the red garments associated with martyrdom in paintings; resting one hand on her escorting officer's sleeve; raising her crucifix high and praying for forgiveness over the sentencing executioners' voices; and pinning her kerchief to her auburn wig so that after the "dull chunk of the axe," when her beheaded face is lifted into the air, both kerchief and wig come off, allowing her head, with "shrunken and withered and gray" stubble on a shrunken skull, to pull off and roll on the platform, a shriveled humiliation that finalizes her thesis—she and her cause are to be pitied. Beware of intentions and misleading implications.

Deductive Analysis

Unlike *Inductive* thinkers, *Deductive* thinkers start with a *thesis* (also referred to as a *major premise*) instead of discovering one through the implications of particulars. Usually the thesis is an established theory or truth that has matured through previous *Inductive* thinking and is now being used as a start-up truth for examining a new experience. For instance, one can start with a previously argued definition of a classical garden as one that uses symmetry and decorous flourishes to imply that nature is beautiful when controlled by humans' sense of order. Logicians would call this statement the *major premise*. On viewing a particular garden, if the writer-thinker finds that all the plant arrangements and walkways of the garden stress symmetry and decorous flourishes, they become *supporting examples* or the *minor premise* for a *Deductive Analysis*. The *major* and *minor premises* can then be brought together *by necessity* (not *probability* as discussed in *Inductive Analysis)* to make a *claim* that this particular garden is a classical garden that implies nature is most beautiful when controlled by humans. Logicians call this order of thinking a *syllogism*.

Thesis. *Deductive Analysis* encourages helpful connections with preexisting ideas. For instance, *Deductive Analysis* helps determine the extent to which a work of art conforms to a definition of an artistic movement; whether a business deal is supported by tested business practices; whether a couple's personal intimacy matches a psychological profile for a healthy relationship; whether a legal case conforms to a legal precedent; or how the mandala, "a design that aids meditation by drawing attention from its borders toward its center," explains the nature of baseball (as Peter Gardella does in *Touchstone*); how a feminist theory clarifies a Shakespearean play; how a painter's manifesto evaluates a greeting card; how a work by Emanuel Kant decides the worth of a Protestant moral stance. For a *Deductive Analysis*, the writer researches different theories and concepts that might help to better understand the *primary source* (see *withheld judgment* under *Inductive Analysis*) and then uses these as a *thesis*, screening in only those details of the *primary source* that have implications which validate the *thesis*. Unlike a biased or a person committing a hasty generalization (see *Logical Fallacies* in this unit), the *Deductive* thinker accepts the *thesis* as a vulnerable, start-up truth that can vanish if not enough of the *primary's* particulars support the *thesis* or if the *thesis* is not helpful in understanding the *primary* material.

English teachers tend to think that an essay is *Deductive* if the thesis is at the beginning of an essay but, just as with *Inductive Analysis*, the thesis can occur anywhere—introduction, body, conclusion—and can even be not stated but implied throughout the essay. *Inductive* and *Deductive Analysis* describe the initial thinking that goes into an essay and not its final organization. In fact, some parts of an essay can be thought through *Inductively*, others *Deductively*.

Kinks. Since *Deductive Analysis* cannot advance beyond its *major* and *minor premises*, it is not as likely to nurture original thought as *Inductive Analysis*. For instance, in the humanities, definitions of intellectual movements and aesthetic theories are often used as the thesis for *Deductively Analyzing* a painting, a poem, or a musical score, and subtle nuances of the work that make it unique are ignored as the thinker focuses only on details that support the chosen theory. Also, there is never a full guarantee that the theory evolved in the past through careful *Inductive* thinking, or if it did, that the circumstances or details that were used to form the thesis have not changed. Worse, weak *Deductive* thinkers start milling material to conform to the thesis, sapping any essay's credibility based on that thesis. The problem with using the *intentions* of the *primary source* as the thesis is explained under *Inductive Analysis*.

Enthymeme Testing. Created by philosopher Stephen Toulmin, enthymemes are miniature *Deductive* arguments that are useful for testing a thesis statement that was reached through *Inductive* or *Deductive Analysis.* They are made up of a *claim* followed immediately by the reason(s) supporting the *claim*, usually connected by the word "because" or "since." For instance, the *claim*, "Students should study the history of landscape design" can use the word "since" or "because" to connect the *claim* to its reason, "they will be able to appreciate history when they travel." Since the reasons supporting this *claim* may be scattered throughout the introduction, if not the entire essay, the act of creating the enthymeme forces the writer to validate the existence of those supporting reasons.

Also, by defining the *claim* and support, the writer can more easily locate the writer's *hidden assumptions* (also called a *warrant).* The essay is only as strong as these assumptions, and if they are not stated and supported clearly, the writer may need to change the thesis. For instance, in the *claim* above, there are at least three *hidden assumptions*: that landscape design truly reflects history, that students will be interested in history when they travel, and that students will encounter gardens when they travel. The essay needs to address the concerns somewhere, and to varying extents, some assumptions perhaps more important than others. *Enthymemes* are primarily a way to test a thesis, but sometimes they may be effective enough to use as a thesis. However, some English teachers require students to have an *enthymeme* before writing a rough draft, in which case the *enthymeme* is tantamount to thinking *Deductively* and excludes *Inductive* discovery.

Claim Cast

After *Inductively* or *Deductively Analyzing* a subject, an essay writer expresses a *claim* to begin organizing the results of the *Analysis*. (A *claim* can also be referred to as a *hypothesis, conclusion*, or *major premise*—all alternative labels for *thesis. Academia can be term-tiresome.) There are five major types of claims*: resemblance, evaluation, (refutation), definition, causal, and proposal. They can be used separately, but many essayists chain several *claims* together for reinforcement.

Resemblance Claim. To varying extents, a *resemblance claim* provides important scaffolding for all the other *claims*. A *resemblance claim* establishes a similarity between two or more subjects and adds significance to the *claim* by then contrasting the differences within that similarity. *Resemblance claims* compare and contrast. Here's an example that demonstrates why *resemblance claims* are so important:

An appealing quality of one of your friends is that he always offers unconditional support, no matter what you do. Over time, you begin to take for granted that this unqualified backing is what makes a good friend. However, this quality is brought quickly into sharp focus when comparing and contrasting these attributes to like qualities in another friend who applauds your moral actions and attitudes, but also offers constructive criticism when you reveal your moral weaknesses.

By comparing and contrasting the two friends on a similar issue, you initiate a dialogue that takes place in your mind about supportive friends. Both friends offer support, but there is a difference in how and when they express it. An essayist would ask, what difference does this difference make? What does this contrast suggest about friends who are supportive? What makes friendship meaningful or helpful or delusional? The conclusions spawned by these questions often become an essay's primary food source.

Sometimes a *resemblance claim* forms the guts of an entire essay. Other times a *resemblance claim* generates details and ideas and then is disassembled after the rough draft of the essay. Other times the *claim* is a quick flash, a *minor premise* supporting a *major premise*. Comparison and contrast are basic critical thinking skills used for *Analysis* of all subjects: two or more business proposals, evil characters, quarterbacks, Italian restaurants, composition instructors, or mosques. A *resemblance claim* argues the differences between two comparable subjects, but usually stops short of overtly expressing a value judgment between the two. That is the work of an *evaluation claim.*

Evaluation Claim. This *claim* builds on a *resemblance claim.* By exploring the implications of the differences between the two friends in the example above, an evaluation begins to emerge. This value judgment is then expressed with a value term: one friend is better, more reliable, more intimate, less honest, less supportive, and more critical than another. Or the essayist might first establish a *criterion* to express what makes a good friend valuable and then argue which friends better meet that *criterion.* If a good friend is someone who spurs your emotional growth, then the friend who criticizes you would be the better friend. However, if the *criterion* changes, establishing a good friend as someone who always makes you feel good about yourself, then, based on that standard, the first friend would be a better friend.

Evaluation claims flood our intellectual lives: arguing that one architectural design better solves the problem of office space than another; that one president has more leadership qualities than another; that one short story better merges the spiritual with the grotesque than another. Or, based on certain established criteria, an *evaluation claim* can be formed stating that Robert Crumb is a master cartoonist, Rubio's has superior fish tacos, Eric Rohmer's *My Night at Maude's* is a great literary film. In establishing one's criteria, the writer's definition of what constitutes "a good friend" or what is meant by the term "humanitarian" or when a film is deemed "literary" may differ from the reader's interpretation. *Definition claims* further clarify those abstract concepts embedded in the criteria of an *evaluation claim.*

Refutation Claim. An offshoot of the *evaluation claim* is the *refutation claim,* whereby the essayist compares and contrasts all his or her major details and implications with those made by another thinker or writer, and with a specific criterion, shows why his or her essay's position is the stronger of the two. Often essayists anticipate or imagine another person's opposition, and thus rebar the essay while crumbling away an opposition's footing before it even has a chance to solidify. For instance, if the essayist above anticipated someone thinking that a good friend is one who will lend money freely, the writer could imagine the arguments for this and then show what is wrong with this friend compared to other kinds of friends, demonstrating how money lending shifts the basis for a relationship to exploitation instead of intimacy or how lending money can create anxiety between two friends.

Definition Claim. Nearly all arguments require defining one's terms. And *definition* arguments take up space in nearly all the other *claims*. This *claim* argues the meaning of an abstract concept or subject. Rewriting the above *claims* into a *definition claim* could result in, "A good friend is one who compliments us for our positive actions and criticizes us for our negative actions and attitudes." Note that again the other *claims* can become components to support this *claim*: a *resemblance claim* with another kind of positive friend, an *evaluation claim* that establishes a criteria as to what constitutes a friend's importance, a *causal claim* that argues the effect of having this friend, a *proposal claim* that argues the necessity of having this friend— all can potentially clarify who this friend is.

Deductive Analysis craves *definition claims* because it starts with a concept and then argues how details from a *primary source* fit that concept. For instance, one could start with one of the following concepts about friendship as a *hypothesis*: "Friends are an answer to existential dread"; "Friends are a result of living in a capitalist society"; "Friends are the essential catalysts in our maturing." An *Inductive Analysis*, like the ones that might originate out of using the strategies under *Encircling*, might yield more unexpected *claims*.

Causal Claim. This *claim* (sometimes called the *cause and effect claim*) argues whether something *causes* something else or whether something is the *result* of something else. An essayist makes a *causal claim* when arguing "friends who not only praise us for positive actions but criticize us for negative actions develop our moral character." *Causal claims* appeal to our need to believe in results: children's behavior causes parents to react to them in specific ways; the formal devices of a novel lead us to a certain understanding of the protagonist; exposure to Italian cuisine makes for better California cuisine; a holy-war mentality inevitably leads to terror.

Proposal Claim. This *claim* argues whether something should or should not be implemented. For instance, the *claim* above can be made into a *proposal claim* by stating, "We should have friends who not only praise us for positive actions but criticize us for negative ones in order to develop moral character." Note that if the word "should" was changed to "will" that part of the *claim* would be *causal*. A *causal claim* is often an essential aspect of a proposal because proposals usually spotlight the effects of taking or not taking a specific action. Note also that if the *claim* were written to say, "We should have friends who not only praise us for positive actions but criticize us for negative ones instead of friends who are always supportive in order to develop moral character," an evaluation *claim* would need to be developed. *Resemblance, evaluation*, and *causal claims* are often components of *proposal claims* because they answer *hidden assumptions* in a *proposal claim*. (See *Deductive Analysis*.)

Forms and Claims. Any of the strategies in the *Form* unit can be used to explore, intensify, and support any of the *claims*. Depending on the subject, some strategies might come more immediately to mind than others. For instance, *Devil's Advice* and *Trojan Horse* would require a *proposal claim*; *Netting* and all the strategies under *Encircling* would power *definition claims*; *Problem Making* and *Pulsing the Tense* would bring life to *causal claims*; *Raising the Dead*, *Mocking* and *Sincerely Yours* seem impossible without *evaluation Claims*; *Masquerading* cannot live without a *resemblance claim*. More likely than not, several *claims* and a few *Form* strategies will exist in any essay. The combinations are endless.

Infer-styling

Verb Connection. Verbs cleanly graft details to inferences; however, the essayist must always decide how definitively or delicately the two should fuse. Note how the underlined verbs below are chosen based on the degree of connective strength between the detail and its inference. Sometimes details *strongly suggest* ideas: rain <u>symbolizes</u> growth; a crown of thorns <u>alludes</u> to Jesus; a long sentence describing the actions of an automobile <u>represents</u> the car's movements; colors <u>signify</u> moods; a hedge of plants <u>exhibits</u> order. Other times details are not strong enough to suggest ideas, but they can *reinforce* ideas established elsewhere: light entering a window in a painting <u>emphasizes</u> the motif of unexpected hope; an unselfish action <u>reveals</u> a person's love for another person; metal furniture <u>underscores</u> the utilitarian mood of a room; a specific word <u>sharpens</u> an essay's sarcastic political perspective.

Sometimes a detail only has the strength to *subtly suggest* an idea: dark clouds in a film <u>hint</u> at an ominous turn of the plot; a legal precedent <u>implies</u> that a law should be overturned; a low ceiling <u>suggests</u> the protection of a cave. Other times the opposite is true, and details *dramatically create* ideas: her throwing out the textbook <u>propagates</u> a thought about her seriousness; yellow sparkles of light <u>unseal</u> a nude's innocence; Jesus' rejection of his family <u>reveals</u> his priority of spirit over blood. Still at other times details *limit* or *qualify* an inference: Le Corbusier's geometric shapes <u>restrict</u> one's awareness of nature's chaos; a melody's B flat in the third measure <u>confines</u> a particular song's sense of joy; a financial proposal <u>focuses</u> on efficiency.

In all these examples, the verb connects the detail on the left side of the sentence with inferences or meanings on the right side. A *thesaurus* will expand the possibility of creating the most compatible connective tissue. When a sentence rejects several verb choices, a good essayist knows to check the initial *Inductive* or *Deductive* thinking that took place before writing the sentence. The thought might be weak.

Flow Connection. When details spread out and away from the thesis they support, the strength of an essay's thesis fades. Essayists never want a reader to wonder, "What's the point of all these details?" Consider the following unfiltered part of an essay:

> I think that the J writer in the Bible's Book of Genesis is trying to depict a world where corruption rules, where deception and greed put certain men on "God's side." God empowers Abraham. When Abraham is in the land of two different rulers, that of the Pharaoh and that of Abimelech, he tells his wife Sarah to pretend like she is his sister. By doing this, Abraham is able to protect himself from rulers who might need to kill him if they think the only way to have Sarah is to get rid of her husband. Abraham comes out ahead by the scheme, receiving flattering gifts from the rulers, but God punishes them because they innocently have adulterous sex with Sarah. Later on two angels visit Abraham's brother Lot. Lot's neighbors in Sodom, both young and old, think these male angels are great looking and want to rape them. Since they are holy guests, Lot wants to befriend the angels, so to take the heat off he offers the gang rapists his own virgin daughters, and God not only refuses to intervene with punishment for Lot but actually helps him get away from the city. Later, Jacob, who is a man of "guile," and his scheming mother, Rebecca, trick Esau and steal his blessing, God doing nothing, so that Jacob becomes one of the next important patriarchs.

This student has a clearly stated, controversial thesis regarding a part of Genesis's satiric nature; however, there are two problems with the *Style*. First, by spreading all the supporting details over several sentences, the reader can easily forget the writer's point. Second, the weakness caused by the spread encourages people who disagree with the thesis to cut into this flab, isolating what appear to be unconnected details, taking them out of context, and then even using them to change the issue or make different points. When the passage is rewritten with the *Flow* and *Pause* techniques from the *Style* unit, details and thesis are pulled closer together, the argument becoming more muscular and difficult to attack:

> In Genesis, the J writer satirically depicts a god who supports injustice: God super-charges Abraham, who schemes by calling his wife his sister, thereby setting up two other rulers to innocently "go into her," thereby each one earning a one-two punch from God while Abraham walks away with riches; God blinks while Lot tosses his virgin daughters to rapists to curry favor with angels; God launders a blessing that was

stolen by Rebecca and her son Jacob, the brother of "guile"—all inequities that suggest empowerment is on the side of cowardice, deception, and greed.

Fusion Connection. Since metaphors always carry a compressed load of associations, in arguments they effectively suggest the inferences of any detail onto which they are fused. (See the *Fusion* chapter in the *Style* unit.) Following are some lines from a *resemblance claim* that compares and contrasts F. Scott Fitzgerald's 1925 novel, *The Great Gatsby,* with Terrence Malick's 1973 film, *Badlands,* both fictional works featuring enigmatic characters, Jay Gatsby and Kit Carruthers, who pursue unrealistic dreams in a promising, distinct American landscape:

> Whereas Gatsby is suave and taps into a mysterious, romantic past for his energy, Kit is impulsive and derives his strength from what he imagines to be dramatic moments in teenage and Western movies. Luxurious clothing symbolizes Gatsby's personality while a James Dean Levi outfit defines Kit.

By using the support details of clothing as *Line-ups* below, the essayist effectively blends inference and detail while avoiding extra modifying phrases that can interrupt the argument's flow and take up space better used for developing more related ideas:

> Gatsby's *silk-shirt* demeanor whispers his mysterious, life-support past, just as Kit's *Levi-jacket* behavior aids and abets his playing out a tough, serial killer movie image.

Aside from using single details from the analyzed subject, quotations related to the subject can be transformed into *Melted-together Line-ups.* (See *Melted-together Words* in the *Pause* chapter of the *Style* unit.) For instance, Kit accuses his girlfriend, Holly, of "just being along for the ride" and Gatsby declares to Nick, his best friend and the novel's narrator, "Can't repeat the past? Why of course you can!" By turning both quotes into *Melted-together Line-ups,* the essayist creates a strong bond between the idea and a supporting quote:

> Kit's just-being-along-for-the-ride accusations and Gatsby's can't-repeat-the-past?-Why-of-course-you-can assertions underscore these two idealists' diminishing senses of reality.

Details from the subject can also provide a list of *Break-up* verbs and possessives to tighten the bond between detail and idea. In the following passage the writer makes use of an important afternoon tea party where Nick's consciousness is raised after witnessing a contrived reunion of Daisy and Gatsby. The metaphors remind the reader of the importance of the tea scene but also remind the reader of the novel's tone, which in turn adds to the commentary's legitimacy.

> After the tea, Nick cannot easily sugar his emotions. He teaspoons his criticisms, pretending to reserve judgment, hoping to avoid even a spot of moral indignation, until the end of the novel when he forgets etiquette: small sips of judgment are replaced with gulps of censure and outrage.

Although the above examples are applied to fictional works, the same process works for creating metaphors in an *Analysis* of a political candidate, a proposal for city planning, an evaluation of a painting, or definition of a new astronomical phenomena. Analyzing any of these *primary sources*, the writer would take dialogue, images, and other details that are examples of points being made and turn some of them into metaphors.

SCRUB:
Ways to Purge Deceit

Facial Pack: Euphemism
War Paint: Euphemism
Jousters: Logical Fallacies

There are people who are paid to swindle and sway audiences. Exposing these "dirty tricks" of persuasion in their handbook *The Thinkers Guide to Fallacies*, Dr. Richard Paul and Dr. Linda Elder warn us that, "those who strive to manipulate you always want something from you: your money, your vote, your support, your time, your soul—something!" Sincere writers scrub deceit from their arguments, scouring away *euphemism*—the use of pleasant or lofty language to replace words that are accurate but considered offensive, unpleasant, painful, indelicate, frightful, embarrassing, or mundane. Principled writers also resist the temptation to take short cuts in their reasoning, abstaining from *Jousting,* known as *logical fallacies.*

Knowing how these propagandists operate will protect you—as a reader, professional, consumer, and voter—from being easily swayed by specious claims and language and also force you to check your own impulses to resort to these fallacious methods (unless you grow so cynical that you think people are always manipulated anyway, or you lack the energy to carefully work through the principles discussed in the *Peel* section). Check the impulse to manipulate by putting on each of the following masks and, for a moment, clown with those spirits instead of being fooled by them.

Facial Pack: Euphemism

For the most part, *Facial Packers* use harmless *euphemisms* to make normal-but-unappetizing realities more pleasing or more important than they really are. No one really cares to hear the details of what pours out of his or her intestines or where it gets poured. That place was once *euphemized* as the "toilet" because a *toilette* was the process of making yourself presentable by applying cosmetics or shaving, but "toilet" went the way of all *euphemisms*, over time losing *euphemistic* force, so that the reality of what it hid seeped back in.

Sex. Sex often gets *euphemized*, such as when two people who have affection for one another call sex "making love" to detract from the more primal aspects of the act and to emphasize their spiritual desires. We accept such *euphemisms* unless we know the couple are merely using each other as live tissue to have an orgasm, in which case the *euphemism* becomes a lie to hide their motivations or fool themselves. The *euphemism* "sexual intercourse" creates a *Facial Packed* term for medical personnel and their patients who wish to perceive the act as outside the realm of both the animal and the spiritual, instead thinking of sex as merely a biological function.

Nature. The animal can even be taken out of animals themselves when guides at Sea World refer to animal sex as "courtship behavior." According to the *Orlando Sentinel*, guides at Sea World are required to use numbing vocabulary, replacing down-to-earth words with multi-syllabic terms, *Facial Packing* the harshness of the experience: "hurt" is replaced with "injured," "captured" with "acquired"; a "cage" becomes an "enclosure," and animals are no longer in "captivity" but in a "controlled environment." Depending on one's position concerning the health of captured sea life, these euphemisms might be thought of as somewhere between harmless and dangerously desensitizing.

Jobs. The business world massages our egos by *Facial Packing* job titles. The secretary becomes an "Administrative Assistant" and garbage collectors upgrade to "Sanitation Engineers"; a teenager in charge of opening the ice cream shop becomes the "manager" (managers become "vice presidents"), and the term "mortician" buries "undertaker," a person easily imagined as someone who pumps dead bodies with chemicals, boxes them, and lowers them into a hole. (Note how *Super-literalism* kicks dirt in *euphemism's* face.) When a sanitation engineer or administrative assistant slips up and must be "fired," the blow is softened by phrases like "right-sizing" or "involuntary separation."

Markets. The marketplace *Facial Packs* products, advertisements appealing to our primal instincts, and the naming of consumer goods designed to protect egos. An airplane vomit bag becomes a "motion discomfort receptacle"; male genital protective devices grow from small, medium, and large to "medium," "large," and "extra large." "Previously owned" cars seem more appealing than "used" cars. Restaurant menus whip up a beef entrée to Wrangler's Steak with Country Gravy, and their fruit dessert becomes Grandma's Apple Pie à la Mode, or both can be upgraded to Steak au Poivre with Pommes Frites and Apple Tarte Tatin.

Academics. The academic world has its own priestly *euphemisms*, rationalized as efficient jargon, but the danger is that the intensity of the subject matter is often lost. In the social sciences, we are concerned with people who live in demolished buildings whose schools are a mess and whose English is almost unrecognizable, who are resentful of people who have money, who have little chance of making substantial amounts themselves without doing back-breaking labor or criminal acts, who are treated unfairly because of their ethnicity. These grim realities are whitewashed with *euphemisms* such as "disadvantaged," "underprivileged," "culturally deprived," or "developing nation," jargon that not only takes away accuracy, but perhaps our sense of urgency in bringing about social change.

The humanities have their own paste. Professors speak through *Facial Packs* such as "symbolic registers," "semiotic discourses," or as Gerard Genette describes in *Narrative Discourse Revisited,* a "heterodiegetic" narrator (a narrator who is not a character in the events he or she recounts) as opposed to a "homodiegetic" narrator (a narrator who is part of the events) or from a "metadiegetic" narrator (a narrator who is part of a narrative embedded within another narrative). Writing for *The New Republic*, Alex Heard discovered the following phrases at a Modern Language Association convention, all designed to "obliterate the layman": "derivation from the deconstruction of Kantian formalism," "The shift from expressive to structured totality cannot ground meditation," and "History can be totalized when being reified only if it moves into the absence of the real." The dangers of relying on *euphemisms* when discussing any of the arts are twofold: First, the language numbs the reader and declares that evaluating literary art can only be articulated with inflated language that is outside the discourse of everyday life; secondly, the language itself becomes the source of study rather than the artistic creator's sense of humor, irony, morality, and the nuances of style, story telling, and characterization, all the elements that language is supposed to clarify rather than obfuscate.

Decorum. *Facial Packers* even soften everyday realities. How harmless these are always depends on the context. Does someone make weak decisions and then hide them as "compassionate" ones? Do our cronies give simplistic advice and then disguise themselves as "friends"? Do we bicker with colleagues out of jealousy but pretend to have a "healthy difference of opinion"? Is a student pretending to "listen well" but really "has no ideas to express"? We also *euphemize* the negative characteristics of the people we want to protect. In Moliere's play *The Misanthrope*, the character Eliante exposes how men decorously describe their women: "The spindly lady has a slender grace; The fat one has a most majestic pace. . . . The haughty lady has a noble mind; The mean one's witty, and the dull one's kind. . . ."

Your turn. To purge, make a list of all your nasty habits or shortcomings as a student, parent, child, lover, employee, or all the above. Then for each of the flaws on your list, create a *euphemistic* word or phrase that puts a prettier face on those unattractive qualities. For instance, instead of saying you "procrastinate," doll up your fault by saying that you "have a unique sense of time." Avoid antonyms, terms that mean the opposite, but instead make unpleasant details more pleasing, retaining the flaw but willfully misleading with language that makes the fault seem a virtue. Then combine this description into a *euphemized* classified advertisement, resume, or online profile.

Another turn. Cleanse yourself of jargon by giving instructions on a ridiculously simple procedure—washing your face, giving someone a kiss—by breaking the procedure into six numbered steps and creating a jargon label for each step by using a thesaurus and thinking in terms of long, multi-syllabic words. Replace all the simple items in the instructions and the title of the directions with created jargon.

War Paint: Euphemism

War Painters kick *euphemism* up a notch several ways: by hiding even more dangerous realities than *Facial Packers*, by intentionally confounding with wordiness, and by misusing diction so that the nuances of words are violated.

Institutional. George Orwell was one of the first writers to look behind the *War Paint* of military atrocities perpetrated by different countries throughout the century to numb the effects of war's horrors on both the soldiers and the public that supports them. For instance, when defenseless villages are bombed, people thrown out of their homes, livestock poisoned, grain supplies torched, women raped, and children murdered, the official anesthesia is "pacification," "neutralization," and "elimination of unreliable elements." When troops kill their own troops, the stupidity and pain is camouflaged with "friendly fire" or "incontinent ordinance."

The military is not the only place with camouflaged dangers. The Church has them too. In an article entitled "Catholic Church Must Lose the Psychobabble" in *The Los Angeles Times*, George Weigel claims that the Church telling priests to "observe the boundaries," was really a *euphemism* for "do not commit grave sin," and that the Church referred to the molestation of young boys as "fixated ephebophilia," the stem word "ephebus" alluding to a youth of ancient Greece who is entering manhood and training for full Athenian citizenship. These are tapestries to cover up references to sodomizing, which is already a *euphemism* for sticking a penis into an anus.

Industry. All culpable institutions resort to cover-ups. The atomic energy industry sedates us with "energetic disassemblies" and "plutonium takes up residence" (Like a good neighbor?) when radiation leaks and spreads cancerous poison; the forests that provide the world's oxygen are brutalized with clear-cutting, referred to as "managing standing inventory through regenerative cutting"; the medical industry pulls sheets over our eyes with "therapeutic misadventure" when someone dies on the operating table; the airlines evaporate responsibility for an airplane explosion with "involuntary conversion"; and the Environmental Protection Agency has buddied up with industry by neutralizing acid rain as "poorly buffered precipitation."

In a lecture entitled "Unethical Contexts for Ethical Questions," Rutgers professor David Ehrenfeld points out just how prevalent *War Paint* can become in any industry. For instance, to have cows that produce more milk, some are injected with the growth hormone rBGH, which leads to an "increased risk of clinical mastititis ([a symptom of which is] visibly abnormal milk)," which means there is pus in the milk. Not an appetizing reality.

Nuance. Aside from obscuring realities that are dangerous for people, *War Paint* trashes the nuances of language. English is one of the most complex languages in the world because it is made up of so many other languages, containing Anglo-Saxon-based words and words of Latin and Greek origins. This allows English to articulate nuances in an attempt to be exact, but *War Paint* abuses this richness. For instance, "say" is an Anglo-Saxon-based word that has come to mean something different from the Latin-based word "indicate" which now implies a response that is less committed, direct, or clear than "say." Putting on *War Paint* abuses this difference. If a teacher "says" for you to do homework, it would be painting over the truth to say she "implies" that she wants you to do the homework, the *War Paint* pretending that the demand is not definite, suggesting this is just a matter of interpreting the teacher's raised eyebrows when mentioning homework.

In fact, abusing nuance is often a sign of avoiding responsibility. For instance, when an attorney for an automobile manufacturer must admit in a recall letter to a customer that the company's poor manufacturing might kill the driver, the writer immediately applies a palette of *War Paint.* The writer makes an admission, but crafted to sound intimidating and beyond reproach, while simultaneously flattening a dangerous situation. The result quiets the customer and shifts blame away from the manufacturer: "Please bring your car in for service. A certain deficiency could adversely affect vehicle control." The word "deficiency," that normally means "a slight lacking," paints over "poor manufacturing"; "adversely affect vehicle control" glazes over "the car could crash, killing you." This is called professional writing, but it is also deceit.

Wordiness. Every student has at one time or another tried to make up for lack of knowledge through redundancy of words. Likewise, lawmakers load laws with enough language chaos for people on opposite political sides to both claim victory. Here is *Congressional Record* with *War Paint:*

> The oil price structure should give the President a substantial measure of administrative flexibility to craft the price regulatory mechanism in a manner designed to optimize production from domestic properties subject to a statutory parameter requiring the regulatory pattern to proven prices from exceeding a maximum weighted average.

The president of the National Council of Teachers of English scrubbed this statement to uncover "Congress should authorize the President to design an oil price structure. The system must encourage domestic production, but outlaw exorbitant prices."

Unfortunately, even English professors can be guilty of *War Paint* wordiness. Here is a description of a graduate literature course at a University of California campus: "If persons are answerable for the characters they construct when they as much as think about a person, writers of stories are no less answerable for their characters—the standard disclaimer about the resemblances between characters and persons being 'purely coincidental': notwithstanding." Is this saying, "All people, including writers, imagine characters based on people they know, even if they claim they do not"?

Your turn. To purge, rewrite a simple adage, nursery rhyme, famous quotation, advertisement jingle, or a description of a dangerous situation into *War Paint* so that each line extends for several lines. Apply three principles to achieve *War Paint*: In some parts, change all simple words to more complicated ones; use several words that mean the same thing; and take simple items and actions and break them into smaller, unnecessary-to-talk-about elements. For instance, in the adage "The grass is always greener on the other side of the fence," break the word "fence" down into its parts, functions, or sources, and then find multi-syllabic or infrequently used words to name all these things. Now fence might be "a separating barrier that is hewn from heavily vegetated terrain and then fabricated for the use of property definition." Using all three abuses, the final *War Paint* will read,

> The growth of minute leaves consistently and invariably exists in a more stimulating propagation, and in a higher realm of verdant hue or vibrant chlorophyll on the territory and confines antipodal to the separating barrier that is hewn from heavily vegetated terrain and then fabricated for use of property definition.

Jousters: Logical Fallacies

The Greek philosopher Aristotle maintained that a strong argument has three persuasive dimensions: *logos* (the organization of claim and support into a clear and *logical* format), *ethos* (the establishment of the writer's/speaker's credibility and reliability), and *pathos* (the ability to entice the audience into an emotional investment). Unfortunately, some writers unwittingly, and some intentionally, abuse these dimensions thus committing *logical fallacies*.

Learning the names and definitions of these *fallacies* helps you avoid making these mistakes and prevents you from being manipulated by others. Since there are so many *fallacies* (below is just a partial list), we have divided them by different abuses of the Aristotelian triad— *fallacies of logos, fallacies of pathos* and *fallacies of ethos.*

Fallacies of Logos.

These *fallacies* abuse Aristotle's idea of *logos*—strong arguments need to provide logical support. Instead, the *fallacies* below all contain a disconnect between the claim and support, sometimes offering *hasty generalizations*—faulty conclusions arrived at with insufficient evidence or *smoke screens*—irrelevant proofs that act as diversions from the claims or issues.

Misapplied Generalization: This *fallacy* wrongly attaches or misapplies support that may be generally true but will not work to support a specific claim.

> One may assert that my English teacher, Professor Stein, is a Democrat because most English professors are Democrats.

Fallacy of Composition/Fallacy of Extrapolation: The inverse of a misapplied generalization, this *fallacy* assumes that what is true for one particular instance can be used as evidence to draw a general conclusion.

> Fabio is a good lover, and he is a Latin man; therefore, one can conclude that all Latin men are good lovers.

Circular Logic (Begging the Question): This *fallacy* occurs when a claim, thesis, or argument is supported with a restatement of the claim, although the support is not usually presented as a verbatim repetition of the claim but buried in synonymous language.

> Pornographic films are offensive because they are distasteful.

Shrink & Grow Fallacy: A temptation in deductive analysis when finding support for a claim, this *fallacy* involves downplaying evidence that contradicts or refutes one's position while also inflating smaller, tangential points.

> The fact that no WMDs have been found in Iraq should not deter our government from aggressively combating rogue nations that threaten the safety of Americans; instead, we should focus on the important and huge gains in Iraq—that some groups have more freedom since we invaded.

Appeal to Statistics: Using statistics that are either irrelevant to the argument, or from questionable sources, to bolster a weak claim. This *fallacy* relies on the premise that people are easily swayed by numbers and a belief that "numbers don't lie." All statistics are subject to interpretation, and the methods of gathering the information can be dubious.

> Based on the Associated Press' Ipsos poll that found that "the chances that an American says the word 'fuck' is 2 out of 3," one can conclude that foul language is on the rise.

False Cause (Post Hoc Propter Hoc): **Often committed in causal arguments, this** *fallacy* **assumes a cause and effect relationship between two events simply because they happened close in time.**

> I complained to the dean last semester about my political science professor, and this semester he is not teaching; therefore, my letter of complaint caused his dismissal.

Slippery Slope (Domino Effect): **Frequently occurring in causal and proposal arguments, this** *fallacy* **claims that taking or not taking an action will cause an undesirable effect. In other words, a prediction of what** *might* **happen is substituted for valid reasons of why a particular claim should or should not be implemented.**

> We should not teach sex education to high school students, because it will encourage students to become sexually active, and there will be a rise in teen pregnancy and STDs.

Leap in Logic (Non-Sequitur): **A missing link between a claim and its support. The claim and support seem related, but a step in the logic has been omitted.**

> Because he sees the ghost of his father, Hamlet's grief makes him indecisive.

Fallacy of Time and Place (Tempus et Locus Peculiaris): **Sup-porting a claim with an undocumented notion of what was acceptable in a particular historic time period (** *tempus* **) or an unverified assumption of what is customary in a particular culture (** *locus* **).**

> We may accept the idea of "taming" a woman because in Shakespeare's time, before women achieved equality, curbing a woman's passionate temperament through starvation, physi-cal abuse, and sleep deprivation was an acceptable practice.

Shifting the Burden of Proof (Ad Ignorantium): **Using the absence of contrary proof as support of the claim. In critical thinking, it's always necessary to provide support for one's claims.**
One may assert that extraterrestrials have visited Earth because there is no proof they have not been here.

Subjectivist Fallacy: **Supporting a claim based on one's limited point of view, personal experiences, or offering as support, "It's just my opinion" or "That's just the way I see it." Critical thinkers always offer facts for support of their opinions and viewpoints.**

> I reject the scientific evidence that supports the theory of global warming because I have not noticed any appreciable differ-ences in weather or temperature where I live.

Appeal to Faith: Supporting a claim with "the word of God," using the Bible, Koran or other sacred texts as support. When arguing issues of faith, support from these sources is acceptable; however, critical thinking is based on the use of factual evidence and outside the purview of faith-based argumentation.

> The death penalty is a moral and effective punishment for the worst crimes because in the Bible God says, "an eye for an eye, a tooth for a tooth." (*Exodus* 21:23-27).

False Dilemma (Either/Or Fallacy, Black and White Fallacy): Reducing a complicated or ambiguous matter to two polarized choices.

> In order to keep ourselves safe from terrorism, we must give up some of our civil liberties and have our government listen in on the phone calls of private citizens because the only other option is to leave ourselves and our loved ones vulnerable to being killed in a terrorist attack.

False Equity: Claiming that an argument is persuasive because both sides were represented or, inversely, that an argument fails to convince because the other side was not presented.

> The documentary *An Inconvenient Truth* fails to persuade audiences that global warming is caused by man-made pollution because the documentary never presents other possible causes for global warming.

False Analogy: While analogies are often used to support an argument, when the dynamics of the comparison do not have enough parallels, then the analogy must be deemed false.

> Being forced to pay higher taxes to pay for universal healthcare is unjust because it is like Rosa Parks being forced to the back of the bus.

Equivocation: Switching the meaning of a key term in the claim (usually an abstraction) without noting the switch:

> We shouldn't teach critical thinking to college students because they are already too critical.

Tu Quo Que (Two Wrongs Don't Make a Right): Justifying an unethical action by claiming that another person did something equally wrong.

> I am justified in stealing from my work because they promised to give me a raise this month and then reneged on that promise.

The Ends Justify the Means (Robin Hood Syndrome): Claiming that an unethical, illegal, or unacceptable action was justified since it resulted in a positive outcome.

> Even though the government lied about Iraq having WMDs, it was still right to invade this country since we removed the dictator Saddam Hussein.

Amoeba Vocabula: Loading an argument with unsure, indefinite, and tentative language in order to absolve oneself from the responsibility for making a claim.

> Though my position has sort of been to support a constitutional amendment to protect the desecration of the flag, I haven't really explored all the arguments for this amendment, and it seems like the other side may have some valid points, and so I might be changing my mind, but I am not sure yet.

Fallacies of Pathos.

While a strong argument should address deeply held values and entice audiences to care about issues, using unscrupulous appeals and taking advantage of emotions is an abuse of Aristotle's idea of *pathos*.

Appeal to Pity (Ad Misercordium): There are justifiable and logical appeals to pity; it is only when someone unjustifiably substitutes pity for support in an argument that it is a *fallacy*. Often committed in proposal arguments, this *fallacy* tries to arouse one's sense of pity in coercing agreement with a position.

> I deserve an "A" in English class because I have a poor self-image due to my underprivileged upbringing.

Appeal to Fear (Scare Tactics): Attempting to scare or intimidate someone into doing something. Employed in both causal and proposal arguments, this *fallacy* often attaches a *slippery slope* element, a catastrophic prediction of what will happen if the plan is or is not adopted or the argument not accepted.

> If we don't fight the terrorists over there, we will have to fight them here.

Joke and Choke Fallacy: Humor and wit are important tools in argumentation, but this *fallacy* uses humor to reduce a position to a joke, mocking and ridiculing an argument to deflect real issues.

My wife has been after me to exercise, eat healthier, and lose weight so that I can lower my cholesterol and blood pressure. Since when did she get a medical degree—he-he-he-he?

Brown-Nose Fallacy: Replacing actual evidence with flattery in an attempt to lower the defenses of the audience so that they won't think critically about the claim and evidence.

You won't vote to legalize marijuana because you're too smart to buy into the other side's weak arguments.

Affective Fallacy: This *fallacy* is committed in evaluation arguments when determining the worth of a work of art (paintings, literature, films). In evaluating art, one uses criteria or a set of standards to logically measure that worth. One's emotional response, however, is not a legitimate criterion. Works of art can be great even if they fail in jerking tears from your eyes, and they can be propaganda pieces and arouse tears.

Troy should have been voted best picture because after I saw the film I was crying my eyes out of their sockets. Any film that makes someone cry that hard must be excellent.

Ego Es Ibi: Like the *affective fallacy*, this *fallacy* employs invalid criteria for judging a work of art. Instead of using the emotional appeal as the criteria, this *fallacy* illogically bases the worth of art on its ability to create verisimilitude.

The abstract paintings of Jackson Pollack cannot be considered great art since they do not depict realistic landscapes or lifelike portraits, but the painting of a horse I saw was great because it looked so real you wanted to reach out and touch it.

Fallacies of Ethos.

Illegitimately establishing one's own credibility or unfairly disparaging the trustworthiness of one's opponent produces this last group of *fallacies* that abuse Aristotle's concept of *ethos*.

Well Poisoning and *Ad Hominem:* The fallacy rejects someone's argument based on the track record of the person arguing or substitutes a personal attack for a well-reasoned argument. How a person lives, skeletons in closets, even selfish motivation cannot be considered in accepting or rejecting one's claim. While we have been taught to "consider the source," in critical thinking, one accepts or refutes an argument based only on an evaluation of the support and logic of the argument.

The country should reject the president's position on global warming because he is an anti-Muslim and once worked for a refinery in a high-oil-yield country.

Rubber-Glue: Accusing your opponent of doing what he is accusing you of.

While my opponent claims that I have not stated my position on the death penalty, I'll reveal my stance when he finally takes a public stand on abortion.

Raising the Ante (Call for Perfection): Agreeing with your opponent's position but then claiming that it is not going far enough or raising all objections despite any agreements.

I agree that we should stop criminals from purchasing weapons, but until the government can assure us that no honest citizen will be prevented from his or her right to bear arms, we must not enact any limits.

Saint's Mask: Bolstering your own position by claiming that you are not motivated by personal gain.

I believe it is the government's obligation to pay for all kids to get a disciplined, religious education, and I don't even have any children.

Appeal to Authority: While it is important to establish your credibility or expertise in a subject being discussed, one cannot substitute their authority—an advanced degree, celebrity status, or seniority—for actual support of one's claim.

My interpretation of *Moby Dick* is correct because Professor Wack, a Melville expert at the University of California, agrees with my interpretation.

Intentional Fallacy: Supporting an interpretation of an artwork by claiming to know the artist's/writer's intentions in creating that work. Sometimes creators speak ironically in interviews, or they do not realize all the effects of their works. Their analysis is subject to the same burden of proof as their audience's.

In his interview, the poet said his poems were intended to be satirical, so his works should be read as satirical.

Minority Privilege (In Margine Immunitas): Used as a rationale, this *fallacy* excuses or cuts slack for a writer's lack of credibility and questionable support because of the writer's minority status.

Though Malcolm X's doctrine of "We want equality by any means necessary" could be interpreted as a call to violence, his quote should be accepted in a positive light since as an

African American, Malcolm X and many other blacks in this country have suffered much racial injustice.

Strawman Fallacy: Often associated with refutation arguments, this *fallacy* purposely misrepresents an opponent's argument in order to make it easier to reject.

> Position Statement: I support state assisted suicide and the right to die.
> Refutation of Position: My opponent believes that doctors should have the ultimate power to decide who lives and who dies.

Bandwagon (Ad Populum): A frequently employed tactic, this *fallacy* uses the consensus of what many people think or desire—the ethos of a group—to support or oppose a claim. Since whole groups or populations can be wrong or guilty of groupthink, this is an illogical and potentially dangerous way to support an argument.

> Most people define marriage as between a man and a woman; therefore, I believe the government should ban gay marriages.

Your turn. Before you can recognize *fallacies* in others' arguments and thwart the temptation to use them yourself, you first need to memorize the names and definitions. Create flash cards by writing the name of the *fallacy* on one side and the definition on the other. Once these *fallacies* are committed to memory, you will start noticing/hearing the *fallacies* being used by family members (who, by the way, will appreciate when you point out the flaws in their argumentation), by politicians and pundits, professors, news commentators, talk-show hosts, lawyers, and coworkers.

A good way to practice recognizing *fallacies* is through literature. Since short stories, novels, and films often deal with characters in conflict, one way to read a story is by explaining the actions of a protagonist or central character through the critical thinking *fallacies*. For instance, one might explain Hamlet's dilemma through the either-or *fallacy* since he thinks he must either kill his uncle, King Claudius, to avenge his father's death, or he must kill himself. Also, an antagonist's (a character who needles the protagonist) actions might be explained through the *fallacies* since this character might be trying to deceive and manipulate the main character.

BASTE:
Ways to Research

Seasoning
Drenching
Presenting

One of the most important ways to test both inductive and deductive thinking is to conduct research. When passionately involved in a subject, research is a pleasure and people do it automatically: A person loves his or her houseplant and based on past experience (past research) with other plants, narrows down to a few places where this new one will get enough light. The person calls the nursery, talks to a friend, consults a few plant books, goes on the Internet, and finally blends and synthesizes all the advice with his or her own experience to place the plant. Research is endless. Now the person studies whether or not the plant thrives and maybe moves it again. Not all research is so thoughtful. A teenager deciding whom to date does research by doing live interviews and phone calls (but maybe without savvy about his or her sources' motivations) and careful field observations (maybe paying too much attention to someone's physical attributes rather than his or her kindness). Even the most acclaimed research can be flawed, scorched by emotions or faulty sources.

Seasoning

Pre-thinking. Before researching your *primary source* (a novel, business proposal, axel, medical procedure, case study, historical document), first try to understand it by inductively analyzing it. (If you have been given a writing assignment on a topic you know nothing about, concentrate on finding primary sources to study first.) The analysis may consist of rough notations and hypotheses that change as you consider the research. In the library you will find *secondary sources*, writers who have commented on your primary source, but now your mind has a context allowing you to compare and contrast your own analysis with the new material you are looking up. You will be able to ask whether the secondary material *adds to*, *argues against*, or *expands* your previous analysis. Without the context of your rough draft notes as a basic recipe, you will library-stew, overwhelmed with information, and your reading of secondary sources can become mindless.

Confident writers never attempt to create a summary or report by omitting the writer's own synthesis of material and by using only secondary sources. Aside from the problem above, one should never rely on secondary sources simply because they are written by authorities. (See *Appeal to Authority* in the *Scrub* section.) There are many published, credentialed writers who are poor writers, lack insight, and argue thoughtlessly. Be suspicious. Use your own rough draft analysis to question what you read. Read critically by studying other writers' use of *exemplification*. (See the *Peel* section on *Inductive Thinking*.) Being open-minded and working inductively means rejecting inadequate and unconvincing evidence or weakly argued positions, and accepting only strongly supported, thoughtful arguments, regardless of whether the source validates or refutes your own position.

Sources. Sources take different plunges into your subject: *Encyclopedias* offer abbreviated, surface-quality information, mentioning subtopics related to the subject that will take the writer to other depths. For instance, if you were writing about Thoreau's *Walden*, encyclopedias and other reference books would mention documents and writings, political and historical events, and other figures or writers you might decide to investigate. Library reference sections are filled with special encyclopedias on subjects such as rock music, utopias, Catholic saints, sports, and film history. Librarians will help you locate these sources. While encyclopedias offer an overview of the subject, they usually do not provide much critical analysis.

For more critical analysis, look for books on the library's computer catalogue, but when you find them, look first at the table of contents in the front and the index in the back and go only to those pages that seem related to your analysis. Use large specialized indexes (librarians will help you) that cover essays in periodicals (*Readers' Guide to Periodical Literature or InfoTrac*), essays written for specialists (*Art Index, Social Science Index,* and other Indexes), and newspaper articles (*New York Times, London Times* and many others) to find more focused and current information than material found in books. Library indexes will do searches for these articles.

Do not forget that most libraries have extensive holdings of documentaries and films. Use them. The Internet provides sources that range from the encyclopedic to the intimate, from ancient to up-to-date, from gospel truth to outright lies. It is better to bring up whole articles on the Internet than abstracts that are too general. Use the Internet to interview professors and other experts. Librarians will help you find out where to find their email addresses.

Drenching

Giving credit.   Academic papers and some journals require a *works consulted* or *works cited list* of all sources used in composing your final draft. Keep a list or *working bibliography* (a rough draft of what will eventually be titled the "Works Cited" or "Works Consulted" page), writing down all the bibliographic details (author, title, publication date, *etc.*) needed to cite each work. Many guidebooks, websites, and CD-Rom programs provide the proper citation procedures for the two most common formats: MLA style (*Modern Language Association*), used in the humanities; and APA style (*American Psychological Association*), adopted by many of the sciences. Beware: citation rules occasionally change. And beware: improper and careless documentation can lead to failing research papers and charges of plagiarism. Some professors demand precise adherence to citation rules. Smoke them and get an up-to-date computer program that will rearrange the entire source material and print up a correct, final "Works Cited" page.

Save time by writing the library call number next to each source in your *working bibliography* in case you need to go back to it for more clarification. Also, assign a made-up code (letter, number, symbol) next to each source and write the same code on each note card (discussed below) generated from that particular source. This cross-referencing quickly places notes with their sources and saves time because the source information only needs to be written once: the code will represent all the fussy but necessary bibliographic information.

When you are finished writing your final paper, you will drop three things from the *working bibliography*: all the library call numbers, all your personalized codes, and any works that you did not end up using in the paper (though remember that works not quoted, but paraphrased, or that have ideas which influenced your final draft, must be included). You will also arrange all the sources in alphabetical order (author's last name first, if no author then editor, if neither, then title) according to the rules of the *MLA* or *APA* that can be found online.

Note-shattering. When taking notes from sources, put each idea on a note card rather than on a page of notebook paper. (Some laptops have computer programs that have note-card set-up programs.) Note cards provide the freedom to psychologically shatter that source into information bits that can be easily rearranged and shuffled among other sources, as opposed to notes written on loose papers with source information all lumped together on one page. Also, the note cards offer space for a writer to absorb and paraphrase the source information, an opportunity to break away from the source's style and organization since the writer will have his or her own.

You will need to put three items on each card: the note, the code that corresponds to your rough draft "Works Cited" page, and the page number or numbers from which you took the note. When you write the note, write down the material verbatim with quotation marks ("__") *only* if the quoted material is quotable, germane to your argument; otherwise, paraphrase or put it in your own words. Many writers think that only quoted material must be cited, but the citation refers to the idea or details you are taking from the source even if you have put those ideas in your own words. Failing to give credit to or cite a source is called *plagiarism* and is tantamount to stealing. Changing only a few words and not citing the source is still plagiarism. That is why every note card must have a code and page number on it.

Presenting

Shuffling notes. Reading each of your note cards, write a personal response to the researched material on the back of every card. Write down as many implications as you can. (See *Inductive* and *Deductive Thinking* in the *Peel* section.) Ask yourself whether the researched side changes, strengthens, or expands your original, pre-research analysis. Write that on the back of the note card as well. Considering either side of the card, now start stacking them according to any commonality: the supporting role they play or topics they relate to. Shuffle and reshuffle these stacks so that clusters evolve that you might use for organizing your essay. In addition, start thinking about all the strategies in the *Form* section of this book. Maybe those strategies will decide the different parts of your paper, and then you will reshuffle cards again to support those forms. Many of your notes will become irrelevant, get shuffled out of stacks, and saved for another project. No matter what happens, the more you shuffle, the more your sources will become integrated, and you will always know where the note comes from by looking at the code on the card and matching it with your source card (which becomes the "Works Cited" page).

Writing and Citing. Once you like the organization created by the stacks, pick up the first pile and start writing the notes into a rough draft essay. Don't worry about starting at the beginning; it's better to write the introduction last after you see how the essay's body is shaped. Use the *Transition* unit under *Form* after you complete all the sections of your essay. Make sure any notes from the sources include inferences with them or use the implications you wrote on the back of the card. Remember, you are primarily writing everything into your own style and quoting only those word-for-word notes that are especially pithy, rich, or shocking. (For quotes that go over four lines, indent ten spaces, block the quote, and omit quotation marks, but still give that parenthetical citation.) Review *Quote Sandwiching* in the *Encircling* unit to gracefully lead into and out of quotations.

Everything, absolutely all notes which come from your sources must be credited as soon as they enter your rough draft, even when not directly quoted. Although most publications prefer footnotes at the bottom of the page, academic style (*MLA*) has made the process sensible by requiring in-text citations in parentheses. For instance:

> Even though the Qunitians fought the Quibblians, they managed to produce art that equaled the best art of Hellenistic Greece (Johnson 21).

By looking at the code on your note card and cross-referencing it to your source card, you know the note comes from Johnson, and the page number comes directly off your note card. Note that the period goes outside the parentheses and, if you mentioned Johnson in your sentence (Johnson says that even though . . .), then only the number 21 would go in parentheses.

There is no punctuation or letters for "page" between the name and page number. If you use more than one Johnson, you will need to include the first names' initials in parenthesis; and if you use more than one source written by the same Johnson, or if there is no author or editor, then you will need to use a key word from the title of the work, but not necessarily the whole title as it is written on your "Works Cited" page: (Johnson, *Spoof* 21). Consult the *MLA* or *APA* style sheets on how to cite properly under different circumstances.

Final draft. Revise, revise, and revise, but always include your in-text citations. Use style (see the *Style* section and *Peel* chapter) to make your paper a pleasure to read, to artfully connect details and implications, to ensure that the research is well integrated with your own ideas and observations, and to make sure that no one can accuse you of being an academic bore. Contrary to popular opinion, "academic" and "boring" need not be synonyms.

THE STIMULATOR:
An Appendix of Sorts

All the strategies in the *Form* unit can be used to organize a strong essay; however, condensed versions of these strategies can be combined in endless ways and used as introductions, body sections, and conclusions. Combining strategies creates shifts in tones and tactics that refuel a longer piece and gives the essay more in common with professional writing, averting the sagging caused by the single-toned, pre-cast parts traditionally associated with academic writing.

All the suggestions for combining strategies can be reinforced with research, these outside sources sometimes used in just one of the strategies, sometimes in all of them. (See the *Baste* chapter in the *Headwork* unit.) The disparate strategies can then be stitched together with *Transitions*. (See *Transitioning* under *Form* unit.) All essays then need to be revised using all the techniques in *Style* unit, but especially *Flow* and *Pause*.

Important: Often it is best to work on only one strategy in the combination without anticipating the others and then not decide on their order until later: this prevents running out of *juju* that typically accompanies writing large essays. Even the order in which the strategies are presented should not be anticipated until all parts are close to final form and the effect of each strategy is fully realized.

Ugly Giants. Undermine a group that seems politically shallow, culturally bankrupt, or emotionally immature.
Mini 1: Describe the breadth of the group using third person singular in *Distancing Lens*. Mini 2: Use the *Scrub* chapter in analyzing the group's rhetoric, drawing inferences from the topics selected, language used (*euphemism*), bad arguments employed (*logical fallacies*) found on their websites, blogs, and in the magazines they read or the group's own publications.
Mini 3: Write a *Devil's Advice* to tease the group's assumptions or an *Anecdoting* if you have had a telling experience with the group.

Talking Words. Choose one abstraction such as a scientific term (*balance, linear, stasis*), or literary term (*romanticism, existentialism, myth*), or political term (*history, democracy,* *pluralism*) or after studying a group of essays or literary works that have a common theme, pick a key abstract word (*abuse, love, betrayal, empathy, sacrifice*) that is central to that theme. (In the last case use only examples from the works to do all the following.)

Mini 1: Write a *Thesauruscoping* on the abstraction.

Mini 2: Write an *Anecdoting* or *Stress Testing* that centers on the abstraction.

Mini 3: Create a *Netting* on the same abstraction.

Live Wires. Pick an insect, architectural or engineering wonder, or machine.

Mini 1: Write a *riddling* version of *Masquerading*.

Mini 2: Write paragraphs using *Problem Making* one to three times.

Mini 3: Write an *Anecdoting* about a personal experience with the subject.

Sensualizing. Pick an action that happens relatively quickly: a car crash you have been in, a kill made by an animal or bird, an athletic action, a cooking action, a burial, a sex act.

Mini 1: Break the action into five parts and use *Splitting the Second* to describe the action.

Mini 2: Write a separate research paper on an issue related to the action you just described. (See *Baste* in the *Headwork* unit.)

Finally, take the two papers and splice them together using Double Exposures.

Flushing Out. Write about a politician or celebrity you want to make fun of in terms of their mentality and values.

Mini 1: Use a fictional *Q&A-ing* with the person.

Mini 2: Analyze one of the person's positions using Inductive Analysis. (See *Peel* in the *Headwork* unit.)

Mini 3: Conclude by telling the person off using *Humbling Lens*.

Fuming. Write about a thing you are angry about (a political party, a workplace, an inane class you are taking, a profession).

Mini 1: Use a *Netting* to list its foibles, disadvantages, upsets.

Mini 2: Write two to three *Stress Tests* about the subject.

Mini 3: Use three different kinds of *Echoing* in your concluding statement.

City Watch. Pick eight topics from the following to write about a city: sports, politics, industry, academia, art, geography, history, food, architecture, crime, recreation, monuments, and celebrities.

Mini 1-8: Write about a city using the *Thirteen Ways* approach but limit the paper to eight ways. For each of the eight ways, use a Mini version of eight different strategies in the *Form* unit. Some *Ways* can be much longer than others.

Updating. Write about a past event (political, artistic, legal, military, or religious). Instead of three parts, use each Mini section to rewrite the same paper.

Mini 1: Describe and discuss three sub-happenings that led up to the event, with the *strip tease* strategy under the *Captions* transition technique to build and connect the events.

Mini 2: Rewrite the essay using the *Personalizing Lens*. Put yourself in the narrative as a minor character or witness although you will need to cite everything important you "know." Everything factual needs to be in-text cited. (See *Baste* in the *Headwork* unit.)

Mini 3: Rewrite the whole essay using *Pulsing the Tense.*

Building. Propose doing something important (environmental, architectural, philosophical, reading a specific kind of literature, having a specific kind of relationship. (See *Peel* under the *Headwork* unit.)

Mini 1: Craft a *Cliché Busting* relevant to the subject.

Mini 2: Use *Problem Making* two times to explain the worth of the proposal.

Mini 3: Write a *Netting* of all the by-products and advantages of the proposal not covered under *Problem Making.*

Reheating. Pick a topic that is related to an important primary source: speeches, declarations, constitutions, poems, historical diaries, and philosophical tracts.

Mini 1: Write a *Stress Test* on how at least two groups would understand the topic.

Mini 2: Take the related important text (literary, philosophical, historical) and rewrite it using *Raising the Dead.*

Mini 3: Then write an evaluation claim (See *Claim Cast* under the *Headwork* unit.) explaining how your *Raising the Dead* is more effective or less effective than the original; explain what is lost and gained.

Light Bulbs. Propose a position (political, psychological, spiritual).

Mini 1: Write a *Trojan Horse*, which means first writing a process paper about absolutely anything and then giving it the subtext of your primary proposal.

Mini 2: Transition to a famous quote that supports your proposal and organizes the quoted line using *Quote Sandwiching*.

Mini 3: Do an *Anecdoting* that supports your proposal.

Bull's Eye. Pick a subject to satirize. Start either with a stale writing format (newspaper, business letter, legal brief) or start with a political or social topic (an institution, the president, a profession). Focus on both the format and the topic but concentrate on satirizing one. For instance, under *Mocking*, see the example of the Wile E. Coyote legal suit: it makes fun of legal briefs and cartoon violence. Only one would be the subject of this essay.

Mini 1: Do a *Riddling* version of *Masquerading* to introduce the subject.

Mini 2: Write a *Pie Slicing* of the target so in this case you would *Pie Slice* either two or three kinds of legal briefs or you would *Pie Slice* two or three different kinds of cartoons that use violence.

Mini 3: Write a *Mocking* that makes fun of your subject.

Sad Blasting. Write a letter to someone whom you could never send the letter without getting into some trouble: your current boss, an instructor where you still attend classes, a parent or grandparent, but not necessarily a politician. This essay involves the sections of *Sincerely Yours*.

Mini 1: Use *Netting* for the *facting* section but withhold judgmental words.

Mini 2: Use *Inductive Analysis* (see *Peel* in the *Headwork* unit) for *interpreting* of *Sincerely Yours*.

Mini 3: For the *delivering* of *Sincerely Yours*, use *Devil's Advice*.

Spicing. Pick any topic about anything, a work of literature, social phenomena, an essay, artwork, business proposal.

Mini 1: Look up a famous quote on the subject and do a *Quote Sandwich*.

Mini 2: Write down key items (at least twenty) from a rough draft essay explanation of the subject, using the words to play *Mix Masters* until you have created fifteen metaphoric sentences. Now revise the explanation with ten of your *Mix Master* sentences.

Mini 3: Use the most important concept from your subject and write a personifying version of *Masquerading*.

Rewiring. Write a researched evaluation claim on anything scientific. (See *Claim Cast* in the *Headwork* unit.)
Mini 1: Use *Martianing Lens* to describe how laymen usually look at the subject.
Mini 2: Rewrite an explanation of the subject using *Super-literalism*.
Mini 3: Write a *Q&A-ing* about an important aspect of the subject.

Bloodflow. Write about something prevalent or omnipresent that is taken for granted such as rat packing or alcoholism.
Mini 1: Write a *Martianing Lens* of what should be, a view of the norm, what one would expect to see without the presence of this omnipresent force.
Mini 2: Write a *Netting* of research and field observation on the subject.
Mini 3: Write a *Sincerely Yours* to a person involved with the subject.

Spit Fire. This involves using the three Minis within the *Sincerely Yours* format.
Mini 1: Use *Echoing* at least four different ways in the *facting* section.
Mini 2: Use the *Distancing Lens* of the kinds of people the addressee could end up joining for the *interpretation* section.
Mini 3: Use the *Humbling Lens* for the *delivery* section.

Booking. Using *Thirteen Ways*, write about a piece of literature using five *Ways*: Mini 1-5: For each of the five *Ways*, use a Mini version of five different strategies in the *Form* unit. One way could use *Deductive Analysis* (see *Peel* in the *Headwork* unit) to look at the work from a specific critical school (mythic, feminist, deconstructionist, *etcetera*); a *Stress Test* using a second work with a similar theme; a *Personalizing Lens* by fictionalizing a dialogue with one of the characters; a *Q&A-ing* or *Humbling Lens* with the author.

Index

249